The Vanishing Jew

A Wake-Up Call From the Book of Esther

The Vanishing Jew

A Wake-Up Call From the Book of Esther

Michael Eisenberg

Translated by Rena Siev

Edited by Elli Fischer

Michael Eisenberg

The Vanishing Jew

A Wake-Up Call From the Book of Esther

ככה יעשה ליהודי

Translation from Hebrew: Rena Siev
Editor: Elli Fischer

Cover: Micky Friedman
Typesetting: Sheffi Paz, Agata

Table of Contents

Introduction

By Rabbi Binyamin Lau

"In much wisdom is much grief, and he that increases knowledge, increases sorrow"

(Kohelet 1:18)

Escaping from the Tree of Knowledge

"A person is obligated to become intoxicated on Purim." There is an important mitzvah for one to become so drunk on Purim that "he cannot distinguish between 'Mordechai is blessed' and 'Haman is cursed.'" A Talmudic anecdote (BT *Megilah* 7b) relates the story of two sages who shared a Purim feast and drank a great deal of wine. When one sage was especially inebriated, he got up and killed his friend. The next day, he petitioned God to have mercy on his friend, and his friend returned to the living. The next year, this same scholar asked his friend to once again join him for the festive Purim meal. His friend replied, "Miracles do not happen every day." This obviously extreme story describes the intense Purim intoxication that was prevalent in Talmudic times. For better or worse, there is no doubt that drunkenness is a symbol of this holiday.

If we examine the inner significance of the practice of drinking until drunk, we can say that it represents the radical renouncement of self-control and the desire to escape to a world that is not governed by knowledge and understanding. This is the religious dimension of Purim: it mocks earthly kingdoms that presume omnipotence. By abdicating control of the body through alcohol and reading the events of the Megilah, the reveler asserts that there is a different Ruler in charge of everything, including one's very own self. Release from the fetters of self-control through drinking is an attempt at self-criticism. It is as though one says to himself: "Stop trying to control everything; you are an insignificant object, acted upon in the immensity of a world concerned with far greater things." R. Shagar z"l articulated this idea as follows: "This drunkenness of destroyed values, of 'cannot distinguish between blessed and cursed,' marks, more than anything else, the postmodern era in which we live: the chaos that threatens culture in general, and Jewish society in particular; the disintegration of the subject and his values; the fragmented nature of postmodernity that is really just the crumbling of society; and its merry and drunken approach to life, a carnivalesque, pluralistic, variegated depiction of reality."[1]

This dimension of Purim is so confusing and confounding that it is itself emblematic of the inability to distinguish between a blessing and a curse. Instead of devoting ourselves to dealing with serious questions and a Jewish self-accounting, we spend our time mocking the significance and magnitude of life. The wine helps us to forget, divert our attention, and pollute our hearts. This is obviously tragic, because every drunken night is followed by a morning hangover. At the end of the night, the sun rises, and with it man awakens to his day, to his job, and to his life. He regains awareness of everything he tried to escape.

---

1 R. Shimon Gershon Rosenberg (Shagar), *Pur Hu Ha-Goral: Drashot Le-Purim*, Beit El 2005, pp. 50-51.

The Pursuit of Understanding

Michael Eisenberg seeks to unmask the holiday of Purim, to sober up from the wine, and to restore awareness and understanding to human life. His down-to-earth reading of the Megilah brings the reader to new insights, and this mindfulness ushers in anxiety and fear. *The Vanishing Jew* was written by a man who is deeply rooted in the real world and connected to the realm of economic and political thought; he draws inspiration from the world of Torah in all of its layers and strata. He beholds Megilat Esther, with all of its ridiculous characters, and does not laugh at all; he identifies in the story's folly the tale of a Jewish nation assimilating in a foreign empire and denying responsibility for itself and its mission. His pen does not spare anyone from criticism, not even Mordechai and Esther.

Eisenberg has reintroduced and sharpened a longstanding disagreement regarding the character, motives, and actions of the Megilah's hero, Mordechai the Jew. This disagreement goes back to the days of the Talmud and was addressed by medieval commentators, as well as the likes of R. Yitzhak Reggio, a leader of the *Wissenschaft Des Judentums* movement in the nineteenth century. Mordechai's character has been treated in contemporary scholarship as well. According to this reading, behind the joyous mask of the Megilah lurks a story of assimilation and destruction. It is a story that exposes self-deprecation in the face of a foreign empire, marked by a loss of Jewish identity and the adoption of the names, customs, and values of the Persians. Eisenberg asks us to try and read the Megilah as if for the first time: to closely examine the words of the Megilah's characters and pay careful attention to the hints planted in the text by the Megilah's author, who wrote this story with an awareness of both the story's place on the continuum of Jewish history, and an intimate knowledge of the Tanakh (the Jewish Bible) and its foundational stories. This reading tears away the Megilah's jolly mask and exposes the author's piercing criticism.

The initial crisis that confronts the Jews culminates in the edict that calls for their destruction. This is the moment where all pretenses are dropped and reality is exposed. This unmasking is the polar opposite of the Purim masquerade; this sobering realization is in complete contrast to intoxication. The phase of drunkenness and costumes is the stage of lost identity and God's concealment. This is the stage in which the Jews seek to assimilate in an alien land, forget who they are, and allow the memory of a glorious past to evaporate. The king's ring that is handed over to Haman transforms Mordechai from a man who sits at the king's gate into a Jew who wears sackcloth and ashes and screams out a loud and bitter cry.

Eisenberg is endowed with an additional perspective: that of a Jew living in Israel who was brought up and educated in the Diaspora, and who maintains many professional and personal contacts there. This unique point of view, from a person comfortably ensconced in two very different worlds, charges his words with pain, worry, and hope, as well as a feeling of urgency and clarity that, perhaps, guided the Megilah's author as well. According to Eisenberg's exposition, the Megilah's author did not withhold his critique from anyone in writing a stinging narrative that cautions Diaspora Jews against the attractions of a rich and contented life that inevitably results in a catastrophic identity crisis.

Every person writes from his own unique perspective and brings his personal background and associations to bear on his writing. Eisenberg is no exception, and he invests his writing with an additional, unique personal element. Most people fall into one of two groups – doers and thinkers. Eisenberg is unusual in this regard. Over the last two decades, he has established himself as a pillar of Israel's hi-tech economy, and in this book he demonstrates the importance of bringing one's life experience to intellectual investigation and scholarship.

The Sages of the Mishnaic period, living under Roman rule in the Eretz Yisrael, brought their political status and life situation to bear both in explaining the Megilah and in their unique emphasis on the *mitzvot* of Purim. Through the *Midrashim* and Megilah commentaries that they authored, the Sages of the Babylonian Talmud express their political and religious sensibilities as subjects of Sasanian Persia. Medieval commentators explained the Megilah in a world plagued by incessant anti-Semitism, which nurtured their interest in the anti-Semitic story of Haman. Eisenberg's reading is informed by the elbow-rubbing, competition, and endless interactions of economics, economic policy, business, and politics, enabling him to identify patterns and nuances in economic cycles and the inevitable struggle for money, power, and control.

This perspective, together with his life experience as a Jew who uprooted himself from the American empire of abundance and affluence in order to build a new life here in Israel, enables Eisenberg to identify the relationship between assimilation that stems from anti-Semitism and economic uncertainty on the one hand, and assimilation that rises from wealth and abundance, on the other.

Eisenberg's commentary is deeply rooted in the Megilah's text, and his skill is clearly evident in the work that you hold in your hands; he has incorporated both new and old scholarship, from traditional *Midrashim*, through R. Yitzhak Reggio, and on to contemporary authors. The variety of time periods and approaches that he includes enriches the story of the Megilah with the story of the Jewish nation through the ages. Above all, he insists that we seriously consider the challenge to Jewish identity in modern times as well as in the time of the Megilah. He forces us to confront the challenge of preserving and enriching Jewish identity in the Diaspora and Jewish identity in Israel, struggles and tensions that existed even 2,500 years ago.

My reading of the Megilah differs slightly from Eisenberg's reading, but we stand in agreement on one central point: the need to tell the story of the Jews who chose to live and remain in a foreign land, to integrate into the local culture, to renounce their connection to Eretz Yisrael, and to attempt to cope as a small minority in a huge empire – this is a chapter of

Jewish history that needs to be studied everywhere in our contemporary Jewish world.

The Mitzvot of Purim as a (Partial) Corrective for Diaspora Jews

The holiday of Purim has four *mitzvot*: reading the Megilah, sending foods to friends (*mishlo'ah manot*), eating a Purim feast, and giving gifts to the poor (*matanot le-evyonim*). The reading of the Megilah is analogous to the mitzvah of recounting the Exodus on Passover. It is not enough to read the scroll and make noise upon hearing Haman's name; one must read it mindfully and knowingly, understanding that our nation has been continually tested in the same way throughout history. Reading the Megilah is a call for relevance, insight, and contemplation.

The Purim feast (which includes the mitzvah of drinking 'until one cannot distinguish') helps man understand his limitations and impermanence. It is a way for each individual to mock the sense of 'royalty' and dominion that punctuates our lives: Not only am I not a king – even the man in me is of limited capacity.

The mitzvah of *mishlo'ah manot* is unique to Purim and is a corrective for the sins of alienation and assimilation, so prominent in the Purim story. This mitzvah recognizes the importance of belonging and identity. Haman cursed the Jewish people, describing them as "scattered and dispersed," and Esther's answer was "go and gather all of the Jews." The Jews therefore sought to enact, already in the days of Mordechai and Esther, the practice of "sending portions, each man to his friend" as an expression of fellowship and brotherhood. The idea that on Purim we must gather together in brotherhood, in mutual attentiveness and rejoicing with our neighbors and friends, is rooted in this aspect of Purim. A drunken man cannot fulfill the mitzvah of *mishlo'ah manot*. He is too self-absorbed. The Talmud avers that, in general, when one gives a gift to a friend, he must inform him: do not hide yourself, but rather show your love and concern. Pertinently, in a world that is so alienating and divisive, the *mitzvot* of Purim come to encourage camaraderie and solidarity between and among people.

The mitzvah of *matanot le-evyonim* is unique to Purim as well. This mitzvah is mentioned in the Megilah only when Mordechai sends a letter to the Jewish people establishing the holiday of Purim (chapter 9). Our Sages instituted that this mitzvah should be fulfilled immediately after the reading of the Megilah, and even instructed that the Megilah be read at times when the poor would best be able to benefit from this charity on that very same day. We are obligated to give *matanot le-evyonim* before the festive meal on Purim, to ensure that every single Jewish person partakes in the happiness and celebration of the day. This mitzvah brings out the good in us and teaches the secret of joy through unity. Celebrations are happiest in the context of community.

The difference between these three *mitzvot* – drunkenness, *mishlo'ah manot*, and *matanot le-evyonim* – is best explained by an inverted pyramid.

With respect to the mitzvah of drunkenness, one is essentially alone, dissociated from the intensity of his ego, either longing for God, or wallowing in his fate.

In the mitzvah of *mishlo'ah manot*, we meet face to face and break down barriers. We experience an ambience of togetherness in happiness, abundance, and fellowship.

In the mitzvah of *matanot le-evyonim*, we strive toward social rehabilitation. There is a demand to narrow the gaps in Jewish society and for inclusion of each member of the community at a holiday feast.

People who are involved in spiritual worship, whether through Hasidism, Kabbalah, or Mussar (for those in the yeshiva world), naturally focus on the first aspect, drunkenness. Most of the inspirational homilies and the Torah that is taught and learned around Purim focuses on the inner world that one discloses and experiences by removing the outer layers and 'masks,' enabling the reveler to engage in true introspection. In *yeshivot*, the mitzvah of *mishlo'ah manot* is performed in a cursory manner, with the exchange of dishes in the dining hall. It is not an essential part of the day. In order to fulfill *matanot le-evyonim*, they view themselves as dependents and rely on their parents' fulfillment of the mitzvah.

People who live in a communal setting focus on the mitzvah of *mishlo'ah manot*. Even though the mitzvah requires only that one send two portions of food to one person, people take this mitzvah to an extreme, often spending much of the day distributing food baskets to friends and neighbors. This expresses the desire for a life that is pleasant and easy, quiet and relaxed. In such environments, drunkenness is considered socially deviant and repulsive.

The apex of this holiday though, as elucidated by Maimonides, is the fulfillment of *matanot le-evyonim*. This mitzvah expresses man's drive to assume responsibility, not just for his own internal world, but also for God's world, improving it to the best of his ability. This is almost diametrically opposed to the mindset of the drunken man, who seeks to mock the superior man who rules everything with his intellect.

An Additional Mitzvah – Reading Megilat Nehemiah

As a whole, the *mitzvot* mentioned function as a corrective, first within the individual, and expanding to encompass the broader community. Megilat Esther's tenth and final chapter concludes with Mordechai as the second in command to King Ahashverosh. This is the enduring image, the final frame frozen in time: Mordechai reaches the pinnacle of Jewish influence in the Persian Empire.

Yet even in this final verse, he is called "Mordechai the Jew." He remains an alien in this kingdom that is not his. He aspires to achieve as much as possible, a level that only a select few will ever reach: to be second only to the king. However, sovereignty and independence will never be his. He is, and will remain, an outsider, ultimately the subject of mockery. This story has been the story of the Jewish people for thousands of years.

The solution that the Megilah presents is not really much of a solution. The return to Zion, the establishment of an independent polity, and the attempt to construct the Third Temple require that we continue on to a "non-existent" eleventh chapter of the Megilah. In truth, that chapter indeed exists, though it appears at the beginning of the book of Nehemiah (chapters 1 and 2). These chapters are an important addition to the Megilah, and they pick up, both chronologically and spiritually, where the Megilah leaves off. Nehemiah approaches the king who has inherited the throne from Ahasheverosh and asks him for permission to build the ramparts of Jerusalem. This wave of *aliyah* to reinforce the Second Temple serves as the corrective of the story of Diaspora Jews who forgot their homeland and obscured their identity. If the story of the Megilah is the story of chance and "the lottery", then the story of Nehemiah is the transition from chance to destiny. Rebuilding Jerusalem and returning the Jewish people to their homeland remains the only viable solution for the nation that craves an eternal role.

Therefore, I suggest that after fulfilling the age-old Jewish custom of reading the Megilah on Purim at night and again in the morning, let us read the first two chapters of Nehemiah at the *minha* (afternoon prayer) service. We express thereby our yearning to be active participants in the vision and destiny of the return to Zion and the reestablishment of the Jewish kingdom of Israel.

Foreword

Every year since my Bar Mitzvah, I have read Megilat Esther on behalf of the congregation. The Megilah is close to my heart, engraved in my memory, and woven into the fiber of my being, my family's story, and my friends' stories.

I grew up in New York. To be more precise, I grew up in Manhattan – the Shushan of the United States. I was educated in New York's Orthodox day schools. Much of my family has lived in New York for generations. My family left Europe for the United States before the Holocaust: We were not refugees, but immigrants. Some of my extended family still lives in the United States, although, to our great joy, many family members have made *aliyah* to Israel. I am in touch with some of those who stayed behind. Other, more distant relatives have completely disappeared; they assimilated and vanished into the vast expanse of America.

This is the story of translucent people, those who are neither seen nor heard. The story of Diaspora Jewry is not just the history of Jewish persecution, the Inquisition, blood libels, pogroms, and the tide of rabid anti-Semitism that led to the destruction of six million Jews by the Nazis in the Holocaust. We commemorate these horrific events with prayers, memorial days, monuments, and museums. Those branches that have been cut off of the Jewish family tree still remain in our collective memory.

But there is another story as well: the story of seeds that were blown off the tree and sown in foreign fields, of a worldwide exile that is fading from Jewish history and from Jewish consciousness. Generations of Jews who have severed their connection with their identity, their heritage, their culture, their people, and their God. They have been pruned away and are gone forever. Their story unfolds between the lines. It remains untold because it is a rather unpleasant truth that is not "politically correct." We know today that more than fifty percent the world's Jews assimilate into their surroundings and are absorbed into their host cultures and nations. After a few generations, they are lost to the Jewish people forever.

* * *

Throughout the centuries, readers and interpreters of the Megilah have found a ray of hope in it – hope for the Jews' eventual triumph over enemies in foreign lands, who rise up to destroy them in every generation. Most Biblical exegetes and Talmudic Sages maintain that this is a story of exile that finds hope and comfort in the previous exile, which lasted seventy years: In each generation, they rise up to annihilate us, but the Almighty saves us from them.

These same readers also view the Megilah as a compelling drama, a tale about the weak rising up to vanquish the mighty. Such stories are so stirring because people naturally identify with the little guy, the underdog. Such stories provide hope for each of us because there is not a person in the world who has no weaknesses, no chinks in the armor, that they dream of overcoming.

The Megilah is also a Cinderella story: A kind-hearted orphan from the wrong religious background not only manages to become the queen of the empire but is also the heroine of the story. And if that were not enough, her cousin, who helps her conceal her nationality and religion, emerges triumphant in front of the king and his kingdom, clothed in regal garb. He manages to gain recognition for his heritage as an integral part of the ethnic mosaic of Persian culture, rises to greatness, and saves his people without sacrificing his loyalty and commitment to his nation and its legacy.

It is hard to imagine a story that would sound better to the ears of Diaspora Jews: the victory of good over evil, the triumph of Jewish wisdom over gentile malice, Jews using wisdom and beauty to overcome those who scheme against them, and the miraculous reversal of the decrees against them.

The vast majority of commentators lived lives quite similar to the lives of Mordechai and Esther, whether in Babylonia, Spain, Morocco, Poland, or elsewhere. In each generation, they faced a "Haman" bent on their destruction: Khmelnytsky and Petliura, the Hep-Hep riots and Kishinev pogroms, the Fez massacre of 1033, the uprisings in Spain in 1391, the May Laws, Kristallnacht, and the Farhud – all of these atrocities bleed into one another and merge into the figure of Haman.[1] Purim was the day of imagined liberation, the day when Jews could dare to hope and dream about a reversal of their current political situation, when they would be treated as equals among equals, or perhaps even gain primacy. Purim became a folk holiday, when the nation could dream, at least once each year, about "the very day on which the enemies of the Jews had expected to get them in their power, the opposite happened, and the Jews got their enemies in their power," or regrettably, the day on which the Jews would fully integrate into their new country.

Other commentators, and certainly the Sages who dated the events of the Megilah to the time period before the return to Zion and the edicts

1 During the long exile, there were many local "Purims" commemorating the salvation of the Jewish community from the latest Haman. For example, Purim Sebastiano was celebrated on 1 Elul and Purim of Rome was celebrated on 3 Iyar. In Frankfurt, the Jews celebrated "Purim Winz" to commemorate their salvation from the persecutions of Vincent Fettmilch; though the celebration was more elaborate in the past, the Frankfurt community does not recite *tahanun* on 20 Adar even nowadays. For more examples and a discussion see chapter 10 of: Elliot S. Horowitz, *Reckless Rites: Purim and the Legacy of Jewish Violence*, (Princeton University Press: 2006).

of Cyrus and Darius, view the events of the Megilah as the first steps in the process of redemption from the Babylonian exile. The Sages saw each of the Megilah's motifs – from "beakers of varied design" to "blue wool, caught up by cords of fine linen and purple wool" – as a veiled reference to the destroyed Temple that would soon be rebuilt through the inspiration of Mordechai and the descendants of Esther. They told the story of the Megilah and interpreted it with numerous references to the Temple's vessels and other Temple-centered elements. They also identified Mordechai as a member of the Sanhedrin, the seat of Jewish justice in Jerusalem, thereby "enabling" him to live both in Eretz Yisrael and Persia.

* * *

The real story of the Megilah, though, is quite different and far more complex. Megilat Esther is the story of the first Jewish exile after the rise and fall of the first Jewish kingdom. This complicated narrative has been with us for 2,500 years. In Spain after the Reconquista, when the victorious Castilians decreed that Jews must either convert to Christianity or be expelled, many chose exile, and many attempted to live as crypto-Jews, but a great many stayed in Spain and assimilated. Through the years, there were those who fell victim to pogroms and massacres, but there were many more who chose to become new citizens in their country of refuge – they literally or figuratively shaved off their beards, removed their head coverings, and adopted the customs of the land.

Spain's crypto-Jews, the *anusim* or Marranos, were persecuted by Grand Inquisitor Tomás de Torquemada, a descendant of a Jewish family of *conversos* – those who had willingly chosen to convert from Judaism to Catholicism. There were many others like him, and so the *anusim* of Iberia have all but disappeared, aside from a few ancient vestiges of Jewish identity that are discovered from time to time in far-flung communities. These apostates were not wiped out in an act of mass murder, but rather through assimilation: some willingly, others through persecution, and still others because they were simply overwhelmed by the local culture.

Many contemporary Europeans can tell of a grandparent or great-grandparent whose Jewish identity was disclosed only on their deathbed. In countless other cases, these people took their secret to the grave, without anyone ever discovering their Jewish identity. Assimilation could be the result of a weakened Jewish identity, of apathy, or of the strengthening of a different national identity.

At the epicenter of the story of Megilat Esther are these two existential threats against Diaspora Jewry. One is spoken aloud in pronouncements and royal edicts. The other is covert, taking place in bedrooms, in the king's court, and along trade routes.

In today's world, identity is **the** issue. It is of paramount importance. Globalization, urbanization, and freedom of movement, destabilize prior identities. The world changes rapidly. Questions of belonging and affiliation have become the most important challenges of this generation – not only for Jewish people, but for the whole world.

Identity is a contemporary issue, but it is also an ethical issue: How does one who grew up in cosmopolitan Manhattan, or in Paris, London, or Sao Paulo, cope with the overwhelming diversity of cultures that inundate him and beckon him with their charms, values, and contributions? These values, which we often call liberal Western values, are both objectively valuable and important in the Western world, of which most contemporary Jews, in Israel and the Diaspora, are a part.

The Persian Empire's age of globalization began with the rise of Cyrus, the grandfather of Ahashverosh of Megilat Esther. Like other kingdoms that became empires, the Persian Empire in its heyday abandoned the approach of ethnic exclusivity in favor of a broader, more inclusive approach. At times, they still asserted the superiority of the ruling tribe over other tribes as well as between ruler and subject. However, Cyrus and his successors fundamentally acknowledged that all citizens of the empire are entitled to their own rights, their own territory, and the chance to secure their place under the sovereign king.[2]

This was the global Persia – the mightiest empire of the ancient world – where Mordechai grew up: two generations after Cyrus's foundational vision of globalization, several decades after multiculturalism had begun to trickle down to the empire's streets, and just a few years after a sparse group of his fellow Jews had returned to Eretz Yisrael to re-establish Judaism and Jewish culture where they could flourish.

The world's greatest superpower and biggest economy invites boundless attractive opportunities. As a child growing up in Manhattan, I dreamed of becoming a U.S. Senator. I even spent a summer volunteering on Capitol Hill. I wanted to be part of the governing body of the empire, to bring my Judaism and my contributions to America's magnificent mosaic. I loved and still love America, and I am grateful for the warm embrace that it afforded my family when they immigrated. In the land of limitless opportunity, a Jew can be anything and do anything.

When I was a college student in the United States, I worked as a volunteer with special needs children in different Jewish communities across America. It was then that I was first exposed to the challenge of Jewish identity in the United States, of maintaining Judaism in a foreign land. The Shabbat experiences that I had in these various communities were like a mirror, reflecting my future back at me. Or perhaps they were like a telescope, allowing me to peer into the future of American Jewry. This is me. This is my upbringing and that of my extended family and my peers. So right after college, I got married and moved to Israel. My wife and I did not want to wait around for that future to become a reality.

Over the past two decades, my daily life has revolved around the worlds

---

2 In *Sapiens: A Brief History of Humankind*, Yuval Noah Harari claims that the Persians were the first to adopt this globalist approach on the large scale. Later on, the Hellenist Greeks also adopted this approach.

of economics and finance, of the advent of the internet, and of innovative technologies that are changing the world and humanity. I am an investor in startup companies as a partner in a venture capital fund that identifies and leverages the profound technological and economic changes of the past two decades and the coming decades, in an effort to gaze at the distant horizon and predict future trends, opportunities, changes, developments – and risks.

I came to realize that money and finance, as averred by the song in the musical "Cabaret," make the world go round. The Holocaust, the greatest calamity that befell the Jews in history, was born from a deep economic depression. The same is true in other instances as well. Behind just about every historic upheaval is an economic story: control of natural resources, slave markets, trade routes, taxes, technologies, economic opportunity, unemployment, underemployment and financial crises. Economic relationships were always the strongest and most important relationships between individuals, states, and peoples. Financial envy rises among the have-nots, fueling and fanning the flames of enmity.

My wife claims that I am predisposed to seeing the world through an economic lens. Perhaps. I try to identify the economic story that lies behind every historical and moral narrative. It is uncommon for anyone to examine traditional and religious texts from an economic perspective, certainly not someone who grew up in a religious home and leads a traditionally observant lifestyle. Yet one who studies Tanakh and *halakha* (Jewish law) closely can see the important role that money and finance play as a basis for discourse and a source of changes that have shaped the Jewish people, its halakhic observance, Scriptural exegesis, and ideology.

In the book of Devarim (17:14-20), our teacher Moshe describes the influence of money, gold, and horses on future kings of Israel. He cautions against the dangers of material wealth: "lest you eat and be satisfied, build luxurious homes and dwell in them" which may lead to an unfortunate outcome: "then your heart will become boastful and you will forget your

God...and you will say in your heart 'my power and the might of my hand has achieved this material wealth'" (Devarim 8:10-14). This, too, is the story of Megilat Esther, perhaps even its central plot.

This economic angle is not just my personal reading of the Megilah; it can be considered the perspective of the author of the Megilah. One who reads the Megilah must address a major question that he encounters in the very first verses: What is the function of the first chapter of the Megilah and its detailed description of the ostentation of the king's palace in Shushan and the jovial, lavish party held there?

The same question can be raised with regard to the Megilah's conclusion as well: What is the meaning of chapter 10, the shortest chapter with only three verses, which discusses the "tribute on the mainland and the islands" that Ahashverosh imposed and "the full account of the greatness to which the king advanced Mordechai"?

At first glance, these two chapters seem irrelevant to the Megilah's plot. Had they been left out, Esther would still become queen, Haman would still threaten to annihilate the Jews, Esther and Mordechai would still fast, the king would still have a restless night, and the Jews would still emerge victorious. Nothing that happens in these two chapters impacts the story's main plot developments.[3]

The Megilah's author, however, chose to bookend the story with these two chapters. The opening chapter provides context for the events that will unfold in the story, and the final chapter summarizes the principal message that the Megilah seeks to impart to the reader. Therefore, any serious attempt to arrive at the main theme of the story must first address the presence of these two chapters, analyze their content, and understand

3 The Galilean Sages who lived under Roman hegemony in the period following the Bar Kokhba revolt contend with the question of where one begins reading the Megilah: "From where should one read the Megilah in order to fulfill his obligation? R. Meir says, in its entirety; R. Yehuda says, from 'A Jewish man' (2:5); R. Yosi says, from 'Sometime afterward' (2:1; 3:1)" (M. Megilah 2:3).

the message that the author is using them to convey. The lavishness, the abundance, "white cotton and blue wool, caught up by cords of fine linen and purple wool" and the taxes are an integral part of the Megilah's narrative and the story of Mordechai and Esther. They are not part of the scenery, but part of the plot itself.

Midrash Abba Gurion on Megilat Esther (Section 1) discusses this time period in Persia:

> There were fruit trees, and fragrant bushes, trimmed in the shape of domes, half the height of the trees. The floor tiles were precious stones and pearls, and shaded by the trees. There were curtains of linen and purple wool and rings of silver secured with cords of linen. Purple wool would be spread beneath the feet of the attendants, and they would dance before those dining on couches.

This picture of abundant, Hollywood-like wealth described both in the Midrash and in the Megilah itself is ostentatious and excessive. King Ahashverosh displays the palace's finest before the people who have gathered for the party. He has rolled out the red carpet, silver ornaments adorn the pillars, and the overall ambience is dreamlike. This description is not incidental: It emphasizes the primary theme of the Megilah – and the story of Shushan's Jews.

* * *

Economics is not only about gambles and risk taking, fortune and misfortune; it is also about opportunity. When I was a yeshiva student in 1989, I was fortunate to be studying at Yeshiva Har Etzion. At the end of the First Gulf War, I sat in the yeshiva's auditorium with a handful of other students for a question and answer session with R. Yehuda Amital, the yeshiva's founder and head. I asked R. Amital whether moving to an underpopulated, peripheral region of Israel is a greater fulfillment of the mitzvah of settling Eretz Yisrael than moving to the population centers of Tel Aviv or Jerusalem. R. Amital stared and me and, in his typical manner and tone of voice, answered: "That is nonsense. Move to Eretz Yisrael and set up a business that will provide 10,000 people with a **decent and honest living**. That is the greatest mitzvah." Until that point in time, I had not seriously considered moving to Israel. At that exact moment, I decided that I would make *aliya*.

R. Amital's 'economic' answer, delivered in his distinctive approach, astonished me and continued to redound in my mind. The rabbi is right, I thought to myself. If we want to establish a state and attract people to settle here, we need opportunity, jobs, and mutual respect. In a well-functioning state that aspires to be a light unto the nations, livelihood is important, as are respect for others and for employees. [4]

Economics makes the world – including this particular nation – go round. If economic opportunity can only be found in Shushan, Jews will not move to Eretz Yisrael. The best minds and the most efficient and skilled workers will stay in New York or Paris, or take their skills and talents there. A strong, stable, growing respectful economy is a prerequisite for the successful development of the State of Israel and the Jewish future. The rapid and welcome pace of change in the world, the abundance, and the lowering of the cost of basic products in the last few generations, are all spurred by financial, economic, and technological development. A strong economy built on respect, technological innovation, and progress is vital for sustaining Jewish identity and for Israel's ability to exert influence on Diaspora Jewry and on the entire world. They are also indispensable in establishing a just and viable Israeli society. R. Amital's message was clear: Behind every significant historical change is an economic element.

4 During 2016, Israel's GDP per capital surpassed the GDP per capita of France. Israel's economy grew an average of 4% from the year 2000 to 2014.

R. Amital did not articulate the idea of the start-up nation,[5] but he identified its core idea.

* * *

My reading and interpretation of the Megilah pays close attention to the text, the style of its author, and the story's manifold characters. Sometimes these are main characters, and sometimes they are secondary characters who serve to direct the reader's attention to the real story that the author wishes to tell. Megilat Esther is filled with literary allusions, often invoking or winking at other texts and Biblical characters. This is one reason that so many different commentaries have been written on the Megilah through the years, and especially for the renewed interest in the book within the last two decades.

We can easily understand why commentators have taken such great interest in the Megilah. In terms of its straightforward meaning, it is a captivating story. On a deeper interpretive plane, intricate webs of meaning are evidence of the work of a literary virtuoso. On an intertextual level, the Megilah is full of allusions and references to other biblical characters and texts, from Yosef to Esav, and from Avshalom to Ezra. Each allusion presents another exegetical challenge.

The question of the Megilah's authorship presents an additional challenge to the would-be exegete. The author is anonymous, making it difficult to ascertain who he was and when he composed the Megilah. My approach assumes that the Megilah was written by a Jew living in Jerusalem, a rough contemporary of Ezra and Nehemiah.[6] One might even

---

5 "Start Up Nation" is a term coined by Dan Senor and Saul Singer who authored a book by the same name, which describes Israel's growth as one of the world's most vibrant high tech economies.

6 There is no question that exegesis, consciously or unconsciously, is informed by the exegete's experience. For example, Aaron Koller maintains that the Megilah's author lived in Persia and is enthused by the exile and the new forms of Judaism

be so bold as to suggest that the author is Nehemiah himself, or one of his close associates, considering the author's deep familiarity with the king's palace and royal protocol. This is information that Nehemiah was privy to, given his role as the royal attendant of King Artaxerxes I, the son of Xerxes I, who is identified with Ahashverosh of the Megilah.

My commentary draws inspiration from the traditional exegetes of the Megilah, such as Rashi, Ibn Ezra, and various *midrashim* authored by the Sages. I also incorporate modern commentators, such as R. Yitzhak Reggio, R. Dr. Benny Lau, Dr. Yonatan Grossman, R. Menachem Leibtag, and Dr. Aaron Koller.

* * *

The Megilah's economic axis swings from a thriving, growing economy at the beginning of the story – an economy that generates opportunities for the Jews – to an economy in a state of recession, which threatens the Jewish exiles in Shushan, and back and forth again, ad infinitum. I read the Megilah's words through my personal experiences. I feel that these events are strikingly familiar to me: the characters, the powerful temptations that Diaspora Jewry must face, the tension between the Jews in exile and the Jewish community in Eretz Yisrael, the results of that tension, and the opportunities that it presents. The people of the Megilah are me. The people of the Megilah are my family and friends.

This new commentary to Megilat Esther has been gnawing at me for many years. The financial crisis of 2008 intensified the impetus for me

---

that can develop there. Koller himself lives in the Diaspora, and it seems to me that this affects his commentary, just as my commentary is impacted by experience of moving to Israel and witnessing the renaissance of Jewish national life here. To take another example, Yoram Hazony, who interprets the Megilah in his book *The Dawn*, reads it as the story of a new mode of Jewish political conduct in a post-prophetic age. Hazony himself is a professor of political science and political philosophy. See also the discussion of chapter 9 of the Megilah, p. 138 ff.

to sit down with myself, work things out, sharpen my ideas, and begin to think of publishing this innovative approach to the Megilah. The "seven good years" that the stock exchange has had since then have also spurred me on: Beneath the encouraging, beckoning, but ultimately deceptive surface, economic problems continue to ferment and bubble up, just like in the Megilah.

* * *

My interpretation of the Megilah relates to it as a distillation of the story of the Jewish people for the past 2,500 years. More precisely, it is a recurring story that repeats itself every few hundred years. The difference between the previous cycles and the one playing out today is that the relationship between Israel and the major Diaspora communities today bears an uncanny resemblance to the relationship between Eretz Yisrael and the Diaspora in the times of Ezra, Nehemiah, Esther, and Mordechai.

Diaspora Jewry, led by Mordechai, was comprised of those who had been the commercial and professional elite of Judah and Eretz Yisrael. They were the upper crust of society, descendants of those who were exiled from Eretz Yisrael eleven years before the destruction of the First Temple. This elite is described in the Books of Yirmiyahu (chapter 24) and 2 Melakhim (chapter 24) as having been the officers and skilled artisans of Judah – the social and professional elite. They were not exiled violently and they were not refugees: They were immigrants. They were later joined by refugees from the destruction of the Temple and the horrific bloody rampage that accompanied it against the Jews of Eretz Yisrael. The elite, those with skills and status, sought a way to integrate into the Persian Empire, its economy, and its institutions. The greatest opportunities can be found in the biggest and most powerful countries. Ahashverosh's Persia was similar to the United States in the time of Roosevelt, Truman, Nixon, Reagan, Clinton, Bush and Obama. And the Jews managed to obtain government appointments and positions of economic importance.

After some time, their impoverished brothers returned to Zion to drain the swamps and rebuild the destroyed Temple. They were joined by a group of exiles who returned to Eretz Yisrael out of ideological commitment. Together, they rebuilt the walls of Jerusalem and restored God's Temple. Others began to establish settlements to defend their homeland. A great deal of tension – economic, philosophical, and religious – developed between the impoverished Jews of Eretz Yisrael and the Jewish elite living securely in Persia. This tension finds expression in the Megilah's pages, where neither God nor Eretz Yisrael is named, suggesting that they are missing from the mindset of Persia's Jews as well. It is also evident from the lack of consent about the canonicity of Megilat Esther and from the hesitation of the Men of the Great Assembly to officially establish the holiday of Purim, even though the Megilah contains an explicit and precise directive to do so.

In spite of all this, later Sages require us to transcribe the Megilah on parchment and with etched lines – just as a Torah scroll is written. According to one of the Sages of the Talmud, other than the five books of the Torah itself, Megilat Esther is the only Scriptural work that will endure forever, even after all the other books of Tanakh are rendered null.[7] The reason for this anomaly is that the Megilah serves as a guide through which we might decipher a certain principle. Therefore, seemingly, the Megilah is as important to the future of Judaism as the Torah itself.

The expression of this principle is not found in the frivolity of Purim; this is merely its external manifestation. Like a Purim mask, the celebration

7 "R. Yohanan said: 'The Prophets and the Writings will be nullified, but the five books of the Torah will not be nullified.' R. Shimon b. Lakish said: 'Also Megilat Esther and the *halakhot* will not be nullified'" (YT *Megilah* 1:5). In Rambam's words: "All of the books of the Prophets and the Writings will be nullified in the messianic era, aside from Megilat Esther. It will forever endure, like the five books of the Torah and the *halakhot* of the Oral Torah, which will never be nullified" (*Mishneh Torah*, Laws of Megilah 2:18).

hides the real principles. R. Meir Simha of Dvinsk articulated this hidden principle in words he wrote before the Holocaust, and which took on a terrible significance in its aftermath:

> From the moment that Israel lived among the nations...this has been the pattern of Divine providence: They will have a period of respite for a number of years, a century or two, and then storm winds will come and wave upon wave will lash out, destroying, wrecking, and overwhelming mercilessly until the lone, scattered remnants flee to a distant place where they regroup, become a nation once more, cultivate Torah centers, and achieve great things using their minds and intellectual resources. But then they forget that they are strangers in a foreign land. They begin to think that is their place of origin, and they stop anticipating the spiritual redemption that God will bring at the appointed time. Then an even harsher storm wind will be visited upon them, reminding them with a deafening roar: You are a Jew! Who made you important? Go forth to an unknown land. This is how Jewish existence among the nations of the world will remain in flux, as the discerning eye will notice in history books...[8]

The author of the Megilah uses a seemingly cheerful and amusing story to tell about the dangers of assimilation in exile and the factors that drive this process. Assimilation begins with a sense of comfort in the host country. Next comes the desire to be accepted and successful in the new society. These steps are natural and shared by all human beings. The next stage of assimilation is the detachment of life from God and His value system. Timeless Jewish values and beliefs are what binds Jews to other Jews and to God. When God's hand is absent, like in the pages of the

---

8 *Meshekh Hokhma* to Vayikra 26:44.

Megila, and when Jewish values are beset by foreign cultures and norms, the sense of Jewish fraternity deteriorates, and the yearning to return to the land of their fathers fades away.

Diaspora Jews have always enjoyed success. They forged close ties with local rulers, built institutions of Torah and Jewish culture, and succeeded in their business endeavors. In the end, though, they remained small in number. Some were killed and some apostatized, but most simply vanished after a few generations, swallowed up by the host nation.

The Megilah's author wrote with a close eye on the other books of Tanakh. He draws on the wisdom of Tanakh and derives from it a sense of foreboding about the bitter end of Jews in exile. He does so from his perch in Jerusalem, without embarrassing Diaspora Jewry explicitly, but with the clear awareness that the clock is ticking for them.

He writes with a sharp pen and subtle cynicism, with allusions that would primarily be understood by the educated Jews who returned to Eretz Yisrael or who remained in exile.[9] The message that he seeks to impart is that Jews must return to their land and recognize the mighty hand of God that directs history. The return of the poor and feeble Jews to Eretz Yisrael was not incidental. Rather, it demonstrated the guiding hand of the God of Israel. Those who noticed returned to Zion, and God was with them. Those who did not discern the hand of God continued with business as usual, building places of worship and Torah institutions, cultivating political connections, successfully avoiding existential threats, and continuing down the path to assimilation and extinction.

The Jewish people have known ups and downs on foreign soil. In its ten chapters, Megilat Esther sets out this entire history: the decades, or perhaps centuries, of the Babylonian and Persian exile, the centuries of

9 It is important to remember that the author did not write the Megilah to be printed or widely disseminated. Presumably, its first readers were educated colleagues and associates who read the autograph manuscript.

the Roman exile, the centuries of the Iberian exile, the centuries of exile in Eastern Europe, and the centuries of the American exile. It opens with a depiction of Jewish assimilation in the third or fourth generation of the Babylonian/Persian Exile. The middle chapters (chapters 3-7) serve as a reminder that it is very hard to disguise Jewish identity over the long term; enemies will always discover it and plot against us. The seventh and eighth chapters remind us of the long arm of God, which intervenes to save the Jewish people. Since the Jews living in exile did not recognize God, they eventually reach their "destiny": The Jews disappear into the fabric of the Persian Empire. Esther's own son eventually succeeded Ahasuerus as emperor. The son of a Jewish mother was the most powerful man in the world, but he had no Jewish identity whatsoever, and history remembers him as a Persian, not a Jew.

To use a contemporary example: In the three centuries of Jewish life in America, very few have fallen victim to violent anti-Semitism. Conversely, millions of Jews have completely assimilated. They are Americans and have lost their Jewish identity entirely. This is what happened to Europe's Jews. Many people like to tell about the charms of "shtetl" life that vanished with the Holocaust. They wax romantic about the Jews, Jewishness, and pervasiveness of Torah of that time. In actuality though, many residents of *shtetlach* dissolved into European and American society long before the Holocaust. The challenge here is existential – even if it is not immediate.

* * *

Every year, I read the Megilah and try to pretend that it is a happy and uplifting story. For years I tried to believe that it is a story of redemption – the salvation of the Jews from calamity – or a story of the return to Zion, as the Sages viewed it.

My heart was telling me something else, though: that Megilat Esther is not a comedy, but a tragedy. It is a tragedy that has repeated itself time and again, in different places throughout history. On the surface, it is a happy story, but beneath the veneer is a story of disconnection, apathy, and loss of identity. People become estranged from Jewish culture, from the Master of the universe, from monotheism, from His nation, and from His land. They disassociate from the Jewish people and its values and develop a national or economic identity that supersedes their moral identity. For me, the Megilah is a story of assimilation and missed opportunity.

When I read the Megilah, wrapped in a *talit*, I can hear R. Meir Simha of Dvinsk in the background, warning the Jews of Berlin that they must not feel so at home in Germany. Berlin is not Jerusalem. Shushan is not Jerusalem. Brooklyn is not Jerusalem. I am wearing a *tallit*, but inside I feel like I am wearing sackcloth, mourning the thousands of Jews throughout history who have vanished in a sea of assimilation. On Purim I think of the hundreds of students who stream into the country with Birthright Israel, to study in *yeshivot* or volunteer on *kibbutzim* here; I fear for their futures, and so I pray that even if they decide to return to the United States, France, Brazil or Argentina, their children will remain Jews. I chant the Megilah in an uplifting melody, but my heart is deep in prayer.

I feel the pain of the Vilna Gaon, who wanted to move to Eretz Yisrael, imagining what he must have felt when he read about Mordechai, who could have joined his nation in Jerusalem, but chose to stay put. I feel the pain of those European Jews who realized too late that Eretz Yisrael is a very, very good land. I lose sleep due to pain and concern for the Jewish world.

Each year, when I read the Megilah, I cannot escape the feeling that it is a story of flagging faith, of lost opportunity, whose end is bitter and confusing. The story itself is in costume, disguising the dread that lies at its center. Its veneer of drunkenness masks its melancholy. In the words attributed to the American writer Mark Twain: "History may not repeat itself, but it does rhyme."

Acknowledgements

I am so grateful to the many people who have helped me in writing this book. First and foremost, my parents, Rabbi Barry and Debra Eisenberg, who raised me and my siblings to be Zionists, to feel responsible for the Jewish people, and to live a life of loyalty and devotion to the timeless Jewish tradition and law. My parents encouraged me to learn to read the Megilah after I became Bar Mitzvah. Without their push, I never would have come to know it as well as I do.

My Megilah teacher, R. Joseph Wermuth z"l, was the devoted Ritual Director and Torah reader at the Jewish Center on the Upper West Side of Manhattan for half a century. He taught countless Bar Mitzvah boys, myself included. Each year when I read the Megilah, I recall his comments about the special tunes that are used for specific verses. In many senses, my reading is his reading.

I am also indebted to my aunt and uncle, Aviva and Marvin Sussman, and to their brother-in-law, R. Dr. Moshe Sokolow, who allowed me to read the Megilah for the very first time in their home, a mere ten months after my Bar Mitzvah; and to my grandparents, Opa Charlie z"l and Oma Els Bendheim, who bought me my first parchment Megilah, which I still read from each year.

I am also thankful to Ori Radler, the editor of the Hebrew edition of this book, who took a raw and disorganized text (written in the Hebrew of an American immigrant!) and transformed it into a book and a story.

With the skill of an expert craftsman, Ori managed to turn a dry text into a vibrant narrative, adding a great deal of depth and gravitas along the way.

This English translation would not have been possible without the excellent work of my translator Rena Siev. I tried a few translators before finding someone who had both the textual understanding and translation skill to bring this together. Rabbi Elli Fischer served as editor and supervisor of the English translation and added both his encyclopedic knowledge of history and Tanakh, as well as his keen wit to the work before you. Candidly, I am sorry I did not let him review the Hebrew manuscript. I am indebted to both of them as well as my cousins JJ Sussman who suggested that Elli would be a good choice for the project.

I would also like to thank my publisher, Rotem Sella, and the person who introduced us, Erez Eshel, the founder of the Ein Prat Israel Academy for Leadership. I am also grateful to the many people who reviewed drafts of the book and made helpful comments, including Josh Rosenzweig and Aviad Friedman.

R. Benny Lau, who is mentioned often in this book and wrote its introduction, devoted a lot of time to this project. Despite the fact that he is so busy, he read multiple drafts and made many constructive and correct comments. R. Lau caused me to reconsider how this book should be written and also generously allowed me to quote extensively from his article on Megilat Esther – an important essay that I had not been familiar with when I wrote the first draft of this book. His patience for a novice author like me is admirable.

Our children and their spouses – Tamar, Yosef, Sonny, Chaim, Sarah, Yehuda, Moshe, Batsheva, and Nili – allowed me to spend my mornings writing, whether at home or in the *beit midrash* at the Shtiblach of Katamon. I am grateful to them, and they are my inspiration for this book. In between the publication of the Hebrew and English version of this book, God blessed us with the birth of our first granddaughter, Anaelle. In a book about generations of Jewish identity, I would be remiss if I did not acknowledge her and the fact that she is the second generation born to our family in Israel. The roots are growing deeper.

Last but not least – what is mine and yours, is really hers. From the bottom of my heart, I thank my wife, Yaffa. She heroically tolerated my locking myself into a room in order to complete this book, as well as all the time that I try to devote to Torah study. She supported my efforts to publish this book, read multiple drafts, and made many important comments about its content and approach. She is the one who introduced me to the quote from R. Meir Simha of Dvinsk that appears above, a quote that spurred her decision, at the age of fifteen, to move to Israel one day. Each year, she tells our children that this passage from R. Meir Simha is the reason that we moved to Israel, before they were born. My dear wife and life partner, we have an agreement not to speak about or compliment one another in public. It must therefore suffice to quote the words of the wisest of all men:

> Live joyfully with the wife that that you love all the days of the life of vanity, which He has given you under the sun, all the days of your vanity. For that is your portion in life and in your work that you labor under the sun. (Kohelet 9:9)

To this I will add the words of Mishlei (18:22):

> He who finds a wife, finds good, and obtains favor of God.

I have found that which is exceedingly good.

Timeline: From the Conquest of Judah to the End of the Persian Era

All dates are before the common era (BCE)

597	Nebuchadnezzar conquers Jerusalem and exiles Yekhoniah; Judahite elites begin to lay the foundation of the Babylonian Jewish community
586	Destruction of the First Temple and the Kingdom of Judah; mass deportations to Babylonia
539	King Cyrus of Persia conquers Babylonia
538	The Edict of Cyrus permits the Jews to return to Jersualem and rebuild the Temple
538-522	The first wave of return to Zion under Zerubavel and Sheshbazzar
522-486	Reign of Darius I
520-515	Haggai and Zekhariah encourage the completion of the Second Temple; Temple begins to function
486-465	Reign of Xerxes I (Ahashverosh)
483	The first banquets and preparation for the campaign against Greece
479	Esther becomes queen
474	Haman promoted, plots against the Jews, and is defeated
465-424	Reigns of Artaxerxes I
c. 458	Ezra's arrival in Jerusalem
445-433	Nehemiah governor of Judah
332	Alexander of Macedon conquers the Judah, ending the Persian Era

Historical Background: From the Lower Classes to the Fleshpots

The events of Megilat Esther transpire at some point during a span of seventy years, between the first wave of *aliyah* in the wake of the Edict of Cyrus and the second wave during the reign of Artahshasta, or Artaxerses I.

The exile of King Yekhoniah and the collapse of Judahite power under Babylonian pressure brought its religious leaders, nobility, warrior class, and skilled craftsmen to Babylonia. Barely a decade later, in 586 BCE,[1] the Temple was destroyed, and Jews of lower social standing were exiled to Babylonia in its wake. Only the most impoverished classes remained in Eretz Yisrael.

About half a century later, with the Edict of Cyrus, Jews were permitted to return to Jerusalem and Judah. But sixty years of exile had transformed the Jews. R. Benny Lau offers a homiletic description of the religious situation that prevailed at that time. Among the Jews of the Babylonian exile, he explains, a dominant faction had emerged:

---

1 As is well known, there is a disparity of c. 165 years between the *Seder Olam* chronology and the accepted historical chronology. We will use the historical chronology, which, as we will see, actually fits better with the plain meaning of Tanakh,

> This group of Jews saw themselves in the land of new opportunities, a "*Goldene Medina.*" The exile of "the locksmith and the artisan," leading financiers and entrepreneurs, and the political leadership (including the royal family) had brought to Babylonia the best and the brightest of Jewish society. Their integration into the Babylonian Empire was swift. They sought new avenues for income, commerce, and wealth.[2]

These Jews, R. Lau suggests, are the same ones that the prophet Yehezkel denigrates for saying, "We will be like the nations, like the families of the lands, worshiping wood and stone" (Yehezkel 20:32):

> This is an assimilationist Jewry, which seeks to escape the antiquated identity that has followed it over from the old country and longs to establish a new identity, as immigrants capable of integrating throughout the East. Unlike Daniel and his peers, these immigrants represent complete assimilation: They change their names and mode of dress. They adapt and assimilate.

> The first generation is the lost generation. They struggle with the language, learn to survive, and dream big dreams for their children. They quietly forge new connections as they wax nostalgic. The second generation renounces their parents, hides their foreign accents, fights for status, and erases their past. The third generation has integrated. They feel at home.... The fourth generation does not even know its origins....

Whether R. Lau is accurately describing the Babylonian exile or a

---

2 R. Benny Lau, *Esther, a Historical Sermon for Purim* (Hebrew).

more contemporary exile, the fact remains that only about 50,000 Jews returned to Eretz Yisrael during the first wave of *aliyah* under King Yekhoniah's grandson Zerubavel b. Shealtiel and the High Priest Yehoshua b. Yehotzadak. Moreover, very few of the returnees belonged to the upper classes, the former Judahite nobility. These were the people who rebuilt the Temple and re-established Eretz Yisrael as a spiritual center. The second *aliyah*, under the leadership of Ezra and Nehemiah, commenced more than sixty years later. This was also era of the "*Anshei Knesset Ha-gedolah*," the Men of the Great Assembly, and during this period, the foundations of Jerusalem and the settlements of Judah were greatly reinforced.

This first *aliyah* was an *aliyah* of the spirit, not of material wealth. It restored the Temple worship, but most Jews preferred the fleshpots. As the rabbi tells the king of the Khazars in R. Yehuda Halevi's *Kuzari*: "If only they would have returned willingly to the land from the start; alas, very few actually returned. Most of them, including their leaders, remained in Babylonia, preferring exile and their professional lives, not wanting to abandon their homes and interests." This is a very familiar picture. As R. Lau writes: Diaspora Jews are established and at home. They love and support the idea of rebuilding Eretz Yisrael, but not right now. It's inconvenient. Maybe when the kids get older and finish college."

We know very little about the Megilah's author or date of authorship. It could have been written fifty, a hundred, or even two hundred years after the events it describes. Ibn Ezra writes, in his commentary to Esther (7:1), that it was written by Mordechai himself. According to Dr. Aaron Koller, the author – who he calls Marduka – was a Persian Jew, and the Megilah was written to convey a sympathetic, supportive message to Diaspora Jews.[3] According to the Babylonian Talmud, the Megilah was authored

---

3 In his book *Esther in Ancient Jewish Thought,* p. 37 n. 8, Koller mentions this point and also notes the opinion of other scholars that the language of Megilat Esther

by the Men of the Great Assembly, a body convened by Ezra or one of his successors in Eretz Yisrael.[4]

It is clear to me that the Megilah's author was deeply familiar with the protocols and terminology of the Persian government but was not a resident of Shushan. He was, rather, a Jew living in Jerusalem and watching its gradual restoration and reconstruction, with the Second Temple at its center. His perspective of the Jews who struck roots in Shushan is intentionally comparative and contradistinctive. It was written decades after the events that it describes – perhaps even by or on behalf of Nehemiah[5] – and it faithfully expresses the attitude of the Jews of Eretz Yisrael toward the Jews of Persia at a specific point in time and under particular circumstances. This attitude, as we will see in the Megilah, was not one of great love and admiration for these Jews.

---

is Late Biblical Hebrew, which bears much similarity to Mishnaic Hebrew. This might place the author in Eretz Yisrael during the Second Temple era.

4 *Bava Batra* 15a.

5 See Rozenson, *Hadassah Hi Esther* p. 225.

It Happened in the Days of Ahashverosh

> It happened in the days of Ahashverosh – that Ahashverosh who reigned over a hundred and twenty-seven provinces from India to Ethiopia. In those days, when King Ahashverosh occupied the royal throne in Shushan the capital... (1:1-2)

"**It happened in the days of...**" These words do not merely introduce the historical setting; they establish a link and allude to parallel passages in Tanakh. The same formula introduces several important Biblical narratives, the most prominent of which are the story of Lot's capture and the book of Ruth – two stories with a significant common denominator.

"**It happened in the days of** King Amraphel of Shinar" (Bereshit 14:1). The story of this war, which involved kingdoms from across the Ancient Near East and is intrinsically connected to the story of the patriarch Avraham and his nephew Lot, is essentially an economic story. For more than a decade, five kings and their subjects labored on the projects and enterprises of King Kedarlaomer of Elam, a Mesopotamian imperialist.[1] At some point, they became disgusted with him and the tributes he imposed on them. But this is not the full story. It is only the political and economic

1 It is suggestive that the city of Shushan itself was originally the capital of Elam before becoming one of the capitals of the Persian Empire. Even today, the corresponding Iranian province of Ilam is alternatively known as Susiana.

background of the story: The city-states of Sodom and Amorah, which were apparently quite prosperous, were defeated by Kedarlaomer and his allies.

Lot, who had left his uncle Avraham's tutelage to find his fortune among the affluent residents of Sodom and Amorah, was captured when the city was sacked. Avraham and his militia attacked the victorious armies and rescued Lot and the other Sodomite captives.

The end of the story attests to its origins: King Bera of Sodom offers Avraham his share of the spoils. Return the captured soldiers to me, Bera says to Avraham, "and keep the property for yourself." But Avraham refuses to take even a shoelace from the spoils, lest the king of Sodom proclaim, "I enriched Avraham." Though the *casus belli* was economic, and despite the affinity of Lot and king of Sodom for money, Avraham sought only to save Lot and his soul.

"**It happened in the days of**..." is a recurring motif in stories that begin with a financial decision, a choice of money over morality, a choice to bind one's fate with unethical people in order to secure a comfortable life.

Megilat Ruth likewise opens: "**It happened in the days of** the judges' rule that there was a famine in the land, and a man from Bethlehem in Judah went to live in the plains of Moab." Like Lot, Elimelech, a leader in his hometown of Bethlehem, fled from the land and people of Israel for his own financial benefit, choosing wealth over sharing the distress of his people.

The same phrase appears at the beginning of the story of Yehoyakim: "**It happened in the days of** King Yehoyakim, son of Yoshiyahu, of Judah." Then, early in the career of Yirmiyahu the prophet, he appears before the king and says: "You have eyes and a heart only for your dishonest gain, for shedding innocent blood, for oppression, and for practicing violence" (Yirmiyahu 22:17). You, King Yehoyakim, choose profit over morality, says Yirmiyahu. You are willing to shed innocent Jewish blood, to destroy Jewish life, for monetary gain.[2]

---

2 I thank R. Benny Lau for the following insight: "The prophet Yirmiyahu likewise

"It happened in the days of..." – these are the opening words of the Megilah. "It happened in the days" that the Jews preferred wealth over happiness, the affluent kingdom over the impoverished of Eretz Yisrael, money over morality, and the good graces of the Persian regime over brotherhood among Jews. The story that the Megilah tells is a critique of the "faction" (as the term is used in R. Lau's essay) that preferred to remain in exile and make it their home rather than joining their fellow Jews who returned to Eretz Yisrael.

Needless to say, the stories of both Ruth and Lot did not end well (at least until they returned to Eretz Yisrael). As R. Ashi states in the Talmud (BT *Megilah* 10):

> R. Ashi said: Instances of "It happened" ("*vayehi*") can go like this or like that. "It happened in the days of" ("*vayehi biymei*") always refers to distress. There are five instances of "It happened in the days of": "It happened in the days of Ahashverosh," "It happened in the days of the judges' rule," "It happened in the days of Amraphel," "It happened in the days of Ahaz" (Yeshayahu 7), and "It happened in the days of Yehoyakim" (Yirmiyahu 1)

Thus, right at the beginning of the Megilah, there are indications of impending tragedy.

> That Ahashverosh who reigned from India to Ethiopia

Here too, the author is not simply offering historical facts about the size of the empire – we know its size, and the Megilah's initial audience certainly did. The author's intention is rather to map out for us the trade

---

uses the Hebrew word '*betza*' (profiteering, unlawful gain) to describe the man he abhors, King Yehoyakim." It thus seems that the author of the Megilah does not love the kingdom of Ahashverosh, despite its opulence.

routes of the ancient world: the Silk Road through India; the Royal Road from Shushan to Asia Minor; and the Spice Routes from India to Ethiopia, back and forth, by way of the Levant.

Ahashverosh controlled these trade routes and generated massive revenues from tariffs and transit fees. The Megilah's description outlines a wealthy kingdom, an economic empire abounding with opportunity, where people can accumulate tremendous wealth: an unlimited market stretching from India in the east, all the way to Ethiopia in the Horn of Africa. As is the case in large empires, proximity to the seats of power translates into immense economic opportunity.

A hundred and twenty-seven provinces

This is no mere number. Many scholars have scrutinized maps and records of the Achaemenid Empire and concluded that the number 127 does not correspond to any political reality. If so, its purpose is to direct our attention to something else. Of course, it immediately recalls the number of years that our matriarch Sarah lived. What is the connection between our matriarch Sarah, wife of Avraham, and the Megilah? Sarah's age at her death is mentioned at the beginning of the episode that describes Avraham's purchase of the Cave of Makhpela from Ephron the Hittite. That is, he invested his money in the acquisition of a homestead in Eretz Yisrael. By burying Sarah there, he established permanent roots in Eretz Yisrael.[3]

The exact same number appears in a description of Ahashverosh

---

3 Yisrael Rozenson comments that there are many points of similarity between Sarah and Esther, even though they are far from parallel characters. Both of them were taken to the palace of the king – Sarah to the house of Pharaoh and Esther to the house of Ahashverosh. In each instance, there was a threat to family member. Both women are described as beautiful. Obviously, the parallels do not need to be perfect. They are meant to provoke the reader to think about the author's intent. See *Hadassah Hi Esther*, p. 229. See also *Bereishit Rabbah* 58:3.

celebrating his wealth in Shushan as the Jews of Shushan experience the vapid and fleeting joy of drinking from his wine instead of buying an everlasting inheritance in Eretz Yisrael, alongside their brothers who have returned to their homeland. The Jews of Shushan prefer the hedonism of the present over the construction of the foundations for the second Jewish commonwealth in Eretz Yisrael.

> In those days, when King Ahashverosh occupied the royal throne in Shushan the capital, in the third year of his reign, he gave a banquet for all the officials and courtiers – the military leadership of Persia and Media, the nobles, and the governors of the provinces in his service. (1:2-3)

This verse is not meant to describe the location of Ahashverosh's throne, but to portray the figure of an exalted king who sits in the grandest of splendor on his magnificent royal throne. This immediately calls forth an association with another king who glorified himself with extravagant grandeur and opulence: King Shlomo, the king with immeasurable wealth of silver and gold. Things function the same way in Shushan: vast sums of silver and gold and forsaking of the Lord your God. This is precisely the same process that occurred in the prosperous Jewish kingdom under Shlomo's rule.

There are several parallels. The structure of these verses is similar to the verses that describe Shlomo's reign: "King Shlomo was king over all of Israel" (1 Melakhim 4:1) – just like Ahashverosh, who rules over all of the surrounding nations, or at least all of the trade routes. In the next verse we are told: "These are his officers…" This is followed by a description of Shlomo's taxation system and tax collectors. Here, too, officers and tax collectors constitute the king's retinue.

The similarities continue. Ancient Persian banquets were the height of sexual and financial decadence. "He shall not have many women"? "He shall not amass silver and gold to excess"?[4] At Persian banquets, they did both. Here, too, there is a parallel to Shlomo: "Judah and Israel were as numerous as the sand by the sea.... Shlomo ruled over all of the kingdoms from the Euphrates to the land of the Philistines and even to the border of Egypt. They brought tribute and were subjects of Shlomo all his life" (1 Melakhim 4:20-5:1).

From the wording, it appears that the banquet took place only when the cavalcade of royal "Brinks" horses, laden with the empire's money, arrived safely in the capital city of Shushan, where the money could be ceremoniously deposited in the subterranean vaults of the royal treasury. It is worth noting the guest list: The king's officers and courtiers; imperial soldiers tasked with protecting royal property; the nobility; and the governors of the other provinces, whose job was to collect taxes from the provinces along the trade routes.

We can hypothesize about the historical background. Khashayarsha I, known to the world by the name Xerxes I, ascended the throne of the Persian Empire in 485 BCE. From the very beginning of his reign, he bore a heavy burden on his shoulders: His father, Darius I, swore vengeance against the Greeks for their burning of Sardis. The Greek chronicler Herodotus tells that Darius was so distraught over the Athenian actions at Sardis that he instructed one of his courtesans to say to him at each meal, "Master, remember the Athenians,"[5] to ensure that he would never forget their treachery.[6]

---

4 There is a series of three commandments to kings of Israel in Devarim 17:16-17: "He shall not keep many horses.... He shall not have many wives.... He shall not amass silver and gold to excess."

5 Herodotus, *Histories* V:105 (all translations of Herodotus are based on Godley, 1920).

6 The identification of Ahashverosh with Xerxes is not certain, but there are several clear indications that this is indeed so, including the name (Xerxes-Khashayarsha-Ahashverosh), the queen's name (Amestris-Esther), and the circumstances of

Yet, instead of sweet revenge, Darius suffered another bitter debacle at the hands of the Greeks in the Battle of Marathon. Herodotus may have exaggerated, as he was wont to do, but it is certain that the Greeks, who dared to defeat the Persians, perpetrated an unprecedented, brazen act against the undisputed superpower of the ancient world.

Darius was determined to avenge the destruction of Sardis and the Greek victory. As Herodotus writes, Darius sent "messengers to all the cities and commanded them to equip an army" (VII:2). This process lasted three years, and reports that the Egyptians, too, had joined the rebellion, strengthened his resolve to launch a campaign of conquest and vengeance.

But vengeance did not materialize. While the royal court in Shushan was preoccupied with the struggles between Darius's would-be successors over who would be acting emperor during the campaign to Greece, Darius died, and "it was not granted to him to punish either the revolted Egyptians or the Athenians" (VII:4).

Xerxes gained the upper hand in the battle for succession. He led a military campaign against Egypt and subdued it, whereupon he returned to the royal court of Shushan. He was still undecided about whether to return to the warpath and accept the counsel of his advisers (who urged him to fight so that "others may beware of invading your realm in the future") – or to exercise caution vis-à-vis the Greeks.

---

the assassination attempt. The book of Ezra (4:5-7) provides a very reliable chronology of Persian kings:

They hired counsellors against them, to frustrate their purpose, all the days of King Cyrus of Persia until the days of King Darius of Persia. And in the reign of Ahashverosh, at the beginning of his reign, they wrote an accusation against the inhabitants of Judah and Jerusalem. And in the days of Artaxerxes, Bishlam, Mitredat, Tav'el and the rest of their cohort wrote to King Artaxerxes of Persia.

This chronology is faithful to the familiar chronology of the Achaemenid dynasty: Cyrus, Darius, Xerxes I, Artaxerxes I. It therefore supports the identification of Ahaseurus with Xerxes.

In the end, the impulse of revenge prevailed. Xerxes decided to attack Greece:

> So I may punish the Athenians for what they have done to the Persians and to my father. You saw that Darius my father was set on making an expedition against these men. But he is dead, and it was not granted to him to punish them. On his behalf and that of all Persians, I will never rest until I have taken Athens and burnt it. (VII:8)

This is not just about revenge, though. Add to this mix a large dollop of megalomania and two helpings of cold calculation. With regard to the megalomania, Xerxes wanted to wipe out his sole remaining enemies, so that "no city of men or any human nation which is able to meet us in battle will be left." As for the cold calculations, the novice emperor wished to demonstrate his might to the Persians ("I have considered how I might not fall short of my predecessors in this honor, and not add less power to the Persians (and enrich the kingdom by means of a "land neither less nor worse, and more fertile, than what we have" (VII:8).

This event, after the campaign to Egypt, occurred in the third year of Xerxes's reign in Shushan (which is "the third year of his reign" described in Megilat Esther). As R. Benny Lau explains: "Anyone who wishes to read the story of the Megila with an open mind and without preconceived notions, will see this story well recorded in chapter 1." And indeed it is:

> In those days, when King Ahashverosh occupied the royal throne in Shushan the capital, in the third year of his reign, he gave a banquet for all the officials and courtiers – the military leadership of Persia and Media, the nobles and the governors of the provinces in his service. For no fewer than a hundred and eighty days he displayed the vast riches of his kingdom and the magnificent prestige of his majesty. (1:2-4)

Xerxes, explains Herodotus, convened "a special assembly of the noblest among the Persians" in Shushan for an intense diplomatic persuasion campaign. Most commentators maintain that Ahashverosh was a drunkard and a foolish king, but in his diplomatic initiative, as R. Benny Lau notes, there is no mention of wine, banquets, or parties. Xerxes addresses those who gathered, makes his case for a campaign of vengeance, and dangles before them a promise that they would be well compensated for participating in the campaign:

> This is how you would best please me: when I declare the time for your coming, every one of you must eagerly appear; and whoever comes with his army best equipped will receive from me such gifts as are reckoned most precious among us. (VII:8)

After this speech by the good and generous King Xerxes, his chief adviser, Mardonius, stands up and swings a big stick on the king's behalf. He explains that there is no choice but war. "It would be strange indeed if we who have subdued and made slaves of…Indians and Ethiopians…for no wrong done to the Persians but of mere desire to add to our power, will not take vengeance on the Greeks for unprovoked wrongs" (VII:9). There is no need to fear the Greeks, for they are weak, but if they are allowed to act out, it will have a negative effect on the other kingdoms of the empire. For the Greeks "are accustomed to wage wars…and they do it most senselessly in their wrongheadedness and folly.… Of the vanquished I say not so much as a work, for they are utterly destroyed" (VII:9).

Another adviser, the king's uncle Artabanus, then attempts to curb the hawkishness of Mardonius. He encourages the king to be cautious about engaging in a war whose results cannot be known ("haste is always the parent of failure, and great damages are likely to arise" [VII:10]). But Xerxes does not accept the sober counsel of Artabanus. Instead, "for four full years…he was equipping his force" (VII:20), raising a massive army for the campaign against Greece.

The Megilah's description of Ahashverosh's banquet is far more spartan than Herotodus's interminable yammering about the buildup to the war. However, Herodotus omits something that the author of the Megilah addresses in his precise, measured, and calculated description of the truly important and essential details. The people who constituted the audience of Xerxes's inveigling ("whoever comes with his army best equipped will receive from me such gifts as are reckoned most precious among us") are none other than "all the officials and courtiers – the military leadership of Persia and Media, the nobles and the governors of the provinces."

Ahashverosh of the Megila convenes all the parties relevant to a military operation for a comprehensive public relations campaign. The ostentatious procession of Xerxes's boastful speeches, as recorded by Herodotus, is presented succinctly in the Megilah: Ahashverosh displays "the vast riches of his kingdom and the splendid glory of his majesty" to those gathered in Shushan. The assembled are the leaders and representatives of the 127 provinces, all of whom must be thoroughly persuaded, "for no fewer than a hundred and eighty days," by means of all the empire's power and glory.[7] Yet these diplomatic overtures, and indeed, the war itself, do not interest the author of the Megilah at all. He devotes his attention to one thing only:

---

7 R. Benny Lau points out an interesting parallel: King Hizkiyahu of Judah receives the king of Babylonia "he showed them all his treasure-house – the silver, the gold, the spices, and the fragrant oil – and his armory, and everything that was to be found in his storehouses. There was nothing in his palace or in all his realm that Hizkiyahu did not show them" (2 Melakhim 20:13). The prophet Yeshayahu chides Hizkiyahu for his foolishness and for choosing to ally himself with Babylon instead of relying on his covenant with his God: "Hear the word of the Lord: A time is coming when everything in your palace which your ancestors have stored up to this day will be carried off to Babylon; nothing will remain behind, said the Lord" (*ibid.* 16-17).

the fantastic wealth of the Persian Empire – and the best demonstration of that wealth is on the day when all of the taxes from the entire empire are gathered in.

One constituency is conspicuously absent among these titans of finance, the senior statesmen of Shushan, and the rulers of the prosperous provinces, all of whom were required to contribute their share toward the upcoming Greek campaign: the Jews. They are not represented at all at this banquet.

The purpose of the banquet was to show off Ahashverosh's wealth. It broadcast one message: "My power and the might of my hand has achieved this material wealth" (Devarim 8:17). Every element in the Megilah's description is attributed directly and solely to Ahashverosh: "**he** displayed…**his** kingdom…**his** majesty." Every regime and every ruler has its own distinct character, and this character is usually established at the very beginning of the term, during the "first hundred days," when priorities are established and declared. Rehavam was a despot. Ahav was cruel. Ahashverosh placed money and conspicuous consumption at the top of his list of priorities.

> At the end of this period, the king gave a banquet for seven days in the courtyard of the king's palace garden for all the people who lived in Shushan the capital city, high and low alike. [There were hangings of] white cotton and blue wool, caught up by cords of fine linen and purple wool to silver rods and alabaster columns; and there were couches of gold and silver on a pavement of marble, alabaster, mother-of-pearl, and mosaics. Royal wine was served in abundance, as befits a king, in golden beakers, beakers of varied design. And the rule for the drinking was, "No restrictions!" For the king had given orders to every palace steward to comply with each man's wishes. (1:5-8)

Here, from verse 5 on, the rest of the people join the king's flamboyant party – Jews included. In this case, the event was far more modest in its duration: only seven days long. However, the location of the party – "the courtyard of the king's palace garden" – compensates for its brevity. Later in the story, the king will storm out to this same courtyard in his rage against Haman (7:6); the courtyard is evidently located within the walls of the palace, and it is here that all the citizens of Shushan were invited. It seems that this is the first time that the Jews of Shushan were allowed a peek into the palace, in all its majesty and grandeur – a first glimpse at the unending feast at the heart of the Persian Empire.

There is an element here that reflects the development of closer ties between the Jews and the king's court. If previously the Jews were the consummate outsiders, those who were left out of the political game and the corridors of power, this time they could get a bit closer – if only for seven days – and experience a taste of the empire's wealth. The sweet smell of the empire's money enters their nostrils, and it is overwhelming, intoxicating.

We cannot overlook the stark contrast between the Jews drinking unrestricted amounts of wine from gold beakers and what was transpiring at the same time in Jerusalem (Ezra, chapters 9-10): The returnees from the exile took up a collection, penny by penny, to restart the sacrificial rite. Ezra prays publicly and reprimands the poorer classes and their leaders for intermarrying. "While Ezra was praying and making confession, weeping and prostrating himself before the House of God, a very great crowd of Israelites gathered about him, men, women, and children; the people were weeping bitterly" (Ezra 10:1). The people of Judah can barely find enough building materials to complete the Temple, and they are sobbing in a combination of happiness for their successes to date and sadness over the nation's bleak condition (Ezra 3:10). In Persia, meanwhile, there is great merriment among people of all ages, national backgrounds, and religions at Ahashverosh's banquet. This contrast is a moral one, and its goal is to reinforce the Megilah's message, as the author sees it.

> [There were hangings of] white cotton and blue wool, caught up by cords of fine linen and purple wool to silver rods and alabaster columns; and there were couches of gold and silver on a pavement of marble, alabaster, mother-of-pearl, and mosaics. Royal wine was served in abundance, as befits a king, in golden beakers, beakers of varied design. And the rule for the drinking was, "No restrictions!" For the king had given orders to every palace steward to comply with each man's wishes. (1:6-8)

This is what the Jews see when they first step into the inner precincts of the empire: the best furniture and utensils, grandeur and majesty, marble tiles and golden goblets. The author of the Megilah describes the six-month long gathering of the empire's upper echelons in a detached, clipped style, as though he did not actually witness the event. When he comes to the second banquet, though, he goes from a general and abstract description ("the vast riches of his kingdom and the magnificent prestige of his majesty") to a highly detailed one. This is what the Jews of Shushan saw with their own eyes, for the first time, and it seems that their amazement knew no bounds. The description of the materials reflects the dizzying and startling sensation experienced by the Jews when they see tapestries that recall the full regalia of the Jewish High Priest – blue wool, purple wool, fine linen – embedded in a completely foreign context, among splendid gold goblets for those who wish to drink wine and drinking beakers and floors of marble and alabaster, inlaid with mother-of-pearl and mosaics.[8]

8 See Shemot 39:2. This is the meaning of the various *midrashim* that state that the goblets were actually spoils from the First Temple and that Ahashverosh himself wore the vestments of the High Priest.

By recalling the destroyed Temple, the reader is also prompted to note the contrast between God's rebuilt Temple in Jerusalem and its paucity of resources, and the Jews of Shushan, celebrating in the magnificent palace courtyard, surrounded by the very things that are meant to remind them of their brothers in Jerusalem.

But even this is not enough to curb their enthusiasm. The sensory overload intensifies:

> Royal wine was served in abundance, as befits a king, in golden beakers, beakers of varied design. And the rule for the drinking was, "No restrictions!" For the king had given orders to every palace steward to comply with each man's wishes (1:7-8)

So many phrases in these verses demand explanations: What is royal wine? What made it "abundant" ("*rav*")? If there was a "rule" ("*dat*") governing the drinking, in what sense was it "without restriction"? People could drink as much or as little as they wished, so why the need for a "rule"? Why didn't they impose minimums or maximums on the drinkers? And how is all of this connected to "each man's wishes"?

The plain meaning of the verse is that the king generously dispensed wine, but in accordance with a "rule" – that is, in precisely measured quantities. It was still possible to bloat the stomachs of the celebrants and quench the thirst of all of the drinkers.

These verses embody every characteristic of the Diaspora, a recurring theme of the Megilah. They struggle to integrate into the kingdom and then enthusiastically adopt its customs. "Royal wine" reminds us of Nehemiah (chapters 1-2), who served as cupbearer to King Artaxerxes in Shushan before emotional turmoil leads him to ask the king for a leave of absence so he could rebuild the city of his fathers' graves. It also alludes to the dream of Pharaoh's royal butler, as told to Yosef in chapter 40 of Bereshit. The unrestrained drinking reminds us of Lot and his daughters, who made their father drunk in order to be impregnated by him. There is a barb aimed at King Shlomo who increased taxes, making it difficult for "each man" to pursue his "wishes."[9]

Even before the plot of the Megilah begins with the story of Vashti, its author seeks to remind us of the negative consequences that await one who is awed by all the golden vessels, silver columns, and mosaic floors in Diaspora sanctuaries. This is the subject of the Megilah. Not for naught are we called to remember Nehemiah's change of heart, Yosef's imprisonment, Lot's incestuous siring of Moab and Ammon, and King Shlomo's yen for women and idolatry.

> In addition, Queen Vashti gave a banquet for women, in the royal palace of King Ahashverosh. On the seventh day, when the king was merry with wine, he ordered Mehuman, Bizzeta, Harvona, Bigta, Avagta, Zetar, and Karkas, the seven eunuchs in attendance on King Ahashverosh, to bring Queen Vashti before the king wearing a royal diadem, to display her beauty to the peoples and the officials; for she was a beautiful woman. But Queen Vashti refused to come at the king's command conveyed by the eunuchs. The king was greatly incensed, and his fury burned within him. (1:9-12)

The focus of the author's interest is revealed clearly by the literary strategy that he adopts here. Until verse 8, it would seem to the reader that there is but one sequence of events: King Ahashverosh prepares for a great war with a banquet for the dignitaries of Persia, and this is immediately followed by a more modest party for the people of the city that had played host to all these dignitaries.

After all of this detailed description of the preparations for the military

---

9 See above, p. 28 ff.

campaign, there is silence. The story continues, but we do not hear another word about the war or its outcome. The author of the Megilah is not interested in the military campaigns of the king of Persia – this is not the story that he wishes to tell, and these are not the lessons that he seeks to impart. He therefore takes the bold step of omitting the war completely.

Nonetheless, in the same way that Judah, Jerusalem, the rebuilt Temple, and the Jews who returned to their land are absent from the Megilah but still very much present, the war against Greece is likewise absent but present. It has major implications on Ahashverosh's conduct: The Ahashverosh we will meet in chapter 2 is not the same confident, ostentatious, boastful Ahashverosh of chapter 1.

Historical sources, Herodotus chief among them, explain that in the year 482 BCE, King Xerxes I of Persia launched his major military campaign against Greece. After the Pyrrhic victory at Thermopylae, where a force of three hundred Spartans led by King Leonidas inflicted thousands of casualties on the Persian forces, there was the Battle of Salamis, near Athens, where hundreds of Persian warships were sunk, forcing Xerxes to return to Persia in humiliation.

Mardonius, the same adviser who had belittled the Greeks, remained behind. He captured Athens and proposed a peace agreement, offering the Athenians autonomy in exchange for recognition that they are subordinate to Persia. The Greeks rejected the offer. Their refusal led to the Battle of Plataea, where the Persians suffered a crushing defeat. The dream of the European Empire of Xerxes I was gone forever.

To all appearances, and according to many commentators, after the Greek debacle, Ahashverosh became a drunken, weak, and indecisive king, confused and detached, in constant need of advice from others. This is how Herodotus, who was hostile towards the Persians, described him. I maintain, like R. Yitzhak Reggio,[10] that the reality was different: The king was neither

10 R. Yitzhak Shmuel Reggio, *Mafte'ah el Megilat Esther* (1841), pp. 31-34. It should

foolish nor fickle. He knew how to lead wars, collect taxes, and issue decrees. The rise of the advisers – a recurring phenomenon throughout the Megilah – is a literary device that directs the reader's attention to shifting cast of characters that surround the king in order to explain the change in the status and influence of the Jews at the royal court in Shushan.

Seven eunuchs, advisers to the king, are mentioned by name: Mehuman, Bizzeta, Harvona, Bigta, Avagta, Zetar, and Karkas. The Megilah's author thereby tells us something important: These are people of stature. They, as well as the people who will replace them in these positions, are an important part of the plot, serving to mark its developments.

Queen Vashti organized a banquet for women in the palace of Ahashverosh. The words "in addition" ("*gam*") establish a connection between the women's banquet, hosted by the queen, and the earlier banquet, but this link is merely a sophisticated literary device, meant to tie together two events – Vashti's banquet and the pre-war banquet for the assembled dignitaries of Persia – that are not really connected at all. The impression generated is that Ahashverosh held a banquet for the men – a party that was not connected to the previous events – and Queen Vashti **likewise** hosted a banquet, to which only women were invited. However, they were not contemporaneous, nor was one banquet for men and the Queen's party for women. The author simply connects them to convey a moral, ethical message.

It is doubtful that Ahashverosh and company would have been content at a lavish banquet with only men for company. This was not the common practice in Shushan. It stands to reason that there were plenty of women at Vashti's banquet as well as Ahashverosh's feast.

---

be noted that R. Reggio, who likewise relies on Herodotus, identifies Ahashverosh as Darius, father of Xerxes I, and maintains that the great works recorded in the Megilah must have come from "the powerful King Darius" and not his son Xerxes, who he presents as a failure.

Both of these celebrations took place in the royal palace. When the king was good and drunk, he requested that Vashti be brought over from her women's banquet. There were many women at the banquet of Ahashverosh, and he wanted to show all those in attendance that his wife was most beautiful of all. But Vashti refused to attend the king's party.

The text gives the impression that the eunuchs, Mehuman, Bizzeta, Harvona, and their colleagues, did not invest much effort to bring Vashti to the king's banquet. When the advisers and eunuchs really want to bring someone to an audience with the king, they know how to be quite persuasive: "The king's eunuchs arrived and hurriedly brought Haman" (6:14). It seems that Vashti's refusal should not have posed much of a challenge. The eunuchs did their work meekly and dragged their feet.

> Then the king consulted the sages learned in procedure. (For it was the royal practice [to turn] to all who were versed in law and precedent. His closest advisers were Karshena, Shetar, Admata, Tarshish, Meres, Marsena, and Memukhan, the seven ministers of Persia and Media who had access to the royal presence and occupied the first place in the kingdom.) "What," [he asked,] "shall be done, according to law, to Queen Vashti for failing to obey the command of King Ahashverosh conveyed by the eunuchs? (1:13-15)

The direct ramification of the eunuchs' failure is the convening of the advisers, those "who were well versed in law and precedent," who "occupied the first place in the kingdom." The issue at hand was too sensitive for the eunuchs to deal with. Their job was to execute the king's orders, and their weakness had been exposed by Vashti's refusal. Harvona in particular learned an important lesson here: the next time he needed to recommend a course of action, he did not hesitate.

It is also possible that the eunuchs "failed" to carry out Ahashverosh's request because they realized that it was a recipe for disaster. It showed a lack of respect for the queen, who was being asked to come to an orgiastic beauty pageant where the wine flowed like water. Perhaps they were conscientious objectors of a sort, and perhaps Vashti's refusal is meant to indicate how the Jews should have behaved: don't mingle with the celebrants at the king's banquet.

Either way, the king was incensed, and his fury burned within him. We sense that Vashti staged a coup of sorts. Her refusal to attend Ahashverosh's drinking party was essentially a rejection of Persian party culture. She organized a modest party for women only (and eunuchs, who could enter because they had been castrated and therefore could not be aroused to passion). The author of the Megilah wants to show how far the Jews delighting in Ahashverosh's banquet had grown from the purity of God's royal palace in Jerusalem, the Temple, whose sanctity demanded separation from sexuality, further reinforced in this era through Ezra's aspirations regarding the purity of male seed.

The character of Vashti can be seen as a literary contrast of sorts: If only the Jews had listened to their voice of conscience, like Vashti, and left the pleasures of Persia, they would have been saved. She is the conscience, and they did not listen to the voice of conscience.[11] The Jews have a long way to go before they can once again meet Harvona; his presence here foreshadows the possibility that the Jewish people will be saved from destruction.

The eunuchs showed solidarity with Vashti's defiant 'Jewish' message, and so the king called the sages who knew soothsaying and law, who were "learned in procedure…who were well versed in law and precedent."

---

11 It is worth noting that later in the story, Mordechai sends Esther to the pageant of the virgins, to precisely the place where Vashti refused to appear before Ahashverosh.

> Then the king consulted the sages learned in procedure. (For it was the royal practice [to turn] to all who were versed in law and precedent. His closest advisers were Karshena, Shetar, Admata, Tarshish, Meres, Marsena, and Memukhan, the seven ministers of Persia and Media who had access to the royal presence and occupied the first place in the kingdom.) "What," [he asked,] "shall be done, according to law, to Queen Vashti for failing to obey the command of King Ahashverosh conveyed by the eunuchs?" (1:13-15)

The king is not confused; he is desperate. He takes action immediately upon Vashti's refusal: The party is not yet over, yet he calls his legal team. He understands, just as his advisers tell him, that he cannot let Vashti's refusal pass without response. The Megilah does not tell us what the king said to his advisers. Rashi says that the words "for it was" indicate that this was the practice, to explain the issue to those who were well versed in law and precedent, so that they could recommend a course of action.

I read the events differently: The author is intimating that the king wanted to tell his advisers something, but he was unable to say what he wants. Accordingly, "the royal practice" ("*devar ha-melekh*," lit. "the word of the king") of verse 13 was retrospective: that is, the king's "word," his order to bring Vashti, was issued in the presence of those who were well versed in law and precedent. Her defiance was public, not private, and so the king could not forego his honor and pardon her. Those zealous and authoritarian experts in law and precedent were sitting right there at the party. The king therefore must ask them "what shall be done according to the law"? It is these jurists who will pronounce sentence on Vashti for defying the king.

> Thereupon Memukhan declared in the presence of the king and the ministers: "Queen Vashti has committed an offense

> not only against Your Majesty but also against all the officials and against all the peoples in all the provinces of King Ahashverosh. For the queen's behavior will make all wives despise their husbands, as they reflect that King Ahashverosh himself ordered Queen Vashti to be brought before him, but she would not come. This very day the ladies of Persia and Media, who have heard of the queen's behavior, will cite it to all Your Majesty's officials, and there will be no end of scorn and provocation! If it please Your Majesty, let a royal edict be issued by you, and let it be written into the laws of Persia and Media, so that it cannot be abrogated, that Vashti shall never enter the presence of King Ahashverosh. And let Your Majesty bestow her royal state upon another who is more worthy than she. Then will the judgment executed by Your Majesty resound throughout your realm, vast though it is; and all wives will pay tribute to their husbands, high and low alike." The proposal was approved by the king and the ministers, and the king did as Memukhan proposed. Dispatches were sent to all the provinces of the king, to every province in its own script and to every nation in its own language, that every man should wield authority in his home and speak the language of his own people. (1:16-21)

Memukhan tells the king and the officers that Vashti has committed a crime not only against the king, but against the heads of every kingdom and every nation under Ahashverosh's rule, and against the general population of the empire. Vashti's coup transpired in a public setting. If word were to get out that Vashti had refused to heed the king's command with no repercussions, it would become the new norm throughout the empire. Women would refuse their husbands, "and there will be no end of scorn and provocation."

In order to prevent this, Memukhan[12] proposed a new royal law: She who refuses to obey her husband will be divorced, and her role will be assigned to "another who is more worthy than she." The situation will thus be rectified, "and all wives will pay tribute to their husbands, high and low alike."

At first glance, it seems that Memukhan was concerned with maintaining family structure and wives' obedience to their husbands in Shushan and throughout the Persian Empire. In the Persian worldview, women were far inferior to men. Herodotus recounts that when the Persian cavalry wanted to humiliate Greek combatants, they would call them women (IX:20). Later, when Xerxes's brother Masistes learned of Persia's debacle, he "reviled the admiral Artayntes very bitterly, telling him (with much beside) that such generalship as his proved him worse than a woman, and that no punishment was too severe for the harm he had done the king's estate. Now it is the greatest of all taunts in Persia to be called worse than a woman" (XI:107).

Memukhan exploits this crisis in order to enshrine men's privilege and the inferior status of women in law: "all wives will pay tribute to their husbands, high and low alike."

But there is something deeper at play here. Many of the women at Ahashverosh's banquets assumed (because they were made to understand) that in coming to the party, they were complying with Persian norms and laws. According to this view, Vashti's party was not only a separate banquet, but the demonstration of a different set of norms, a different tradition, and perhaps even a different set of beliefs and values.

Vashti's defiance, in the presence of all the women at the party, went well beyond a simple act of refusal. Unchecked, there would be risk not

12 Some commentators identify Memukhan with Haman. If that is so, then we see another way in which he was eventually hoist by his own petard: he was eventually dismissed from his job and replaced by someone more worthy.

only of rebellious women, but that the status of Persia's religious priests would be undermined by women who display independence of thought or adherence to a different religion. The king's enactment, then, was not just some order that could be canceled. It was an enshrined religious law, which could never be altered.

There is a definite economic aspect of this story as well. Vashti was clearly a rebellious wife, but she was not killed as a dissident of the kingdom. Perhaps she had a certain amount of her own power and status. Perhaps her status as queen indicates that she was matched with the king for political and financial reasons, and so the king could not just kill her. However, the religious law that Ahashverosh publicizes enables him to enshrine the inferior status of women as well as the superior financial status of men: "all wives will pay tribute to their husbands, high and low alike." Women's liberation threatens the men who control the money and the kingdom,[13] and it is critical to quash this financial rebellion at all costs and restore the status quo: "that every man should wield authority in his home."

Chapter 1 of the Megilah closes with Ahashverosh and his religious advisers differentiating men from women and fixing their separate statuses in society. In contrast, Persia's Jews are not undergoing differentiation but assimilation. They have already crossed the boundaries of their society and absorbed Persian customs out of desire for the same "tribute" and the same imperial grandeur.

One who separates himself from the group protects himself. One who mingles with others eventually assimilates. As it is recorded in the book of Ezra (9:1-2):

---

13 See the more comprehensive discussion of "paying tribute" ("*yekar*") on pp. 96-99. As we will see, economic superiority and the rights to the empire's money play an important role in the Megilah. Vashti's story serves as a literary device, as sort of microcosm of the entire Megilah.

When this was over, the officers approached me, saying, "The people of Israel and the priests and Levites have not separated themselves from the peoples of the land whose abhorrent practices are like those of the Canaanites, the Hittites, the Perizzites, the Jebusites, the Ammonites, the Moabites, the Egyptians, and the Amorites. They have taken their daughters as wives for themselves and for their sons, so that the holy seed has become intermingled with the peoples of the land; and it is the officers and prefects who have taken the lead in this trespass."

In Shushan the Capital Lived a Jew

> Sometime afterward, when the anger of King Ahashverosh subsided, he thought of Vashti and what she had done and what had been decreed against her. The king's servants who attended him said, "Let beautiful young virgins be sought out for Your Majesty. Let Your Majesty appoint officers in every province of your realm to assemble all the beautiful young virgins in Shushan the capital, in the harem under the supervision of Hege, the king's eunuch, guardian of the women. Let them be provided with their cosmetics. And let the maiden who pleases Your Majesty be queen instead of Vashti." The proposal pleased the king, and he acted upon it. (2:1-4)

The beginning of the second chapter marks the first major turning point in the plot: not the change in the king's mood, but the change in the identity of his closest advisers. Perhaps, as R. Benny Lau suggests, after the Greek debacle, Ahashverosh wants to change advisers, seclude himself at home, and devote himself to pleasure-seeking. This explanation is supported by descriptions of Xerxes I in other ancient sources. Perhaps the defeated king longingly remembers the grand banquets from the days that preceded the war, incidentally remembering Vashti, her actions, and their aftermath: his decision to depose her.

The obvious question is: Why does Vashti's absence distress Ahashverosh? Kings in ancient times, most certainly Persian kings, had access to a harem full of concubines. He never lacked a consort for the evening. Perhaps Ahashverosh felt that his decision to depose Vashti brought bad luck, causing him to lose to Greece. Perhaps he felt lonely without her. Perhaps his reawakened fury was actually directed at his officers and advisers. Either way, several years later, he understood that he had erred in his decision to depose Vashti. His officers had incited him to take extreme measures against his wife for a relatively minor infraction. All she had done was resist participation in the pleasure-seeking environment of Shushan.

This may be why the Megilah's author tells us, right at the beginning of the chapter, that the king had new advisers. Essentially, this was the second time that Ahashverosh removed his advisers from their job – he did so on account of their flawed advice about Vashti and on account of their defeat in battle, which led to the loss of many soldiers. In any case, one thing is certain in the Megilah: when new advisers appear on the scene, the narrative is at a turning point.

These servants, literally "*ne'arim*" (young men), eagerly jump at the opportunity created by the dismissal of their predecessors. The author of the Megilah always chooses his words carefully. Dr. Yonatan Grossman demonstrates[1] that the text of the Megilah is highly intertextual, filled with veiled references and allusions to other biblical narratives. These allusions can provide context, thicken character descriptions, and even contain concealed criticism. I maintain that there is a particular message that emerges from each story to which the Megilah alludes.[2]

---

1 Jonathan Grossman, *Esther: The Outer Narrative and the Hidden Reading* (Winona Lake, IN: Eisenbraun's, 2011), Introduction, pp. 1-8, and Conclusion, pp. 218-233.

2 In his conclusion, Dr. Grossman deals with what he calls "dynamic analogies." He cites a scholar, Paul Noble, who argues that "in order to establish the probability of an analogy, corresponding analogues must remain constant," but then states

It seems to me that these *ne'arim*, the servants of Ahashverosh, are actually Jewish advisers. The word "*na'ar*" appears often in Tanakh to describe Jews, including those who serve leaders:

- Yosef: "and there with us was a Hebrew *na'ar*" (Bereishit 41)
- Yehoshua: "and his servant Yehoshua bin Nun was a *na'ar*" (Shemot 33)
- Shmuel: "and the *na'ar* served God before Eli the priest" (1 Shmuel 2)

The story of Vashti is a turning point because it gives the Jews an opportunity to begin the process of establishing closer ties to the monarchy. In chapter 1, the Jews saw the palace from the inside only as invitees to a brief banquet. Now they have the opportunity to influence policy. These servants were no more than junior advisers, of course, but the failure of the senior advisers (Mardonius, the chief voice who called for war, fell in battle against Greece) created an administrative vacuum that the new advisers could fill, as happens in every political or bureaucratic system.

These events happened more than a century after the exile of Yekhoniah, and finally their status in the Babylonian and Persian exile was beginning to improve. This is typical of immigrant groups, and especially Jews: They demonstrate their intelligence to the host country, and in time they start to become enmeshed in the bureaucracy and in the corridors of

that although "Noble's argument makes sense in general...it must be broadened to consider instances in which the analogical shift serves a literary purpose.... This phenomenon occurs often in biblical analogies; however, the book of Esther especially epitomizes it" (Grossman, pp. 218-9). The instability of intertextual analogues is thus not a mistake or evidence that the analogy is accidental, but in fact a deliberate literary device "employed by the author to convey a sense of capriciousness and instability" (p. 232). However, whereas Grossman suggests that "the narrative is deliberately presenting situations and characters as...full of confusion and hardly understood," I maintain that the allusions are not meant to function as analogies or templates, but to stimulate the reader's imagination by indicating that a different biblical narrative contains an important message for the Megilah.

power.[3] It does not seem incidental that this improvement of their status comes after they participated in Ahashverosh's banquet. Their presence there demonstrated their willingness to prioritize the celebrations of Ahashverosh over the Jewish festivals that occurred at the same time. This was how they began to establish closer ties with the government.

> Let Your Majesty appoint officers in every province of your realm to assemble all the beautiful young virgins in Shushan the capital, in the harem under the supervision of Hege, the king's eunuch, guardian of the women. Let them be provided with their cosmetics. And let the maiden who pleases Your Majesty be queen instead of Vashti." The proposal pleased the king, and he acted upon it. (2:3-4)

Here too there is a hint that the king's servants are Jews. The expression that the author adopts ("*ve-yafked ha-melekh pekidim*"/"Let your majesty appoint officers") is borrowed from the story of Yosef's rise to power: "Let Pharaoh take steps to appoint officers (*ve-yafked pekidim*) over the land, to take one fifth of the land of Egypt in the seven years of plenty" (Bereishit 41:34). There is clearly a nod to the story of Yosef here. Yosef was the first Jew to achieve great political power in exile, and he was the one who saved Egypt from disaster. ("There was a famine in all of the lands, but in the entire land of Egypt there was bread" [*ibid.* 54].)

These *ne'arim* who serve the king aspire to rise to the eminence of Yosef, and it is with this in mind that they make their proposal: They wish to gather "**all** the beautiful young virgins" – the word "**all**" includes young

3 The timing does not seem incidental. The first Jews arrived in the United States at the end of the eighteenth century, but the first Jewish senator was elected only at the end of the nineteenth century. The first Jewish member of the United States Cabinet was Secretary of Commerce and Labor Oscar Strauss in 1906, about 110 years after the beginning of significant Jewish immigration to the United States.

Jewish women as well. After all, what would improve the status of the Jews in the Diaspora more than having a Jewish queen? Strategic intermarriage with other nations was the best way to develop close ties with government, exactly like King Shlomo had done when he married the daughter of Pharaoh as a symbol of alliance between the two kingdoms.[4]

> In Shushan the capital lived a Jewish man by the name of Mordechai, son of Yair son of Shimi son of Kish, a Benjaminite (*ish Yemini*),[5] who had been exiled from Jerusalem in the group that was carried into exile along with King Yekhoniah of Judah, which had been driven into exile by King Nebuchadnezzar of Babylon. He was foster father to Hadassah – that is, Esther – his uncle's daughter, for she had neither father nor mother. The maiden was shapely and good-looking; and when her father and mother died, Mordechai adopted her as his own daughter. (2:5-7)

In a sharp change of pace, the Megilah takes a break from the chronological presentation of the plot and offers an exposition on the background and pedigree of a main character. Incidentally, this raises some important questions that significantly impact our understanding of the entire story and of the true intentions of the Megilah's author.

Mordechai is presented as "a Jewish man" ("*ish Yehudi*"). The word "Jew" (Yehudi) in the Megilah had a relatively new meaning: Until the Babylonian exile, a Yehudi was someone from the tribe or kingdom of Judah (Yehuda). Only after the exile did this word gradually come to apply

---

4 It is possible that this idea originates in the book of Daniel, which tells about Daniel, Hanania, Mishael, and Azaria, who were groomed from childhood to serve as attendants before the king.

5 The Hebrew word for Bemjaminite, *Yemini*, recalls the verse "If I forget you, O Jerusalem, let me forget my right hand (*yemini*)." As will become clear, this allusion is apt with respect to Mordechai.

to a member of any tribe of Israel, regardless of whether he was from Judah or a different tribe, whether from the kingdom of Judah or the kingdom of Israel, and whether he went into exile or stayed put.

Likewise, the use of the word "man" (*ish*) is also not incidental. In Biblical Hebrew, the term "*ish*" indicates a person of stature, a main character in the story. Not only that, but Mordechai is called "*ish*" twice in one sentence (the second being "*ish Yemini*"/"a Benjaminite).

The word "*ish*" appears three times in Bereishit, in two different stories. A close look at how the word functions there can help clarify its meaning here.

"He wrestled with a man"

The word "*ish*" first appears at a key point in the life of Yitzhak (Bereishit, chs. 25-27). The two children of Yitzhak, Yaakov and Esav, are entangled in an ongoing struggle for Yitzhak's love, the privileged status of being his firstborn, and his blessing. Toward the end of his life, Yitzhak decides to bless Esav, but his wife, Rivkah, manipulates the situation to ensure that Yaakov receives the blessing.

Esav, who had married two Hitite women, to his parents' great chagrin, cannot accept what has befallen him ("He took my birthright; and now he has taken my blessing!?"). He schemes against his twin brother: "Esav said to himself: The days of mourning for my father draw close; then I will kill my brother Yaakov."

Rivkah learns of Esav's plan and instructs Yaakov: "Arise and flee to my brother Lavan in Haran." She comforts Yaakov by telling him that his escape will only be "for several days." However, knowing though that his absence might last much longer, she wisely enlists Yitzhak to forbid Yaakov from marrying Canaanite women, as his brother had done:

> And Rivkah said to Yitzhak: I am disgusted with my life because of the daughters of Het: If Yaakov takes a wife from the daughters

> of Het, such as these, of the daughters of the land, what good shall my life be to me? And Yitzhak called Yaakov and blessed him, and charged him, and said to him: You must not take a wife from the daughters of Canaan. Arise, go to Padan Aram, to the house of Betuel, your mother's father, and take a wife from the daughters of Lavan, your mother's brother. (Bereishit 27:46-28:2)

After twenty years of hard work for Lavan, Yaakov finally departed with great wealth, married to two of Lavan's daughters and their maidservants, and with eleven sons (his youngest son, Binyamin, had not yet been born). He anticipated an imminent reunion with his brother Esav. Yaakov did not know much about Esav's frame of mind, though. Does he still seek revenge? The messengers that Yaakov sent do not reassure him. They reported that Esav "is also on his way to greet you, in the company of four hundred men" (Bereishit 32). Panic-stricken, Yaakov turns to God in prayer ("Save me from my brother, from Esav, for I am afraid") and prepares for the eventuality of Esav attempting to harm his family. On that very night, when he crosses the Yabok River, transporting his entire family and all of his possessions to the other side:

> And Yaakov was left alone and he wrestled with a man ('*ish*') until daybreak. And when he saw that he could not prevail against him, he touched the hollow of his thigh; and the hollow of Yaakov's thigh was put out of joint as he wrestled with him. And he said: "Let me go as it is daybreak." And he said: "I will not let you go until you bless me." And he said to him: "What is your name?" And he said: "Yaakov." And he said: "Your name shall no longer be called 'Yaakov,' but rather 'Yisrael,' for you have struggled with God and with man and prevailed." And Yaakov asked and said to him: "Tell me please your name." And he said: "Why do

> you ask my name?" And he blessed him there. And Yaakov called the name of the place Peniel, for I have seen God face to face and my life was saved. And the sun rose as he passed Penuel, and he limped upon his thigh. (Bereishit 32:25-32)

Yaakov survives the fight with this mystery man who stands in his way on his journey to Eretz Yisrael and tests his readiness to meet up with Esav. Yaakov acquires a new name, but he still limps, a physical testament to his upcoming spiritual transformation: He is about to settle in Eretz Yisrael.

"A man found him"

Seventeen years later, we find Yaakov living securely in the land of Canaan. He sends his beloved son Yosef, born to him by his wife Rachel (who died while bearing her second son, Binyamin), to inquire about the welfare of his older brothers, who are shepherding Yaakov's flocks (Bereishit 37).

Yosef and his brothers are in conflict due to Yaakov's love for Yosef, which arouses the brothers' jealousy and hatred ("They hated him and could not speak to him peaceably"). Their feelings are compounded by Yosef's dreams about ruling over them ("His brothers said to him: 'Will you reign over us? Will you rule over us?' So they hated him even more, on account of his dreams and on account of his words.")

When Yosef went to search for his brothers, at his father's directive, he lost his way, until:

> A man (*ish)* found him while he was wandering in the field. The man asked him: "What are you looking for?" He answered: "I am looking for my brothers. Tell me, please: where are they pasturing?" The man said: "They departed from here, for I heard them say: 'Let us got to Dotan.'" So Yosef followed his brothers and found them in Dotan. They saw him from a distance, and

> even before he came close to them, they conspired to kill him. They said to one another: "Here comes that dreamer! Let us go and kill him and throw his body in one of the pits, and say that he has been eaten by a savage beast. We will see what will become of his dreams." (Bereishit 37:15-20)

The mysterious man that Yosef met, seemingly at random, led him to his brothers, who sent him into exile in Egypt. The Sages explain that "they departed from here" means that "they departed from brotherly love." That is, they were disconnected from familial and national unity and brotherhood. This "man," "*ish*", led Yosef to his brothers, and from there to schism and exile.

"The man who is the lord of the land spoke"

Yosef was sold to Midianite merchants and brought to Egypt, where he rose through the ranks of Potiphar's household. He was imprisoned, but from there he rose again, thanks to the Divine inspiration that enabled him to interpret dreams, to become second in command of all Egypt. Twenty years after his sale, there was a terrible famine all over the region, drawing people to Egypt to buy food, for Yosef had prepared for these bad years. ("All the land came to Egypt to buy food from Yosef, because the famine was heavy throughout the land.")

Among those who came to Egypt to buy grain are the ten brothers of Yosef. They did not recognize their brother, who had risen to a position of great power, and they bowed down to him, just as Yosef had prophesied in his dreams ("The brothers of Yosef came and they bowed down before him, with their faces to the earth"). Yosef identified them and he spoke to them menacingly, accusing them of espionage ("You are spies!").

The brothers vigorously denied this charge, but Yosef said that the veracity of their words must be tested. If indeed they are innocent brothers who just came to buy food, they will leave one brother in prison and return with their tenth brother who has remained with Yaakov: the youngest brother, Binyamin.

Unbeknownst to them, Yosef overheard their conversation, learning that Reuven was the one who had warned them against conspiring to hurt their brother ("Did I not tell you: Do not sin against the child!"), and the brothers bemoaned the travesty that they had perpetrated ("We are guilty concerning our brother, in that we saw his anguish when he pleaded with us, but we did not listen; that is why this trouble has come upon us").

Yosef supplied the brothers with Egyptian grain, surreptitiously returning their money to them. The brothers returned to the land of Canaan and described their experiences in Egypt to their elderly father, Yaakov:

> They came to Yaakov, their father, in the land of Canaan, and told him all that had befallen them, saying: "The man (*ish*) who is the lord of the land spoke roughly to us, and accused us of spying on the land." We said to him, "We are truthful men; we have not spied. We are twelve brothers, sons of our father; one is gone, and the youngest is now with our father, in the land of Canaan." The man (*ish*), the lord of the land, said to us: "Here is how I will know whether you are truthful men: leave one of your brothers here with me, take food for the famine of your households, and go, bring your youngest brother to me. Then I will know that you are not spies, that you are truthful men. I will give you your brother, and you can do business in the land." (Bereishit 42:29-34)

Yaakov refused to send Binyamin with the brothers, expressing bewilderment:

> "Why did you treat me so badly, as to tell the man that you have another brother?" They said: "The man (*ish*) asked us about

> ourselves and our homeland, saying: 'Is your father still alive? Do you have another brother?' We answered his questions. Could we have known that he would say: 'bring your brother down?'" (Bereishit 43:6-7)

Only after Yosef put his brothers through a series of tests did the masks finally fall away; the viceroy, who had been blinking back his tears this entire time, ultimately broke down crying and revealed himself: "Yosef said to his brothers: 'I am Yosef! Is my father still alive?'"

These three instances of the word "*ish*" have a common denominator: the mysterious identity of the characters. We do not know who fights with Yaakov; we do not know who sends Yosef to Dotan; and the brothers do not know who this tough Egyptian ruler really is. The other common denominator is that, in all three episodes, the "*ish*" is a divisive and intimidating element.[6]

Given that the Megilah's author often alludes to Bereishit, it is not difficult to see that the use of the word "*ish*" indicates obscurity; Mordechai is a man of mystery. Appearances can be deceiving. Perhaps "Mordechai" is not even his real name; perhaps he is an agent of divisiveness and discord. The author is planting suspicion about Mordechai and his importance to the Jewish people.[7]

---

6 My father and teacher, R. Barry Eisenberg, explained in the name of R. Joseph B. Soloveitchik that "the angel of Esav" is an external threat; the man who sent Yosef to Dotan offers advice in what seems to be a gesture of friendship, but ultimately causes harm to the Jewish people; the third episode is one of internal Jewish strife. These represent three different types of threats to the Jewish people.

7 It is possible that this is another allusion to Megilat Ruth. It says there: "It happened in the days of the judges' rule that there was a famine in the land, and a man (*ish*) from Bethlehem in Judah went to live in the plains of Moab." The "*ish*" is in fact Elimelech, husband of Naomi, an important personage who leaves Eretz Yisrael to pursue economic opportunity; his sons then marry Moabite women there who enjoy a close relationship with the governing authority. In the story of

The mystery man, the Megilah tells us, "lived in Shushan the capital," center of government and power for the empire. The Megilah insinuates that this mystery man sought access to the sources of power. Perhaps it is no accident that he is mentioned immediately after a characterization of the king's "*ne'arim*": The mystery man strove to become like these "*ne'arim*," and that is why he lived in Shushan.

At this point, the mysterious man is introduced. His name is "Mordechai, son of Yair son of Shimi son of Kish, a Benjaminite." This genealogy befuddles many commentators, because it is shortened. It skips many generations on the family tree and does not coincide with the Benjaminite genealogy listed in 1 Divrei Hayamim 8. The names that are chosen, though, are hardly arbitrary.

Presumably, Yair was an ancestor of Mordechai. The mention of his name recalls another Yair, the son of Menashe, about whom it is said: "he took the entire region of Argov" (Devarim 3:14) – numerous cities and homesteads in Gilad, on the east bank of the Jordan River. Yair did not continue with his brothers to live in Eretz Yisrael.[8] By using the name Yair, the Megilah alludes to the fact that Mordechai, like Yair the son of Menashe, did not ascend to Eretz Yisrael along with his brothers who returned from Babylonia.

Nor is the name "Shimi" mentioned incidentally. Shimi, son of Gera (2 Shmuel 16), was a Benjaminite who "went out and cursed" David in his moment of weakness, during the tormented king's flight from his son

---

the Megilah: "It happened in the days of Ahashverosh … there was a Jewish man in Shushan the capital" – Mordechai, an important personage, adopted Esther because he saw in her an opportunity to get close to the ruling authority.

8 It is important to note that the half-tribe of Menashe did lead Bnei Yisrael into battle prior to returning to the east bank of the Jordan. In the case of Yair, not only did he not live on the west bank of the Jordan with the majority of the tribes but his cities on the east bank were even named for him. See Bamidbar 32:41 and Yehoshua 13:30.

Avshalom. Right then, when David could not risk endangering his meager fighting force in unnecessary combat, Shimi cursed him: "God is returning upon you all of the blood of the house of Shaul, who you replaced as king. God has given the throne to your son Avshalom." Later on, after Avshalom is killed and Shimi's prophecy/curse thus disproved, Shimi goes to meet David "together with a thousand men" as the latter returns to Jerusalem to reestablish his kingdom. Shimi ingratiates himself to David, in a bid to avoid death ("See, I am the first from the entire house of Yosef to come down today to greet my lord, the king"). Mordechai, living in the capital city of Shushan and ingratiating himself with the king, behaves similarly: He, too, gathers large crowds of Jews and poses a threat to the kingdom of David that is being restored in Jerusalem, in the early days of the Second Temple period.

Kish is obviously the father of the dynasty of Shaul, from the tribe of Binyamin. Many are puzzled by the fact that Kish is mentioned while Shaul is not. Some explain that Mordechai was not a direct descendant of Shaul, but rather descended from a different son of Kish. I maintain that there is a different, more intentional reason. Kish was the one who sent Shaul to look for the donkeys, beginning the process that culminates in Shaul's enthronement. Kish stood behind the scenes, preparing the next generation for dominion. The same is true of Mordechai: He never became king, but he sought to join the government and gain power so that someone from the next generation – namely, his relative, the son of Esther, could become king.

At the end of this genealogy comes Mordechai himself. All the names that precede him on his family tree are Hebrew names, but Mordechai bears a foreign name – the name of the god Marduk, chief god in the ancient Mesopotamian pantheon. The first generation of readers of the Megilah would not have needed any more than this name to conclude that this character was assimilated. It would be akin to introducing a Jewish-American character named Chris or Jésus.

The passage of time since the events described in the Megilah, coupled with the customs that the Jewish people developed during the long exile, may confuse the reader. As R. Benny Lau explains, exegetes of the Megilah attempted to cleanse the names of Mordechai and Esther from the taint of assimilation. The Sages, he writes, presented Mordechai as "one of the Men of the Great Assembly and thus a transmitter of the Oral Torah and one of Israel's spiritual leaders." Some even hyped up his connection to Eretz Yisrael. However, this approach is inconsistent with a historical reading of the Megilah and, it seems, with the author's intent.

Another confusing element is the chanting of verse 2:6 to the mournful tune of Eichah. The exile of Yekhoniah, the exile of "the artisan and the locksmith," was certainly a tragic event in Jewish history, but the author of the Megilah had a different objective here: He wishes to situate Mordechai among the economic elite of Babylonia and Persia. Mordechai was a fourth generation diaspora Jew, living over a century after the exile of Yekhoniah and the emigration to Babylonia and Persia. He was so embedded in the elite that he has taken the name of a foreign deity, Marduk. The impoverished classes of the nation were returning to Jerusalem as the Jewish Persian elite, "the assimilationist faction" in R. Benny Lau's words, was completing its integration into the sources of political and economic power of Persia's capital.

> He was foster father to Hadassah – that is, Esther – his uncle's daughter, for she had neither father nor mother. The maiden was shapely and good-looking; and when her father and mother died, Mordechai adopted her as his own daughter. When the king's order and edict was heard, and when many girls were assembled in Shushan the capital under the supervision of Hegai, Esther too was taken into the king's palace under the supervision of Hegai, guardian of the women. (2:7-8)

Verse 7 seems to tell an entire story in just a few short words: Hadassah, daughter of Mordechai's uncle Avihayil, loses her father and mother, and Mordechai adopts her. Embarking on her new life as Mordechai's adopted daughter is marked by other changes as well: Mordechai himself is already well integrated into the Persian political landscape. His adopted daughter though, still carries the name Hadassah, one of the four species,[9] which reflects her family's loyalty to Eretz Yisrael. Under Mordechai's influence, Hadassah undergoes a "Persianization" process. Her name is changed to Esther, for the Mesopotamian goddess Ishtar.[10]

One source of puzzlement remains, though: The Tanakh is extremely economical with words; there are never any extra descriptors, so when one is used, there is always a good reason. Rachel, daughter of Lavan, is the only character described with the double description, "shapely and beautiful" ("*yefat to'ar ve-yefat mar'eh*"), which helps us understand why Yaakov was willing to work for Lavan for seven years for "Rachel, your younger daughter." Esther is described as a "maiden shapely and good-

---

9 The four species taken on Sukkot are the *lulav* (palm frond), *etrog* (citron), *arava* (willow), and *hadas* (myrtle).

10 In this context it is interesting to note the mirror image of this phenomenon: the Hebraization of names. In the early years of the State of Israel, Prime Minister David Ben-Gurion insisted that people, especially officials, Hebraize their names. In Ben-Gurion's view changing a name was a symbol of changing one's essence: from a generation of exile to a generation that was being built up in its land. David Ben-Gurion himself was David Grun, and his successors likewise were no more than one generation removed from European surnames (Shertok-Sharett, Shkolnick-Eshkol, Meyerson-Meir, Rubitzov-Rabin, Persky-Peres, Yezernitsky-Shamir, Mileikovsky-Netanyahu, Scheinermann-Sharon, and Brog-Barak). Army officers, Foreign Ministry workers, ministers, Knesset members, and senior government employees used Hebraized names, as did many prominent cultural figures (Ephraim Kishon [Ferenc Hoffmann], Haim Gouri [Garfinkel], Haim Hefer [Feiner], Amos Oz [Klausner] and hundreds of others).

looking" ("*yefat to'ar ve-tovat mar'eh*"). This description is likewise neither excessively figurative nor an embellishment; it has a purpose.

The structure of verse 8 is unusual. Prima facie, it should have read: "When they publicized the king's order and edict...." Instead it reads: "When the king's order and edict was heard." The significance here is as follows: The decisive moment was not the publication of the king's order, but the fact that someone heard it and recognized the huge opportunity this "maiden shapely and good-looking" represented. We are told here that "Esther was taken," and it seems that she was taken against her will. This begs the question: Who forced her?

R. Yitzhak Reggio, a major figure in the *Wissenschaft Des Judentums* movement, offers a bold answer in his commentary to the Megilah:[11]

> We have no choice but to accept the commentary of R. Avraham ben Ezra, who writes: "There are those who say that Mordechai was worried that the king would not take her if he knew that she was from the exile." This is consistent with the plain meaning of the subsequent stories in the Megilah; Mordechai wanted nothing more than to see the royal crown on Esther's head. It is on account of this hope that he would walk each day before the harem courtyard, to see what was happening with her and if she had succeeded in her bid for the throne, as he hoped. This despite the fact that the remnants of Israel in each generation, those who truly understand the destiny of the Jewish nation, do not seek temporary positions of power, neither for themselves nor for their families, and certainly not to sit on the royal throne in order to rule over a nation that serves multiple deities and be associated with a king that bows down to the sun. Moreover,

11 My thanks to Ariela and R. Hillel Novetsky for bringing R. Reggio's commentary to my attention.

> it is certainly inappropriate for a Jew to abandon his faith and become repulsive through forbidden foods just to gain power.

In other words, Mordechai himself was the "someone" who heard about the edict and recognized the chance to get a beautiful young Jewish woman into the throngs of virgins and perhaps onto the throne, even though the young woman, Esther, did not understand his machinations and did not want to partake in this beauty pageant. Her Jewishness yet pulsed within her, but Mordechai, her adopted father, pushed her into it. She was thus taken, against her will, obeying her guardian.

> The girl pleased him and won his favor, and he hastened to furnish her with her cosmetics and her rations, as well as with the seven maids who were her due from the king's palace; and he treated her and her maids with special kindness in the harem. (2:9)

Esther's pleasant mannerisms recommended her, and she found favor in the eyes of the eunuch Hegai. This statement is a point of contrast with Mordechai's approach, which only recognizes Esther for her beauty. In the verse where Mordechai is mentioned, Esther is described as a "maiden shapely and good-looking." In the verse where Hegai is mentioned, Esther is described as having a graceful and winning personality. She earned the favor of Hegai, who had discerned her Jewish character. He values more important traits, like grace and kindness, and he encourages her to enhance her beauty with cosmetics.

> Esther did not reveal her people or her kindred, for Mordechai had told her not to reveal it. Every single day Mordechai would walk about in front of the court of the harem, to learn how Esther was faring and what was happening to her. (2:10-11)

Esther concealed her identity and her nationality because Mordechai instructed her not to reveal them. Mordechai was already identified as a Jew. He may have even held some status and had some stature within Persia's elite institutions. If Esther's identity were discovered, it could have sparked a hostile response from those who did not look kindly on the rapidly increasing eminence of the Jews. The path to the throne had to be acquired quietly and with finesse. Mordechai therefore worked assiduously to conceal Esther's identity and present her as a thoroughly Persian woman.

> When each girl's turn came to go to King Ahashevrosh at the end of the twelve months' treatment prescribed for women (for that was the period spent on beautifying them: Six months with oil of myrrh and six months with perfumes and women's cosmetics, and it was after that that the girl would go to the king), whatever she asked for would be given her to take with her from the harem to the king's palace. She would go in the evening and leave in the morning for a second harem under the charge of Shaashgaz, the king's eunuch, guardian of the concubines. She would not go again to the king unless the king wanted her, when she would be summoned by name. When the turn came for Esther daughter of Avihayil – the uncle of Mordechai, who had adopted her as his own daughter – to go to the king, she did not ask for anything but what Hegai, the king's eunuch, guardian of the women, advised. Yet Esther won the admiration of all who saw her. Esther was taken to King Ahashverosh, in his royal palace, in the tenth month, which is the month of Tevet, in the seventh year of his reign. The king loved Esther more than all the other women, and she won his grace and favor more than all the virgins. So he set a royal diadem on her head and made her queen instead of Vashti. (2:12-17)

Once again, there is a contrast to Mordechai. Even the king, who cavorted with his concubines and fed his appetite for wine, recognized Esther's refined Jewish character virtues. And he fell in love – not out of lust, but because he discerns her grace and kindness.

This point may also explain the king's regret for what he did to Vashti: He may have been in love with her, but the partying, the wine, and the many women caused him to lose his mind, lose his conscience, and lose Vashti.

So when Esther arrived, the king recognized that she is a woman, not just a sex object, and he fell in love with her, crowning her queen in place of Vashti. The Megilah never suggests that Ahashverosh was righteous, but he certainly was not entirely bad, and was clearly no fool. R. Reggio points out: "It is obvious that Ahashverosh was not a foolish, indecisive, or cruel king." He made a reckless decision at the behest of his advisers, but his true inclinations and intuitions were rather decent.

Even though Esther spent six months slathered in oil of myrrh and another six months immersed in perfumes, she still radiates Jewish grace, and this is what the king finds attractive. Mordechai put his hopes in Esther's beauty, but what actually wins the king over is her kindness and grace.

Empire in Crisis

> The king gave a great banquet for all his officials and courtiers, "the banquet of Esther." He proclaimed a remission of taxes for the provinces and distributed gifts as befits a king. (2:18)

The war in the west was a disaster for the Persian Empire. King Xerxes I returned home after losing the naval Battle of Salamis, where the Persians lost much of their fleet. He left his army in the command of Mardonius, who did not succeed in reaching an agreement with the Greeks and was later killed in the Battle of Platea.

The signs of this defeat are discernible in the Megilah. The grand banquet that Ahashevrosh hosted in the third year of his reign was attended by all of his officers and courtiers, "the military leadership of Persia and Media, the nobles, and the governors of the provinces in his service." After this banquet, Ahashverosh hosted another banquet for the residents of Shushan, who were exempt from paying taxes.

At the banquet in Esther's honor, however, the Persian military brass, noblemen, and governors are conspicuously absent. The first banquet celebrated the collection of massive amounts of taxes from the vast expanses of the Persian Empire, hosted the governors of the provinces that paid tribute to the king and many soldiers preparing for the military campaign that would soon be fought in the west.

In contrast, Esther's coronation banquet was a far more modest affair. The king no longer displayed his ostentatious wealth, "the vast riches of his kingdom and the magnificent prestige of his majesty." There was not much of a crowd to impress: Only the "officials and courtiers" participated in this banquet. His wealth was not nearly as impressive as before. Herodotus explains (III:96) that the king used to melt down the gold that was brought to him and pour the molten metal into earthen vessels. When he needed to make expenditures, he would break the vessel and coin the requisite amount of gold. The military campaign in the west caused Ahashverosh to break quite a few jugs.

The provinces under Persian rule did not send representatives to this banquet, nor do they bring taxes or pay tribute: The war has depleted their resources. Ahashverosh is well aware of this. "He proclaimed a remission of taxes for the provinces"; Rashi explains this to mean that "in Esther's honor, he absolved them of their tax obligations." The decision to grant a tax break to the satrapies under Persian rule was indeed an expression of his love for Esther, but there are practical considerations as well: Given the difficult financial situation, with Ahashverosh still licking his wounds from the failed campaign in Greece, the king could not risk being forced to make war against another rebellious province. He therefore won the provinces over with a generous, populist economic policy. Economic populism is often a near-term solution for a restless populace and power hungry politician. There is no doubt, as R. Benny Lau writes, that the wind had been knocked out of his sails and he did not have much desire to go to war. He preferred to devote himself to pleasure-seeking for the time being.

The residents of Shushan also lost out here. The first chapter describes a seven-day celebration "for all the people who lived in Shushan the capital, high and low alike," that featured "royal wine [that] was served in abundance, as befits a king." This time, at the banquet in Esther's honor, only the king's officials and courtiers participated. The only display of wealth was that he "distributed gifts as befits a king." In Persia, it was customary that the king could not send guests away empty-handed. There was no wine at this celebration, so the king had to emphasize the gifts that he dispensed to those in attendance.

> When the virgins were assembled a second time, Mordechai sat in the palace gate. But Esther still did not reveal her kindred or her people, as Mordechai had instructed her; for Esther obeyed Mordechai's bidding, as she had done when she was under his tutelage. (2:19-20)

This is the second mention of Mordechai's position at the palace gate. This repetition is not incidental: It highlights Mordechai's important status in the royal court. He was a figure of renown, but he did not rest on his laurels. He was on alert, and his ears were open. His sharp hearing is what got Esther into the palace in the first place, and now he was anxious that someone might reveal that Esther is a Jew. When the virgins were assembled in Shushan for a second time,[12] apparently not long after

12 My good friend Aviad Friedman explains this verse with a bureaucratic joke:

Esther's coronation and the banquet in her honor, it raised Mordechai's suspicion that someone would try to ruin the celebration and harm his improved status. He again insisted that Esther not divulge her homeland or her nationality, so as not to risk provoking protest against Jewish closeness to the government.

> At that time, when Mordechai was sitting in the palace gate, Bigtan and Teresh, two of the king's eunuchs who guarded the threshold, became angry, and sought to do violence to King Ahasuerus. Mordechai learned of it and told it to Queen Esther, and Esther reported it to the king in Mordechai's name. The matter was investigated and found to be so, and the two were hanged on beams. This was recorded in the book of annals at the instance of the king. (2:21-23)

Mordechai's position at the palace gate alludes to another character who went into exile and then rose to a prominence in the new locale, to the point of sitting at the gate: "Lot sat in the gate of Sodom." The Sages understood that Lot did not just happen to be sitting by the gate of the city, but had rather been chosen as a judge in the corrupt city of Sodom.

Sitting in the gate of the city was very significant in terms of finance and security. One who sat in the gate was close to the corridors of power; he had his finger on the pulse. He knew who entered and left, who delivered produce and in what quantities, how many sacks of gold dust arrived in taxes for the king, who was sent on an urgent royal mission, and visited the king.[13]

Why do all of the virgins assemble for a second time if a queen has already been chosen? Because the officials had already received their instructions, so the bureaucracy continued on, even if the goal had already been reached.

13 It is worth mentioning Avshalom, who conspired to rebel against David and who stood in the gate in order to judge Israel, in this context. "Avshalom rose early

Mordechai sat in the gate of the king like one of the noblemen, but he was listening carefully to every rustle of doubt or slight hesitation – like every court Jew who knows how precarious his position is. Coincidentally, this is how he found another opportunity to improve his status: His ears prick up when he hears a rumor that Bigtan and Teresh, two of the king's eunuchs, want to assassinate the king. He communicates this to Queen Esther, who in turn tells the king "in Mordechai's name." The rebellion has been exposed, the insurgents hanged, and the entire episode duly recorded in the king's chronicles.[14] The term "who guarded the threshold" is striking. Bigtan and Teresh are eunuchs of the king, but the author of the Megilah chooses to describe them as guardians of the threshold. Similar figures appear in the book of Melakhim, in events that transpired during the days of King Yehoash and King Yoshiyahu, more than 150 years before the events of the Megilah:

> In the eighteenth year of King Yoshiyahu, the king sent the scribe Shaphan, son of Atzalyahu, son of Meshullam to the House of

---

and stood by the path to the gate. Avshalom called out to every man who had a controversy and came to the king for judgement, saying: "Which city do you come from?"... Avshalom did like this for all of Israel who came to the king for judgement and thus stole the hearts of the men of Israel." (2 Shmuel 15)

14 R. Benny Lau points to the literary role of the conspiracy of Bigtan and Teresh, contrasting it with the Sages' view of Mordechai. Mordechai's sitting in the king's gate "teaches us about Mordechai's elevated status among the upper class of Persian society. It is impossible to imagine a publicly observant Jew, a head of the Sanhedrin, leading the isolationist faction of those who are faithful to Torah, all while sitting 'in the palace gate.' Mordechai is not anonymous. He is well known and he has the stature of one who sits in the gate." This is why his information about the assassination attempt is taken so seriously. R. Lau adds: "The literary role of this episode is to serve as an introduction to the king's insomnia in chapter 4, but from a historical perspective, it speaks of Mordechai's status as an honorable person whose words are taken seriously."

> the Lord, saying: "Go to the high priest Hilkiyahu and let him weigh the silver that has been deposited in the House of the Lord, which the **guards of the threshold** have collected from the people. And let it be delivered to the overseers of the work who are in charge at the House of the Lord, that they in turn may pay it out to the workmen that are in the House of the Lord, for the repair of the House: to the carpenters, the laborers, and the masons, and for the purchase of wood and quarried stones for repairing the House. However, no check is to be kept on them for the silver that is delivered to them, for they deal honestly." (2 Melakhim 22:3-7)

They appear again in chapter 23:

> Then the king ordered the high priest Hilkiyahu, the priests of the second rank, and the **guards of the threshold** to bring out of the Temple of the Lord all the objects made for Ba'al and Asherah and all the host of heaven. He burned them outside Jerusalem in the fields of Kidron, and he removed the ashes to Beit El. (*ibid.* 23:4)

Also in the days of Yehoash:

The priest Yehoyada took a chest and bored a hole in its lid. He placed it at the right side of the altar as one entered the House of the Lord, and the priestly **guards of the threshold** deposited there all the money that was brought into the House of the Lord. Whenever they saw that there was much money in the chest, the royal scribe and the high priest would come up and put the money accumulated in the House of the Lord into bags, and they would count it. Then they would deliver the money that was weighed out to the overseers of the work, who were in charge of the House of the Lord. These, in turn, used to pay the carpenters and the laborers who worked on the House of the Lord, and the masons and the stonecutters. They also paid for wood and for quarried stone with which to make the repairs on the House of the Lord, and for every other expenditure that had to be made in repairing the House. (*ibid.* 12:10-13)

In all of these contexts, the guardians of the threshold were responsible for the Temple's revenues, in one way or another. *Targum Yonatan* translates "guardians of the threshold" ("*shomrei ha-saf*") as "*amarkalia*" – treasurers, financial officers. Or as Radak comments in 2 Melakhim: "the chief treasurers who had others working under them." It emerges from here that Bigtan and Teresh guarded the threshold of the national treasury or were responsible for tax and money collection points.

From their vantage point as guards of the treasury for King Ahashverosh, Bigtan and Teresh clearly saw the gradual emptying of the empire's coffers. They, perhaps more than anyone else, understood that Persia was entering a period of economic difficulty and hardship: Expenditures increased while revenues dwindled. Perhaps they reached the conclusion that Ahashverosh was making financially irresponsible decisions and thought that this was triggered, at least partially, by his choice of Esther as queen. As eunuchs – people without children or families – their sole priority was the national treasury and kingdom's fiscal health. They decided to do something about the situation: kill the king and restore Persia and Media to their past glory, or, to borrow from contemporary parlance, to "make Persia great again."

It is not clear whether Mordechai or Ahashverosh understood the full background of this conspiracy. At this stage, it is unlikely that Mordechai knew much about the kingdom's financial state. Ahashverosh knew but perhaps did not grasp the connection between his dwindling resources and Bigtan and Teresh's plot. Either way, the impending financial depression was the backdrop of the conspiracy.

It is also possible that the author of the Megilah is offering subtle criticism. The original, true guards of the threshold were hard at work in

Jerusalem at this time, building the Temple – the house of the supreme King of Kings – with the limited resources of the Jews there. But this does not concern Mordechai. His ears are attuned only to the words of the Persian threshold guards.

The king and the officers trusted Mordechai's statement about Bigtan and Teresh. The Megilah records, "the matter was investigated and found to be so." Action was taken quickly and definitively. And then, "this was recorded in the book of annals at the instance of the king." This is the ultimate purpose of this story; recording something in the king's chronicles is no small thing. This book functions as a journal of events for the king himself. The most important book of all is "the Annals of the Kings of Media and Persia," which is mentioned in chapter 10 of the Megilah. It records the events that have significance for the history of the empire. Nevertheless, the king's annals sat on the same bookshelf and recorded important events and individuals. In short, Mordechai's prestige had grown tremendously in the eyes of the king and his officers. His stature grew just as the economy entered a downward spiral.

This episode also presents a threat. By exposing the conspiracy against the king, Mordechai has also exposed his connection to Esther. Mordechai was seemingly close enough to the guardians of the threshold, the gatekeepers of the treasury, to detect their subversion, and he also is a blood relation of the queen. This level of proximity to the king and the treasury is a troubling sign in the eyes of many people, specifically those who are powerful in the king's court. Haman begins to cultivate a plan to deal with this new nuisance.

Mordechai Would Not Kneel or Bow Low

> In the aftermath of these things, King Ahashverosh promoted Haman son of Hammedata the Agagite; he advanced him and seated him higher than any of his fellow officials. (3:1)

The obvious question is: In the aftermath of which "things" did King Ahashverosh promote Haman "higher than any of his fellow officials?" Later in this chapter, we learn that we are now in the twelfth year of Ahashverosh's reign – that is, five years had passed since Bigtan and Teresh's conspiracy was exposed and Esther was chosen as queen. In this not overly lengthy span of time, Haman – who according to some approaches descended from an immigrant family, just like Mordechai – had risen from unknown entity to Ahashverosh's top adviser.

The reason for his rapid advance is not entirely clear. According to Dr. Yonatan Grossman, Haman was a bodyguard of sorts, promoted in the "aftermath" of the assassination attempt. Rashi, taking a midrashic approach, also links Haman's promotion to the foiled plot. He explains "in the aftermath of these things" to mean that Haman was only promoted "after the remedy that would bring salvation to the Jewish people was prepared." Both of these explanations are conjectural; one is based on a plausible sequence of events, and the other, perhaps, is based on the author's intent.

> All the king's courtiers in the palace gate knelt and bowed low to Haman, for such was the king's order concerning him; but Mordechai would not kneel or bow low (3:2)

If the meteoric rise of Haman to power seems unclear, Mordechai's conduct is positively incomprehensible. R. Benny Lau raises a series of hypotheses to explain Mordechai's defiance. Firstly, he assumes that the conflict between Haman and Mordechai derives perhaps from the emerging rivalry between two royal officials with growing influence in the king's court: One depends on his influence over the king, the other on his familial and political connections to the king.

Another theory, rooted in traditional exegesis, is that Mordechai's refusal to bow before Haman was an act of self-sacrifice, to avoid prostrating before an idol. In a similar vein, albeit without the overtly religious aspect, is the approach that emphasizes national pride. This approach views Mordechai as a contrast to the patriarch Yaakov, who exhibited a yielding, submissive attitude in his conflict with Esav and his anxious disavowal of Shimon and Levi after their decimation of the inhabitants of Shekhem. Yaakov thus exemplifies a policy of surrender, deception, and survival. Mordechai, in contrast, stands up straight, willing to sacrifice his life to sanctify God's name and restore the flagging pride of his subjugated nation.

Another possibility, based on a somewhat opaque *midrash*[1] and developed in other *midrashim* as well, puts forth an elaborate backstory in which Mordechai and Haman were among the top brass in the army of Ahashverosh. Haman became indebted and subservient to Mordechai, which led to unavoidable hostility between the two when they returned to Shushan and began climbing the political ladder.[2]

---

1 BT *Megilah* 15a

2 According to R. Benny Lau in his essay on Megilat Esther.

Once again, I will adopt an economic explanation. This seems to be the most natural explanation, especially given that the author of the Megilah chose to begin and end the book with blatantly economic issues. This explanation also fits better with the amount of time that elapsed from Bigtan and Teresh's plot until Haman's rise to power, since financial depressions do not happen overnight, but rather develop slowly over time. To explain what the Megilah is telling us here, we will skip back and forth a bit between four verses from three different passages, each of which can point us in the right direction and which together offer a complete picture of Haman's rise to power. Chapter 2 states:

> The king gave a great banquet for all his officials and courtiers, "the banquet of Esther." He proclaimed a remission of taxes for the provinces and distributed gifts as befits a king. When the virgins were assembled a second time, Mordechai sat in the palace gate. (2:18-19)

The second assembly of virgins raises questions. Ahashverosh had just completed a contest to elect a new queen and had even celebrated the new queen's coronation with a banquet, a festive declaration of tax cuts ("a remission of taxes for the provinces"), and distribution of "gifts as befits a king." Suddenly, without any explanation, we find that right after the first contest ends, a **second** one begins.

A bit further along in the story, Haman made a promise to the king:

> If it please Your Majesty, let an edict be drawn for their destruction, and I will pay ten thousand talents of silver to the stewards for deposit in the royal treasury. (3:9)

Haman attempted to persuade the king to call for the destruction of the Jews by promising to supply him with "ten thousand talents of silver." This is an astronomical sum of money. In order to understand the significance of this amount, we turn to the Greek historian Herodotus, who tallies the taxes paid by various kingdoms under Persian rule (III:89 ff.). For instance, Herodotus states that Phoenicia, Eretz Yisrael, and Cyprus together paid 350 talents of silver for an entire year. The total tax revenue of the empire, with the exception of the state of India (which paid in gold ore, which was more valuable), was 9,880 talents of silver. That is, Haman promised to give Ahashverosh an entire year's worth of imperial tax revenues – so that he could kill all the Jews.

All of the commentators attempt to explain how Haman could recoup the unbelievable sum of 10,000 talents of silver from killing the Jews. Some assume that Haman was just blowing hot air and making vague promises. Others suggest that he expected to acquire the requisite sum by pillaging wealthy Jews after killing them. It is not known whether such an amount could be extracted from all of the Jews, but the immediate consequence of Haman's request was:

> The couriers went out posthaste on the royal mission, and the decree was proclaimed in Shushan the capital. The king and Haman sat down to feast, but the city of Shushan was dumfounded. (3:15)

Here it is explicit: Haman had only just brandished the massive financial reward, and the couriers were already traveling at high speed. Indeed, it seems that 10,000 silver talents could persuade a king to change his mind, especially when that king's empire is in the midst of a financial depression in the aftermath of a military debacle and the capital's culture of conspicuous consumption, as exemplified by the pageant to find a new queen.

Haman's rise to power was rooted in an economic reality and political machinations concerning the national treasury, but like all biblical stories, the author is not only interested in telling us what happened, but also **why**.

This story has a Jewish moral dimension that the Megilah's author alludes to and seeks to reveal.

Others have noted that the structure of the verses that tell of Haman's rise to power are strikingly similar to the verses that describe the rise of King Yehoyakhin (Yekhoniah) of Judah in Babylonian captivity.[3]

> In the thirty-seventh year of the exile of King Yehoyakhin of Judah, on the twenty-seventh day of the twelfth month, King Evil-merodach of Babylon, in the year he became king, took note of King Yehoyakhin of Judah and released him from prison. He spoke kindly to him, and gave him a throne above those of other kings who were with him in Babylon. His prison garments were removed, and he received regular rations by his favor for the rest of his life. A regular allotment of food was given him at the instance of the king – an allotment for each day – all the days of his life. (2 Melakhim 25:27-30)

Thirty-seven years after the exile of Yekhoniah, and twenty-six years after the destruction of Shlomo's temple (after eleven years of Tzidkiyahu's reign), Yekhoniah was granted a unique opportunity. His improved status (possibly) enabled the Jews to return to Eretz Yisrael even before the end of the seventy years of exile prophesied by Yirmiyahu. There was precedent for this: God had promised four hundred years of exile in Egypt, but shortened the actual exile to 210 years. Likewise the Babylonian exile, the first exile after the Egyptian exile, could have been shortened, but the Jewish people did not jump at the chance. Yekhoniah did nothing, the Jews did not act, and the possibility of capitalizing on the venerable Yekhoniah's improved status slipped through their fingers.[4]

---

3 Grossman and others have noted this similarity, but their goals and interpretations differ from mine.

4 In the book *Shivhei Ha-Arizal* the following story is told about R. Yitzhak Luria,

Something similar happened in the days of Mordechai and Esther. The author of the Megilah therefore uses similar language and similar sentence structure to describe Haman's ascent to power. The Jews of Shushan and of the Persian Empire were given one chance, during the Vashti episode, to understand that their values are not Persian values and that their long-term place is not among the Persians. When Esther achieved greatness, and Mordechai rose to prominence at the king's gate, the opportunity to flip the script and return to Eretz Yisrael was within reach. This is exceedingly similar to Yekhoniah, who missed his chance in Babylonia, and diametrically opposed to Moshe, who capitalized on it in Egypt.

But five years passed, and the Jews apparently decided that the political and financial centers of control of Persia are not the means, but rather the ends. They missed another opportunity, just like Yekhoniah's eighty years earlier. As often happens, one who disregards opportunity ultimately must contend with a more difficult fate: Immediately after missing their chance, the king promotes Haman "higher than any of his fellow officials." The sign from God has been given – the Jews had political power and opportunity at their disposal – but they chose not to make use of it. When the Jews refused to return to their land and their birthplace, the punishment came in the form of bourgeoning anti-Semitism.[5]

The financial background that prepared the ground for Haman's

---

the Ari Ha-Kadosh: One Shabbat eve, shortly before the evening prayer, he turned to his students , and said: "My friends, do you wish to travel to Jerusalem before Shabbat, and celebrate Shabbat in Jerusalem?" After a few of the students began to ask if they might first consult their wives, the Ari clapped his hands and said: "How unfortunate that we are not worthy of redemption. If only we would have responded as one that we would happily go, Israel would have been immediately redeemed, because now if the time of redemption. Since you held back, the exile has returned to us."

5 Many commentators search for the ethical statement and prophecy hidden within the Megilah. To my mind, this is its very essence: One who squanders opportunity may ultimately be punished.

success now comes into sharper focus: The empire's tax revenues were flagging, and the tax breaks and "gifts" from the banquet in Esther's honor certainly did not help fill the kingdom's coffers. The regathering of the virgins is a clear sign that Haman and company were working behind the scenes to undermine Esther's status, which they viewed (or scapegoated) as the proximate cause of the empire's financial troubles. The king had chosen Esther and, relative to its dwindled capacity, spent an outsized portion of the imperial budget on her coronation, so his advisers were beginning to think about putting a new queen on the throne. To that end, they assembled a second group of virgins.

This issue is also linked to Esther's ancestry, because "when the virgins were assembled a second time" is juxtaposed to the author's second mention that "Esther still did not reveal her kindred or her people." Esther did not say a word, but the suspicions of the king's officers and advisers had certainly been aroused.

I maintain that Haman rose to power by virtue of his efforts to stabilize the Persian economy. Perhaps he was quite wealthy before, or perhaps he acquired great wealth during over the course of the previous five years, when he was a close affiliate of the king. He may have procured certain material benefits from business deals that brought money to the empire's reserves, thereby building his private wealth as well. Haman was personally financially successful but was still working to reestablish the king's economic standing and stabilize the Persian Empire's treasury. The king therefore believed that Haman would manage to bring 10,000 silver talents into the kingdom's coffers.

For this same reason the Megilah's author points out at the end of the chapter that "The king and Haman sat down to feast." The sense shared by Haman and Ahashverosh is that, after a five-year hiatus during which there were no feasts, the glory days were returning, and they could go back to the good times, when "the rule for drinking was: no restrictions!" The king had known difficult years since then – five years of military defeat and economic recession. But Ahashverosh and Haman were beginning to believe that things were about to change for the better.

The bewilderment felt in Shushan had several contributing factors. Firstly, the imminent financial relief that Haman and the king were celebrating was unknown to the rest of the city's population. The money had not yet made its way to the treasury, and certainly had not trickled down into the local economy. They wondered, like Kohelet (2:2), "what does pleasure accomplish?" In typical anti-Semitic form, Haman managed to blame the Jews for the economic decline and promise economic salvation though the plunder of Jewish property, but the masses had not yet internalized this message. They still liked the Jews; they still worked for and alongside Jews. When anti-Semitic leaders arise, they first identify a scapegoat, and the rest of the people eventually come on board.

The script did not play out quickly, and indeed, it never does. Historical examples demonstrate that persecution usually follows a period during which the people are "groomed" to participate actively in, or at the very least to condone, the persecution. Even under Nazism, the persecution of the Jews did not reach its crescendo when Hitler first gained power. The situation escalated gradually, as the Nazi regime "experimented" with public reaction in Germany during its first seven or eight years in power.

Ahashverosh's directive that everyone must bow down to Haman had a concrete meaning and an allegorical meaning. Power resides with whoever controls the purse strings. The king was in his palace, out of sight. The public face of the regime was the treasurer, the source of livelihood and budgetary allocations for all the king's officials and attendants. Mordechai, an affluent Jew, was not willing to accept Haman's economic authority.

Here again we are reminded of the story of Yosef in Bereishit. At the beginning of his story, Yosef tells his brothers about his dream:

> We were binding sheaves in the field, and suddenly my sheave arose and stood upright. And then your sheaves gathered round and bowed down to my sheave. (Bereishit 37:7)

Already in his very first dream, Yosef explained to his brothers that ruling the economy (bread and wheat) will bring them to bow down to him. Then, in his second dream, his future exalted status becomes evident: "the sun and the moon and the eleven stars bowed down to me."

Yosef predicted in his dream that Yaakov and his sons would bow down to him, and this is exactly what happened: Pharaoh appointed Yosef over the Egyptian treasury, including all of the attendant honor and prestige accorded to one who succeeded in providing for the economic and fiscal needs of the kingdom.

> He paraded him in the second chariot which he had, and they called before him, "On your knees!" He put him in charge of the entire land of Egypt. Pharaoh said to Yosef, "I am Pharaoh and without you no man shall lift up his head or foot anywhere in Egypt." (Bereishit 41:43-44)

Everyone bowed reverently to the finance minister: All would genuflect, their hands and feet reaching the ground.

> Then the king's courtiers who were in the palace gate said to Mordechai, "Why do you disobey the king's order?" When they spoke to him day after day and he would not listen to them, they told Haman, in order to see whether Mordechai's resolve would prevail; for he had explained to them that he was a Jew. When Haman saw that Mordechai would not kneel or bow low to him, Haman was filled with rage. But he disdained to lay hands on Mordechai alone; having been told who Mordechai's people

> were, Haman plotted to do away with all the Jews, Mordechai's people, throughout the kingdom of Ahashverosh. (3:3-6)

Yosef and Haman both achieved positions that put them in charge of providing sustenance for their respective kingdoms.

Haman's behavior did not initially stem from Jew-hatred or religious motives. Rather, he was convinced that he, as finance minister, was deserving of having everyone bow before him. With Mordechai's defiance, he had more substantive and urgent reasons: He already suspected Esther of being a Jew, and now it had become evident that Mordechai – also a Jew, as the king's officers divulged – was refusing to bow down and accept Haman's financial authority.[6] Haman was certainly aware that Mordechai saved the king several years earlier from the sedition of Bigtan and Teresh, "guards of the threshold," the previous treasurers, and that this fact gave Mordechai a certain degree of personal immunity and even some power in the struggle to win the king's graces.

The struggle between them was national, but also, and perhaps primarily, personal. As they say, "Everything is personal." Mordechai uses Jewish attendants, "*ne'arim*," to acquire political clout and influence with the king and access to the wealth of the kingdom. Haman, too, aspires to promote himself and his nation, and he, too, has confidants in the royal court. As in every turning point in the Megilah's plot, here, too, the author introduces a new type of adviser, the "king's courtiers (*avdei hamelekh*) who were in the palace gate," who are loyal to Haman.

These servants of the king bow before Haman without reserve

6 It is worth noting that the author of the Megilah says explicitly that Haman did not know for certain that Mordechai was a Jew. That is, Mordechai had been circulating in the corridors of power and at the palace gate for quite a few years already, yet Haman – the king's prime minister – did not know for sure that Mordechai was a Jew. This state of affairs demonstrates the degree to which Mordechai had assimilated into Persian culture.

whenever he passes the gate. They then turn to Mordechai and admonish him: "Why do you disobey the king's order" by not kneeling and bowing down? Mordechai answers them, or doesn't answer them, but it is clear to these courtiers that he has no intention to bow down, and they attribute this to his Jewishness ("for he had explained to them that he was a Jew").

They decide to conduct an experiment. They tell Haman that Mordechai has no intention of bowing down to him. Haman verifies this and finds "that Mordechai would not kneel or bow low to him," leaving him in a fitful, destructive rage.

Modern commentators, such as R. Benny Lau, R. Yaakov Medan, Dr. Yonatan Grossman, and others, basing themselves on the *midrashim* of the Sages, debate the nature of Mordechai's defiance of Haman. It is clear that there is no religious injunction against bowing down to a person. It was customary in Persia, as in much of the Ancient Near East and much of the contemporary Far East. On the contrary, when Yaakov met Esav "with four hundred men," he bowed seven times on his way to embrace his brother – for obvious practical considerations, but also because it was the customary practice. Some modern commentators therefore centered their discussion on the word "*kara*" (kneeled), which may imply an act of religious service or worship.

It seems to me that the Megilah's author did not intend to relate to issues of idolatry, but rather to economics: As noted earlier, several verses are meant to invoke and remind us of Yosef's appointment as viceroy and finance minister of Egypt. It is hard to view this as the Sages did, namely, as Mordechai's religious struggle against idolatry. There was, perhaps, a national struggle – possibly indicated by the identification of Mordechai as a Jew – about independence and economic influence, but this struggle, at its root, was not religious.

Haman's status was quite similar to the status of Yosef in Egypt, in terms of both his actual power and the potential danger one who disobeys the ruler can expect. Ahashverosh appointed Haman as the highest official:

> In the aftermath of these things, King Ahashverosh promoted Haman son of Hammedata the Agagite; he advanced him and seated him higher than any of his fellow officials. (3:1)

This is exactly what happened to Yosef:

> So Pharaoh said to Joseph, "Since God has made all this known to you, there is none so discerning and wise as you. You shall be in charge of my court, and by your command shall all my people be directed; only with respect to the throne shall I be superior to you." Pharaoh further said to Joseph, "See, I put you in charge of all the land of Egypt." (Bereishit 41:39-41)

Neither of them attained royal status ("only with respect to the throne shall I be superior to you"), which alone could have assured that their status would be inherited, but everything else was in their hands as viceroys to the king and chief financial officers of the kingdom. The king gave them his signet ring, a symbol of his authority. They could do as they wished:

> And removing his signet ring from his hand, Pharaoh put it on Joseph's hand; and he had him dressed in robes of fine linen, and put a gold chain about his neck. (Bereishit 41:42)

Haman's new authority and empowerment are no less obvious:

> Thereupon the king removed his signet ring from his hand and gave it to Haman son of Hammedata the Agagite, the foe of the Jews. And the king said, "The money and the people are yours to do with as you see fit." (3:10-11)

Yosef was granted the honor that all would bow before him:

> He paraded him in the second chariot which he had, and they called before him, "On your knees!"[7] He put him in charge of the entire land of Egypt. (Bereishit 41:43)

And a similar honor was accorded to Haman:

> All the king's courtiers in the palace gate knelt and bowed low to Haman, for such was the king's order concerning him (3:2)

The author's intent is quite clear. All bowed before the man with the keys to the treasury – whether in Egypt or in Persia. They were in charge. Haman's economic rehabilitation plan brought stability to the king, and refilled, at least partially, the kingdom's coffers. Yet Haman's position was far from secure. Like Yosef, he had been promoted to the rank of second-in-command and the head of the king's court on account of his successes, but his status was always tenuous, threatened by any power not subservient to him. In Haman's estimation, Mordechai's independence, like the sovereign status of the Jews in Shushan and in all of Persia – including the liberated craftsmen ("the artisan and the locksmith") – present a danger.

---

7 The Hebrew "*avrekh*" appears only once (a hapax legomenon) in the Tanakh, which obviously prompts many different explanations. The primary intent of the word is clear: No man will dare to raise his hand or his knee before Yosef. Seforno explains "like the word knee (*berekh),* meaning that every man will bow down on his knee." This explanation appeals to me as well, and we have thus translated it as "On your knees!" We find a similar term in the episode of Avraham's servant: "He made the camels kneel (*va'yavrekh*) by the well outside the city at dusk." This is also the explanation of *Da'at Mikra* in the name of the *Sifrei Devarim*: "R. Yosi b. Dormoskit has already made the meaning plain: '*avrekh*' refers to knees, meaning that everyone would come and go by his authority." Likewise, "this word also contains the sense of kneeling." Yaakov Etzion's more detailed discussion of this point can be found at daat.ac.il.

Haman's fury here is not all that different from the rage of rulers and kleptocrats everywhere who enjoy close ties with government. They respond wrathfully and seek to eliminate strong, independent, wealthy people who they fear have the capacity to undermine them.

Moreover, the risk of economic recession is never that far from the gates of the palace. The kingdom's revenues depend on trade, taxes and conquest, elements that are rather volatile. One rebellious province can threaten an entire empire. One year of drought can cause trade to collapse. The crown is never secure on the king's head, and his signet ring can easily slip from the finger of the viceroy or the thug who has risen to power.

In such a situation, with economic distress looming, wealthy, independent minorities that had once been close to the ruling powers become easy victims. That is what happened in medieval England, for example. Jews there enjoyed independence and great wealth. One Jew in particular, Aaron of Lincoln was even wealthier than the king himself. When England was eventually struck by economic hardship, the Jews were accused of shaving down the coins. They were murdered and expelled from the country. In another instance, when Germany was defeated in World War I, General Erich Ludendorff, acting dictator of Germany during the final years of war, quickly resigned from his position. Shortly thereafter, he fabricated a story wherein he accused the Jews of stabbing the nation in the back.

> But he disdained to lay hands on Mordechai alone; having been told who Mordechai's people were, Haman plotted to do away with all the Jews, Mordechai's people, throughout the kingdom of Ahashverosh. (3:6)

It is instructive to pay attention to the structure of this verse. The words "he disdained" ("*va-yivez*") immediately recall Esav: "Esav disdained (*va-yivez*) the birthright." Aside from the straightforward meaning (disdain), there are two additional connotations. The first is that he made a reckless decision that was motivated by external, marginal reasons. Esav later regretted his decision, as Rashbam explains in his commentary on Bereishit (chs. 25-34). Esav gave up his birthright for a mess of pottage, and this impudent decision came back to haunt him. Secondly, it seems that "he disdained" (*va-yivez*) always relates to money. Ibn Ezra points this out in his comments to the verse "Esav disdained the birthright," commenting: "Esav disdained the birthright because he saw that his father was not wealthy."

Haman disdained the idea of killing Mordechai alone. When he learned of Mordechai's nationality, and knowing of the Jews' great wealth and independent economic status, he decided to destroy all of the Jews in Ahashverosh's empire – to fill the kingdom's coffers, bring additional wealth to his personal bank account, and rid himself of a looming threat. Thus, the wealthier the Jews became, the greater the risk that their status would boomerang against them.

The singular phrase "Mordechai's people" does not seem incidental. In the book of Yehezkel, the prophet, who himself lived in Babylonia, describes the desecration of God's name that stems from exile:

> When they came to those nations, they desecrated My holy name when it was said of them: "These are God's people, but they have left His land." (Yehezkel 36:20)

The author of the Megilah calls our attention to the fact that "God's people" who had been in exile, where their very presence constituted a desecration of God's name, had already returned to Israel. The people who chose to remain in exile were not "God's people" but "Mordechai's people." They were not forced to remain in exile; rather they chose to remain in Persia because they had achieved great economic and political success there. "Mordechai's people" now stood at the brink of annihilation, God forbid, because they chose to tie their fate with the kingdom of the exile instead of the kingdom of God. In the words of Disraeli: "Man is not the creature of circumstances, circumstances are the creatures of man." And one who ties his fate ("*goral*") to lot-casting (likewise, "*goral*")…

> In the first month, that is, the month of Nisan, in the twelfth year of King Ahashverosh, *pur* – which means "the lot" (*goral*) – was cast before Haman concerning every day and every month, [until it fell on] the twelfth month, that is, the month of Adar. (3:7)

Lotteries and lot-casting were accepted customs in Persia, as in many other places, but from the viewpoint of the Megilah's author they are also the inevitable outcome of choosing to remain in exile. Mordechai concealed his Jewish identity, preferring to remain close to power and its trappings. He surrendered Divine providence, thereby exposing himself to fate and chance.

Furthermore, this lottery "was cast before Haman concerning every day and every month" – in sharp distinction to the lottery that was determined in the Tent of Meeting and in God's Temple (Vayikra 16) – "one lot for God and one lot for damnation (Azazel)" – or the lotteries that determined the division of Eretz Yisrael into homesteads (Yehoshua 17-18). The lots cast before Haman were linked to the monthly zodiac, come what may. The lots cast before God were dependent on the will of God and intrinsically connected to Eretz Yisrael: The lots for God and for damnation were cast in the Temple, whereupon the goat for Azazel (the original "scapegoat") would be sent to barren land beyond Jerusalem ("and he shall cast away the goat in the wilderness"). The same applies to the case of Achan, who committed sacrilege by taking from the prohibited spoils of Jericho, leading to the Israelite defeat at the hands of Ai and endangering the entire enterprise of capturing the land.

The lottery cast before Haman was one of fate and fortune. Mordechai, who chose money and identification with paganism (after all, he was named for a Mesopotamian deity) over his Jewish identity, condemned himself to be at the mercy of those deities, fortunes, and constellations – as well as the cash payment that Haman pledged.

> Haman then said to King Ahashverosh, "There is a certain people, scattered and dispersed among the other peoples in all the provinces of your realm, whose laws are different from those of any other people and who do not obey the king's laws; and it is not worth it for Your Majesty to tolerate them." (3:8)

In just one sentence, Haman encapsulates the claims of anti-Semites everywhere and in every era, from the Crusades, to charges of well-poisoning, the Spanish expulsion, the Khmelnytsky massacres, and an unending succession of riots and pogroms, up until the Holocaust, and even beyond.

The Jews are one nation, "scattered and dispersed among the other peoples," a furtive network that spreads its tentacles all through the empire. This nation, singular and unique, is mysterious, different: "Whose laws are different from those of any other people." Haman's claim touches on the root of hostility and resentment towards the Jewish people in the ancient world: Neither the Babylonians, nor the Assyrians, nor the Greeks, nor the Romans could understand why the Jews clung to their monotheistic faith, unwilling to adopt additional gods into their pantheon and worship them as well. In Haman's case, the Jews seemed doubly alien: Adherence to one God was strange, and refusal to worship additional gods is equally strange.

People are naturally afraid of the unknown, the mysterious, and the alien. Haman fully intended to exploit this fear when he explained their differences as grounds for suspicion: "It is not worth it for Your Majesty to tolerate them."[8]

---

8 R. Benny Lau discusses an interesting *midrash* (*Esther Rabbah* 7 s.v. "*yeshno*

Once again, the Megilah's economically-inclined mood comes to the fore. The expression, "It is not worth it…to tolerate them" ("*ein shoveh le-haniham*") is unique to Megilat Esther. Kings, despots, and rulers throughout history understood that the Jews make important contributions to the economy. At times, though, the religious fervor, envy, and hatred of the ruling powers caused them to lose their rational faculties. Thus, Haman maintained that there was no economic justification for tolerating the Jews, neither in the empire's various provinces nor anywhere else that they had influence over the economy.

These statements precede Haman's bewilderingly generous proposal:[9]

> If it please Your Majesty, let an edict be drawn for their destruction, and I will pay ten thousand talents of silver to the stewards for deposit in the royal treasury. (3:9)

These points relate to a central theme of the story: control over the Persian treasuries, the status of finance minister, and holding the authority to act in the king's name.

> Thereupon the king removed his signet ring from his hand and gave it to Haman son of Hammedata the Agagite, the foe of the Jews. And the king said, "The money and the people are yours to do with as you see fit." (3:10-11)

---

am ehad") in which the rabbis of the Roman era reflect on one of the typical allegations of anti-Semites in that time, namely, that the Jews are idlers given their refusal to work on various and frequent holidays. A similar, more concise *midrash* appears in BT *Megilah* 13b: "'Who do not obey the king's laws' – they leave at any time, saying 'Shahi! Pahi!'" Rashi explains that "Shahi" and "Pahi" are acronyms for "*Shabbat ha-yom*" and "*Pesah ha-yom*" ("Today is Shabbat; today is Pesah"). That is, Jews take off at least one day each week, so they cannot be trusted to sustain the country's economy.

9 See the discussion above, p. 2.

There is something very perplexing about the king's reaction. If he wanted to refill his coffers, certainly with such a tremendous sum of money, it is hard to understand why he refused, apparently, Haman's offer to bring such a huge amount of cash into the king's treasury. One possible answer is that Ahashverosh did not refuse the offer but readily accepted it. Accordingly, the expression "the money…is yours" means that Ahashverosh authorized Haman, in his capacity as finance minister or treasurer, to deposit the money himself. That is, Ahashverosh instructed Haman to credit the money to the treasury because Haman anyway bore responsibility for doing so in his capacity as treasurer. This once again echoes the relationship between Pharaoh and Yosef:

> He paraded him in the second chariot which he had, and they called before him, "On your knees!" He put him in charge of the entire land of Egypt.

Alternatively, this chapter and the following chapter are constructed in a way that highlights their contrast to the situation in Eretz Yisrael and illustrates a major feature of the story's plot: the continued presence of Mordechai and the Jews in Shushan and their assimilation among the nations of the world due to the temptations of money. Therefore, the author of the Megilah spotlights the giving of money to the king, which sharply contrasts with a different fundraising campaign happening at the very same time in Eretz Yisrael.[10]

> On the thirteenth day of the first month, the king's scribes were

---

10 R. Menachem Leibtag correctly, in my opinion, accentuates the irony and sarcasm of Megilat Esther. Under the veneer of a story about Esther is a veiled critique of the Jews in exile in Shushan and Persia, who did not return to live in Eretz Yisrael and rebuild the Temple. See his study at http://www.tanach.org/special/purim/purims1.htm.

> summoned and a decree was issued, as Haman directed, to the king's satraps, to the governors of every province, and to the officials of every people, to every province in its own script and to every people in its own language. The orders were issued in the name of King Ahashverosh and sealed with the king's signet. Accordingly, written instructions were dispatched by couriers to all the king's provinces to destroy, massacre, and exterminate all the Jews, young and old, children and women, on a single day, on the thirteenth day of the twelfth month – that is, the month of Adar – and to plunder their possessions. The text of the document was to the effect that a law should be proclaimed in every single province; it was to be publicly displayed to all the peoples, so that they might be ready for that day. The couriers went out posthaste on the royal mission, and the decree was proclaimed in Shushan the capital. The king and Haman sat down to feast, but the city of Shushan was dumfounded. (3:12-15)

When Ahashverosh gave his ring to Haman, he granted him additional powers. The Agagite could now enlist soldiers to deal with those who were eroding the empire's economy and cash reserves. The addressees of this edict, the people who were expected to carry out this action, were not from the king's inner circle – those who were at the banquet in Esther's honor. They were provincial officials and governors, in charge of the peripheral provinces of the Persian Empire. Haman did not want to run the risk and therefore did not attempt to carry out his scheme near Mordechai's power bases. Rather, he sought allies in the outlying kingdoms that had suffered massive economic hardship, where bitterness ran deep, and which consequently were quicker than the capital to find a scapegoat for their resentments.

The couriers depart, carrying the king's edict "to destroy, massacre, and exterminate all the Jews" on account of their economic independence. The provinces were baited by the phrase: "and to plunder their possessions."

The capital city Shushan was dumbfounded. Its residents had not received "the text of the document" and did not understand what precipitated all of the commotion. They saw the king and Haman sitting and drinking, as if they had just come into a great deal of money, but they did not see the economic prosperity that would warrant a banquet.

At the beginning of the next chapter, we find out that "Mordechai learned everything that had happened." That he "learned" implies that he had not yet seen Haman's edict with his own eyes, as it had not been sent to Shushan or its officials. It would take some time for him to get ahold of an official copy. A decree of destruction loomed over the head of each and every Jew in the Persian Empire. It would not be long before Mordechai took the actions necessary, or at least pretended to.

Do Not Imagine that You Will Escape With Your Life

> Mordechai learned of all that had happened, Mordechai tore his clothes and put on sackcloth and ashes. He went through the city, crying out loudly and bitterly, until he came in front of the palace gate; for one could not enter the palace gate wearing sackcloth – Also, in every province that the king's command and decree reached, there was great mourning among the Jews, with fasting, weeping, and wailing, and sackcloth and ashes were proffered to the masses. (4:1-3)

As R. Benny Lau describes, chapter 4 contains the major turning point of the Megilah as well as its most significant character development – the moral and spiritual transformation of Mordechai. The man who bore the pagan name Mardukh, who meticulously concealed his and Esther's nationality, was forced to proclaim himself a Jew in the face of national catastrophe.

R. Benny Lau draws a parallel between Mordechai's story and the story of Yosef in Egypt. Yosef, like Mordechai, begins to acclimate and live a 'past-free' life. He becomes Egyptian and assimilates into his new land. But when Potiphar's wife tries to seduce him, Yosef recoils at the last second, understanding "that he is part of something greater, deeper, and more significant." Accordingly, when he is thrown into jail, he remembers his father's home and presents himself as a Hebrew, not an Egyptian.

It is difficult for me to accept this explanation of events. Mordechai, from the vantage point of the Megilah's author, did not undergo a deep and comprehensive transformation; he persisted in his ways. His changes were behavioral and purely external. They were not fundamental. We do not find Mordechai tearing off his mask of assimilation. If anything, his assimilation intensified. To my mind, this is the approach of the Megilah's author. His intention is not to point to a deep transformation in consciousness.

> Mordechai learned of all that had happened, Mordechai tore his clothes and put on sackcloth and ashes. He went through the city, and he cried out loudly and bitterly (3:1)

The author of the Megilah does not relent from Mordechai, and in this verse, he takes a particularly provocative attitude toward him. The author could have easily borrowed any number of expressions of pain. He could have alluded to the profound grief of King David[1] or the repentance of the Israelites at the time of King Yoshiyahu.[2] Instead, he chooses to use the expression "he cried out loudly and bitterly," which precisely parallels none other than Esav:

> When Esav heard his father's words, he cried out very loudly and bitterly, and he said to his father, "Bless me too, Father!" (Bereishit 27:34)

Of all the expressions of grief and loss that appear in Tanakh, the author of the Megilah specifically borrows the words of Esav at the

---

1 2 Shmuel 15, where David reacts to the rebuke from Natan (the parable of the poor man's sheep).

2 2 Melakhim 22.

moment he realizes and laments his loss of the blessing of prosperity that his father, Yitzhak, gave to his brother Yaakov in his stead: "May God give you from the dew of the heaven and the fat of the earth, an abundance of grain and wine" (*ibid.* 28). This is not the dual blessing of "offspring and land" (*ibid.* 28:4), the additional blessing bestowed upon Yaakov and the people of Israel,[3] that Esav laments, but rather the blessing of material prosperity. This allusion implies that Mordechai lamented being cut off from the imperial gravy train. He was more concerned with the wealth and prosperity of the Jews of Shushan than about the Jewish lives. It was the lament of Esav the Edomite and not Yaakov the Jewish patriarch.

There is a sharp difference between the description of Mordechai's mourning and the description of Ezra's mourning upon his arrival in Jerusalem from the exile. Ezra expresses grief when he learns from the noblemen that the people of Israel had begun to assimilate among the peoples of the land and that "it is the officers and prefects who have taken the lead in this trespass."

> When I heard this, I rent my garment and robe, I tore hair out of my head and beard, and I sat desolate. Around me gathered all who trembled at the words of the God of Israel because of the returning exiles' trespass, while I sat desolate until the evening offering. At the time of the evening offering I ended my fast; still in my torn garment and robe, I got down on my knees and spread out my hands to the Lord my God. (Ezra 9:2-5)

---

3 The blessing of offspring and land is the blessing that was given by God to Avraham, which he then passed on to Yitzhak, and Yitzhak to Yaakov. This blessing includes the promise of Eretz Yisrael to the offspring of Avraham, Yitzchak and Yaakov, as well as the protection and prosperity of said offspring. See the lecture on *Parashat Toldot* by R. Menachem Leibtag, available at: http://www.tanach.org/breishit/toldot/toldots1.htm.

Ezra does not merely rend his clothing; he also plucks out the hair from his head and his beard. This is an extreme act, certainly for a *kohen*, who is not allowed to pluck his hair.[4] In other words, Ezra is so deeply distressed that he loses control. His mourning is so intense that he must be alone with his pain. He isolates himself from the world until those who share his horror about assimilation assemble around him. He then spreads out his hands and prays to God.

In contrast, Mordechai turned outward: He did not grieve in his home. Rather, he donned sackcloth and goes out among the people, publicly demonstrating his mourning so that others will take note and be affected – so that everyone will hear his "loud and bitter cry." Only One was not in Mordechai's intended audience: He did not raise his hands towards God. He did not pray at all.

Mordechai did not undergo pain, atonement, and repentance. He expressed grief outwardly and attracted a following, but he did not internalize the problem and its roots. Moreover, he neither understood nor internalized his personal responsibility for creating the problem. R. Reggio explains this well:

> When Mordechai learns of the evil pronouncement that has been decreed upon the Jews, that they will be slaughtered like sheep, women and children in one day, what does he do to save them from their fate? Does he pour out his heart in prayer and penitence before the God of the world, that He should have mercy on the remnants of Israel, like Daniel did when Nebuchadnezzar sentenced all the sages of Babylonia to death? Is it not a great aptitude of our sainted fathers, prophets, and righteous men to pray before God in troubled times? Even at the point when Darius decreed that no man could pray for a period

4 "[The *kohanim*] shall not make baldness on their heads" (Vayikra 21:5).

> of thirty days, Daniel nonetheless put his life in jeopardy and prayed to God, blessed Him and thanked Him, three times each day. Did [Mordechai] confess his sins and the sins of his people like Daniel did in the first year of Darius's rule (Daniel 9), Ezra at the time of the evening sacrifice (Ezra 9:6), Nehemiah in Shushan (Nehemiah 1:6), or the Levite noblemen after the holiday of Sukkot (Nehemiah 9)? This is most certainly one of the important prerequisites of repentance: to dispel God's anger against Israel by confessing the sins of the nation, as it is written: "They shall confess their sins and the sins of their fathers" (Vayikra 26:40).

The Megilah continues to describe the mourning of Mordechai:

> He came in front of the palace gate; for one could not enter the palace gate wearing sackcloth (4:1)

Mordechai could not pass through the palace gate in sackcloth, as it was explicitly prohibited by law. However, the very mention of the palace gate alludes to two things: Firstly, the author indicates that Mordechai's main interest was still his close ties with the governing authorities;[5] his feet carried him to the source of his power as if of their own will. Secondly, despite his heavy grief and his loud and bitter cry, Mordechai remained well aware of the rules, of what is permitted and what is forbidden. He was not one to pluck hairs from his beard or head. He would obliviously not enter the palace gate.

> Also, in every province that the king's command and decree reached, there was great mourning among the Jews, with fasting,

5 And not to God.

> weeping, and wailing, and sackcloth and ashes were proffered to the masses. (4:3)

This verse calls out for an explanation. The plain meaning of the verse makes it seem that when the terrible news reached the different provinces of the kingdom, the Jews cried over their bitter fate. But what is added by the statement: "sackcloth and ashes were proffered to the masses"? Why was there a need to **offer** people sackcloth and ashes? And why to the masses?

The key word here is "proffered" (*yutza*) – someone offered the sackcloth and ashes to the Jews. That is to say – Mordechai proffered these items to them. This was not a spontaneous process, as with Ezra, where "all who trembled at the words of the God of Israel" gathered around their religious leader. Mordechai was not a religious leader. It is questionable whether the Jewish people thought of him as a leader at all. He organized a demonstration: Come one, come all, bring signs, and wear sackcloth; Mordechai will provide you with ashes at the registration desk. The Hebrew word "proffered" (*yutza*) is a passive causative verb. The Jews were not taking action; rather, Mordechai was attempting to organize them.[6] This was a protest, a demonstration, and not a spiritual transformation.

There is an additional oddity: The Jews did not attempt to understand the reason for the decree. After all, something very terrible happened:

---

6 It is hard not to detect an element of cynicism in the words of *Midrash Rabbah* (§8): "Is there 'great mourning' as opposed to 'minor mourning'? Rather, under normal circumstances, grief subsides gradually for seven days. The first day is intense, but it weakens through the course of the year. The mourning about Haman gradually increased in intensity…." In this verse, the mourning is called 'great' already on the first day, which means it should have subsided. Yet this *midrash* asserts that it actually intensified. This means that it only seemed to intensify, but in truth only Mordechai's demonstration on the first day was a "great mourning." It is thus difficult to accept the *midrash* at face value.

The king issued an edict to completely eradicate all of the Jews. Yet no one wondered what caused this evil to befall them. They did not undergo a process of repentance or introspection.[7] All of their grief was directed at the loss of their social status. It is instructive to recall the example of the king of Nineveh in the book of Yonah: When Yonah comes and declares before the people of Nineveh that "in forty days Nineveh will be overturned," the townspeople believe him, because he speaks the word of God. They pray and repent:

> Let everyone turn back from his evil ways and from the injustice of which he is guilty. Who knows but that God may turn and relent? He may turn back from His wrath, so that we do not perish. (Yonah 3:8-9)

At its core, mourning is not a set of customs or a way of dressing, but an inner state. One who exhibits great piety and is scrupulous about the practices of mourning does not necessarily have greater faith. The author of the Megilah suggests here that the main element of mourning was absent in the case of Mordechai and Haman's decree; there was no real repentance. There was an exhibition of mourning – the "virtue signaling" of grief, as it would be called today – but no internalization of the spiritual and national challenge. The Jews' did not behave as though their lives were at stake, only as if their livelihoods were at risk. Once again, the emphasis is on how the Jews of Shushan clung to their fleshpots, even as their lives were in danger.[8]

---

7 Obviously, on a human level, people under the threat of annihilation cannot be blamed for not thinking of repentance instead of how to escape their plight. However, the stories in the Tanakh, from Nineveh to Ezra seem to suggest that the Biblical expectation is, in fact, to repent through introspection. This is obviously a high bar.

8 My wife often tells of German Jews who, on the eve of World War II, shipped their

Esther, sitting securely in the palace, likewise did not grasp the gravity of the situation:

> When Esther's maidens and eunuchs came and informed her, the queen was greatly agitated. She sent clothing for Mordechai to wear, so that he might take off his sackcloth; but he refused. (4:4)

Esther did not yet believe that the Jews' status would be undermined because everything seemed just fine: She was still queen, still enjoyed a close relationship with the governing powers, and still lived in the palace. Moreover, Haman made sure to send the edict to kill the Jews specifically to the outlying periphery of the empire.

The author of the Megilah tells us that Esther was "greatly agitated," but her response was to send clothing to Mordechai, as though to make it clear to him that this is not the way to achieve results in the royal court and in Shushan. It is quite obvious that the lesson and the threat had not yet been internalized.

When Mordechai refuses to accept the clothing that Esther had sent him and to remove his sackcloth, she called for Hatakh:

> Thereupon Esther summoned Hatakh, one of the eunuchs whom the king had appointed to serve her, and sent him to Mordechai to learn the why and wherefore of it all. Hatakh went out to Mordechai in the city square in front of the palace gate; and Mordechai told him all that had happened to him, and all about the money that Haman had offered to pay into the royal treasury for the destruction of the Jews. He also gave him the written

---

art collections out of Germany while they themselves remained in what would soon become a killing field. Like the Jews of Shushan, they were unaware of the gravity of what was happening around them.

> text of the law that had been proclaimed in Shushan[9] for their destruction. [He bade him] show it to Esther and inform her, and charge her to go to the king and to appeal to him and to plead with him for her people. (4:5-8)

There are many perplexing aspects in this exchange. Firstly, from where did Hatakh suddenly appear? Who was he? We have explained previously that it is important to pay close attention to the appearance of new advisors on the scene. To this we can add another question: What does Hatakh contribute to the story?

Secondly, a death warrant loomed over the Jews of Persia, yet Mordechai chose to tell the story in the following order:

- Mordechai began by recounting "all that had happened to him" personally.
- He then spoke of "all about the money that Haman had offered to pay into the royal treasury".
- Finally, he told of "the written text of the law that had been proclaimed in Shushan for their destruction."

This description certainly follows the chronology of events, beginning with the cause (Haman's anger at Mordechai's defiance), continuing with Haman's reaction (bribing the king to issue the edict), and concluding with the royal edict to annihilate the Jews.

Yet in a more concrete sense, this description reflects a skewed set of priorities. Mordechai buried the lede, like an article with a banner headline that reads: "Ukrainian President Refuses to Shake Hands with Russian Premier," and then buries the news of a Russian nuclear strike on the Ukraine in the seventh paragraph. The city was burning, but instead of yelling "Fire, brothers, fire!" Mordechai began specifically with his

9 I.e., it was legislated in Shushan but disseminated outside of Shushan proper.

personal issues and troubles. Only at the very end of his report did he address the edict calling for the destruction of the Jews.

In verses 8 and 9 we again encounter something strange, at least from a literary perspective. Mordechai made three separate requests of Hatakh, and they are described with three separate verb clauses:

- "show it [the written text of the law] to Esther"
- "inform (*lehagid*) her" – unclear as to what he will tell her
- "charge her to go to the king and to appeal to him and to plead with him for her people"

In verse 9, Hatakh follows through on Mordechai's directives but in one action, the second one:

> Hatakh came and told (*va-yaged*) Esther Mordechai's words.

From Esther's response we learn exactly what Hatakh said to her:

> Esther told Hatakh to take back to Mordechai the following reply: "All the king's courtiers and the people of the king's provinces know that if any person, man or woman, enters the king's presence in the inner court without having been summoned, there is but one law for him – that he be put to death. Only if the king extends the golden scepter to him may he live. Now I have not been summoned to visit the king for the last thirty days. (4:10-11)

This means that Hatakh delivered Mordechai's message to Esther that she must beseech the king, but it is not clear that he showed her the text of the edict or actually commanded her to intervene with the king. It is obvious from Esther's response that she still did not grasp the threat in all of its severity. Hatakh, who we have not encountered until this point in time, turns out to be a rather undependable and even disloyal courier.

Hatakh was "one of the eunuchs whom the king had appointed to serve her." By contrasting the detailed instructions that Mordechai gave Hatakh with the thoroughly inadequate rendition that Hatakh transmitted to Esther, the author indicates that Hatakh was not faithful to Esther and might have even sought to harm her. Perhaps he was even a secret agent who sought to send Esther to her death in the king's chambers.

This is the danger that awaited Esther according to her understanding of events: Mordechai gave the official text of the edict to Hatakh, but Hatakh did not deliver it to Esther. It would seem that Hatakh softened Mordechai's message to Esther. He told her that Mordechai asked her to go before the king, but he did not explain the reason for the great urgency here. Perhaps he told her only of Mordechai's anxiety regarding "all that had happened to him," or maybe only "all about the money that Haman had offered to pay into the royal treasury," or perhaps neither. Esther had no context and no real grasp of why Mordechai wanted her to go to the king, but she was well aware of the fate that awaited one who went unbidden to the king. It is conceivable that the one who placed Hatakh in this sensitive position with the queen was non-other than Haman, who suspected that Esther is a Jew.

The message that the author of the Megilah seeks to convey is clear: If Mordechai the courtier and Queen Esther had thought they were safe given their personal standing, they could now understand the degree to which the status of Jewish Persian elite was on shaky ground: Word of the threat they faced had spread; it had even reached the eunuchs of the queen.

In verse 12 we encounter another exegetical challenge that traditional commentators struggle with:[10]

> They told Mordechai what Esther said. (4:12)

---

10 See, for example BT *Megilah* 15a Ibn Ezra, Malbim, and others *ad loc.*

In verse 10, Esther directed Hatakh to communicate to Mordechai that she has not been summoned to the king, and that entering the king's chambers could cost her life. Hatakh does **not** deliver this message to Mordechai. Mordechai rather learns about this from an anonymous group of people ("**They** told Mordechai"). It seems that these unknown people might be the young Jewish boys or girls who serve the king or queen but maintain their loyalty to the Jewish people.[11]

It emerges from this sequence of events that Esther did not receive an answer from Mordechai via Hatakh. She therefore sent her (Jewish) servant girls (*na'arot*) or servant boys (*na'arim)* with the message. Once they had a secure communication channel, Mordechai could lay all the cards on the table – his Jewish identity and that of Esther:

> Mordechai had this message delivered to Esther: "Do not imagine that you, of all the Jews, will escape with your life by being in the king's palace. On the contrary, if you keep silent in this crisis, relief and deliverance will come to the Jews from another quarter, while you and your father's house will perish. And who knows, perhaps you have attained to royal position for just such a crisis." (4:13-14)

---

11 BT *Megilah* 13a: "'The seven servant girls (*na'arot*) who were her due from the king's palace' – Rava says: She would use them to count the days of the week. 'He treated her and her servant girls (*na'arot*) with special kindness in the harem,' she would give them kosher food to eat...." That is, according to the Talmud, these Jewish '*na'arot*' knew about Judaism and knew about Shabbat, because they were from Jewish homes. This is why they are called "*na'arot*" and not slave-women (*shefahot*), slaves (*avadim*), or eunuchs (see the discussion above, p. 58). I am inclined to think that Rava is casting a positive light on Esther and Mordechai and their Jewish observance, although it seems the approach of R. Reggio is more correct. He explains (page 6) that Mordechai did not charge Esther to keep the commandments or stay away from idolatry.

Mordechai urged Esther to sacrifice herself to save the Jewish people. After a dialogue of the deaf, Mordechai and Esther could finally communicate securely. The truth finally came out. The Persian mask was finally torn away. Mordechai, who had pushed Esther towards royalty so he could get close to money and power, internalized that there is something far greater and far more critical at hand: saving the Jews of the kingdom of Ahashverosh.[12] He implored Esther unequivocally and ominously: "Do

---

12 Just a few days before this book went to print, I learned of a lecture about this turning point, delivered several decades ago by my teacher and master, Rabbi Dr. Aharon Lichtenstein of blessed memory. R. Lichtenstein would perhaps not agree with the continuation of my commentary, but either way, I felt it appropriate to quote extensively from this lecture extensively here (I thank Dr. Aviad HaCohen for referring me to this lecture; Dr. HaCohen told me that he can still hears R. Lichtenstein shouting: "DO I CARE OR DON'T I?"):

Mordechai knows well that all of Esther's anxiety and hesitation are peripheral. Someone who really cares, someone whose consciousness is deeply rooted in the collective experience of the Jewish people, someone whose destiny is bound up with that of the nation, disregards any consideration of danger.... Such considerations arise, whether consciously or subconsciously, out of a perception that everyone else may perish, but I will manage to save my own skin...

Know that your calculations are mistaken. Not only does your response exhibit moral and ethical rottenness, but you are mistaken in a practical sense as well. Do you believe that everyone will perish and you will remain there, in the royal palace, just because you have succeeded in entering the king's bedroom? Is that how you think God runs His world? Someone who avoids any responsibility, who doesn't care, who isn't prepared to risk himself, who gives his personal ambitions priority over the interests of the nation - is that the person you think will survive? Will he be the one to succeed? Will all values just disappear? "You and your father's house will perish."

...this is also the turning point. For the doubtful, hesitating, fearful Esther at whom Mordechai directs this terrible accusation, pushing her back to the wall and demanding that she stop making excuses and abandon her calculations - these are the real calculations: "Look deep into your soul and see what lies behind your hesitation. Do not try to trick either me or yourself. Do not try to trick God. There are no calculations or considerations, no fears or hesitations, no orders or rules.

not imagine that you, of all the Jews, will escape with your life by being in the king's palace!" He told her (and essentially also told himself) that she must not think that her connection to the throne will save her. His conclusion is dramatic: "And who knows, perhaps you have attained to royal position for just such a crisis." With these words, Mordechai revealed the secrets of his heart – he thought that he sent Esther to the palace in order to improve his own standing; he now understood that they faced an existential threat.

In the safety of the palace, Esther might not have understood the enormity and urgency of the matter. Mordechai's words were an attempt to spur her to action. He feared that she had become too accustomed to her Persian ways and to her intermarriage with the king of Persia. He was concerned that she would not stand with the Jews in their hour of need, so he felt the need to awaken her by whatever means necessary: You will not

---

What lies behind all your excuses is APATHY. What you have to decide is, DO I CARE OR DON'T I?"

...It is now that the young, passive, powerless Esther faces her moment of truth, and she prevails. She passes the test. And it is now that she rises to her full height and reveals herself – not just in title, but in essence – as Queen Esther...

We are all, to some degree, Esther. Each of us, for whatever reason, has doubts as to his ability to accomplish. We, too, are hesitant.... I don't want to use Mordechai's words, but I do want to at least pose the question: how much of our resignation is motivated by supposed "inability" and how much is a result of the fact that our concern simply doesn't run deep enough?

Herein lies the ultimate question. It is directed to each and every one of us. Let each person do as Esther did: stand before himself, stand before God, and once the situation is quite clear to him, ask himself, "Where am I, who am I, what comes first, what is vital and what is secondary?".... A person must ask himself not only whether what he is doing is good and worthy, but whether it is the best and most worthy thing that he could do. He has to keep asking himself, "Is this really what the circumstances require? Is this the best that I can do at this time?" (For the full lecture, see http://www.vbm-torah.org/en/esthers-moral-development-and-ours.)

escape this fate by virtue of your relationship with the king; if you abandon us – me – at this time "you and your father's house will perish," and we will find a different channel of salvation. Ultimately, this is the role that you were selected to play: "And who knows, perhaps you have attained to royal position for just such a crisis." According to R. Benny Lau, this is the defining moment of the Megilah:

> Mordechai knows that there is a possibility that Esther will remain a captive of her delusions, that she will imagine that she can escape the fate of the Jews by remaining in the palace. She is so alienated! The distance between her and the fate of her people is unbridgeable.
>
> Esther is shaken by Mordechai's rebuke, and she awakens from her slumber. She understands what he understood just a few days before: I am part of a whole. I am not alone, and I have not been absorbed into the empire. For better or worse, I stand with the Jewish people and share their fate.
>
> This is how two great people awaken from the fantasy of assimilation in a foreign land and become God's emissaries in the salvation of His people.

I agree with much of R. Lau's Megilah commentary, but it is difficult for me to agree with his two final statements here. Did Esther really understand that she is "part of a whole"? Did Mordechai and Esther really "become God's emissaries"? It seems that the author of the Megilah contradicts these two assertions: Mordechai responded with urgency only when he understood that he faced personal danger, and Esther got the message only when her family was threatened directly.

Like R. Lau, R. Reggio understands the need to internalize the personal element of the danger that Esther faces here, but he reads her motivation in a very different way:

> We see that just as Mordechai initially made every effort to get Esther to become the queen, he was now filled with anxiety and worry that she will lose her status, **that she and her father's house would lose power – and the house of her father, was the house of Avihayil, the brother of Yair, and it included Mordechai**. [Mordechai] therefore portrays the great danger that she and her family face, in order to impress upon her that she must do everything in her power to annul Haman's decree. By doing so, she would retain her status.

In R. Reggio's explanation as well, God was not one of the factors motivating Esther and Mordechai. Even simple motivations like saving the nation are absent: Only Esther and her family – including Mordechai, of course – will survive. According to R. Reggio, Mordechai was preoccupied only with his loss of status and power, and this was why he urged Esther to act. It is difficult to see Esther and Mordechai as God's emissaries, as R. Lau asserts, given that God is absent from the text even at this critical moment. This is no coincidence: Mordechai employed every promise and threat at his disposal, but the Lord, the God of Israel, was not part of his arsenal.

As a point of comparison, let us return to Ezra. In his prayer, Ezra does not see himself as one who is condemning the sin of others, but rather someone who has sinned himself ("everything that has befallen us is on account of our evil deeds and great guilt"). He turns in prayer to God to beg forgiveness on behalf of the blameless as well, because Jews all bear responsibility for one another.

Mordechai, in contrast, asks Esther to plead with the king on behalf of the Jews of Shushan who enjoy close ties with the palace ("the written text of the law that had been proclaimed in Shushan"), and this is how Esther perceives it as well, seeing this distress as something that affects primarily the Jews of Shushan ("Go, assemble all the Jews who live in Shushan"). The two of them do not see themselves as naturally responsible for the Jewish people as a whole – in contradistinction to the guiding principle of Ezra and those who returned from the exile. The Jews of Shushan take care of themselves, of their own *shtetl*, but not the Jewish people as a whole. The author of the Megilah emphasizes their isolation and its assimilationist features.

The events of the Megilah transpired at a dramatic, historic moment for the Jewish people. The sign had been given to return to Eretz Yisrael after the Babylonian exile and to establish a nation there, based on Jewish values and principles. Establishing a nation does not happen overnight; it requires dedicated workers and great thinkers to rehabilitate the nation from their lowest point. There was a need for political, economic, and social leaders.

But most of these potential leaders chose to remain in Shushan. The author of the Megilah does not look kindly upon them. He explains their motives and the ramifications of their decision to remain. He places their leaders in the spotlight. It is as though he says, in the Megilah: You did not come, so the decree of your destruction hangs over your heads; in your time of distress, you do not even think to join your people. You do not even care about them.

> Then Esther sent back this answer to Mordechai: "Go, assemble all the Jews who live in Shushan, and fast in my behalf; do not eat or drink for three days, night or day. I and my maidens will observe the same fast. Then I shall go to the king, though it is contrary to the law; and if I am to perish, I shall perish!" So Mordechai went about [the city] and did just as Esther had commanded him. (4:15-17)

When Esther finally understood the looming threat of annihilation, she took action. She fasted together with her Jewish *ne'arot*, instructed that the

Jews of Shushan should be gathered together, and prepared to risk her life to save her family and people.

But even in the description of Esther's fast there is a veiled criticism that one who is well-versed in Tanakh can detect. When Ezra declares a fast, he says:

> I proclaimed a fast there by the Ahava River to fast before our God to beseech Him for a smooth journey for us and for our children and for all our possessions.... So we fasted and **besought our God for this, and He responded to our plea**. (Ezra 8:21, 23)

In Megilat Esther though Esther requests:

> Go, assemble all the Jews who live in Shushan, and fast in my behalf; do not eat or drink for three days, night or day. I and my maidens will observe the same fast. **Then I shall go to the king, though it is contrary to the law**; and if I am to perish, I shall perish!" So Mordechai went about [the city] and did just as Esther had commanded him. (4:16-17)

The starkest difference relates to what comes after the fast. In the book of Ezra (as well as in the book of Yonah and elsewhere), the purpose of the fast is to repent and beg for forgiveness from "our God." The purpose of Esther's fast is so that she may survive her audience with a mortal king, Ahashverosh. The author adds to his list of accusations against Mordechai and Esther: You did not return to Zion; when you are threatened with annihilation, you do not care about the Jewish people as a whole; and **you have forgotten God**."

The Jews who return from exile with Ezra gather by the Ahava River, where Ezra calls upon them to "fast before our God to beseech Him for a smooth journey." He emphasizes that he asks for repentance innocently: He refused to request a royal escort as he made his way back from the exile ("For I was ashamed to ask of the king for a band of soldiers and horsemen to help us against the enemy on the road") on account of his deep faith that his fate was ultimately in the hands of God alone: "The hand of God is upon all of those who seek Him for good; but His power and His wrath are against all those who forsake Him."

Things are very different in the case of Esther. In contrast to Ezra, who places himself in the hands of God and asks Him for a smooth journey, Esther was required to appear before the king and "to appeal to him and to plead with him for her people" and for her family. Ezra is confident that God will answer his call ("He responded to our plea"), whereas Esther was scared and anxious that no matter what she does, she is in the hands of fate and fortune – "and if I am to perish, I shall perish!"

The Megilah's author alludes to us that the repentance of Esther, Mordechai, and the Jews of Shushan was not genuine. Esther's anxiety was quite justified. Ezra does not ask a mortal king to provide him with a security detail to escort him from the exile, and he does not request his assistance in building the Temple either. Rather, he places his faith in God, Who will provide safe passage for those who believe in Him ("The hand of God is upon all of those who seek Him for good"). Esther, in contrast, feared the human king upon whom she depended for everything.

We can detect an additional element of irony in the calendar dates of these two episodes. Ezra's encampment along the river (Ezra 8) lasted, it seems, for three days ("and we encamped there for three days"). From there, the returning exiles travel onward, toward Jerusalem: "We traveled from the Ahava River on the twelfth day of the first month, going to Jerusalem." That is, this stopover lasted from the ninth to the twelfth of Nisan (the first month), and they arrive in Jerusalem at a later point, perhaps as early as the very next day, the thirteenth of Nisan. On that very same date, the thirteenth of Nisan, albeit in a different year, Haman cast his lot. The Megilah's author is not interested in dating the events much as he is trying to create a literary contrast.

The ironic message is clear: On the very same date that the exiles, on their way to Jerusalem, enjoy God's good grace – "the hand of our God was upon us and He delivered us from the hand of enemy and ambush along the way" – it was decreed in Shushan "to destroy, massacre, and exterminate all the Jews, young and old, children and women, on a single day, on the thirteenth day of the twelfth month – that is, the month of Adar."

The exiles later arrive in Jerusalem: "And we came to Jerusalem and we stayed there for three days." In a parallel universe, in Shushan, on those very same dates, the Jews of Shushan must fast "for three days." At the end of the three days in Jerusalem, Ezra begins taking action toward the critical goal of stopping the intermarriages that plagued the returnees from exile, for "it is the officers and prefects who have taken the lead in this trespass." In the exile, the leaders of the nation married non-Jewish women, just as Esther the Jew married King Ahashverosh. Now she must beg her husband, the Persian king, on behalf of her people.

If it Please Your Majesty

> On the third day, Esther put on royal apparel and stood in the inner court of the king's palace, facing the king's palace, while the king was sitting on his royal throne in the throne room facing the entrance of the palace. As soon as the king saw Queen Esther standing in the court, she won his favor. The king extended to Esther the golden scepter which he had in his hand, and Esther approached and touched the tip of the scepter. (5:1-2)

Esther wore "royal apparel," the very same splendid clothing that she received as a symbol of her intermarriage with Ahashverosh. According to Rashi, she went to seduce the king, to sleep with him again.[1]

---

1 4:16, s.v. "*asher lo ka-dat*" and "*ve-ka'asher avadeti*" (based on BT *Megilah* 15a): "'**Though it is contrary to the law**' – it is against the law to enter the king's chambers without being called. And a *midrash aggadah* states: 'contrary to law' indicates that until this point in time, [her sexual encounters with the king] were by force, but now she would be willing." "'**And if I am to perish, I shall perish!**' Just as I have begun to slip away, I will indeed perish. A *midrash aggada* explains: Just as I am lost to my father's home, I will now be lost from you (=Mordechai, to whom Esther was married according to the *midrash*), because now that I am willingly going to have intercourse with a non-Jew, I will be prohibited to you." The book's English editor, Elli Fischer, suggests that Ahashverosh's scepter is a phallic symbol, a reading that further reinforces the sexual dimension of this encounter.

Esther was terrified of entering the inner chambers of Ahashverosh. She was concerned about her complete dependence on him and about her precarious and fragile position, since she had not been called to the king for a full month. She feared, perhaps, that Ahashverosh suspected that she is a Jew. She definitely feared that Ahashverosh had grown tired of her.

But then, unexpectedly, the king who first chose Esther because she found favor in his eyes, once again noticed that same charm – Esther's unique quality, which Hegai, the king's eunuch, had noticed as well – the personal qualities that he had discerned previously. This charm was the distinctly Jewish aura that emanated from Esther, her true identity that Mordechai instructed her to hide. Her physical beauty had faded after three days of fasting, allowing the charm and grace (*hen va-hessed*) that had shone through during the beauty pageant to break forth once again. The author of the Megilah is offering us an implicit lesson: When everything looks bleak, we can overcome our distress by returning to our origins, our Jewish roots.

We are once again reminded of Yosef who, by God's grace, finds favor in Egypt, first in the eyes of Pharaoh's courtier Potiphar, then in the eyes of the prison warden, all because, as Scripture states repeatedly, "God was with him."

The secret of Yosef's success is the grace of God. This is why both Potiphar and the officer of the prison take a liking to him, "whatever he did, God made succeed through him." This is true of Esther as well: The author of the Megilah gently winks at us, reminding us that even though she still had not prayed to God or exhibited concern for her people, it was not yet too late. She would still have an opportunity to show her courage, to disclose her identity, and to beg Ahashverosh and the Master of the Universe for her life and her people. But in her first test, she stumbles:

> What troubles you, Queen Esther?" the king asked her. "And what is your request? Even up to half the kingdom, it shall be

> granted you." "If it please Your Majesty," Esther replied, "let Your Majesty and Haman come today to the feast that I have prepared for him." (5:3-4)

Commentators and scholars are rather perplexed about the steps that Esther takes here. Why did she not plead for her life immediately when the king extended the scepter to her and she was given the right to speak? Why did she choose to invite Ahashverosh to a banquet? The story continues, and these questions grow stronger:

> The king commanded, "Tell Haman to hurry and do Esther's bidding." So the king and Haman came to the feast that Esther had prepared. At the wine feast, the king asked Esther, "What is your wish? It shall be granted you. And what is your request? Even up to half the kingdom, it shall be fulfilled." "My wish," replied Esther, "my request – if Your Majesty will do me the favor, if it please Your Majesty to grant my wish and accede to my request – let Your Majesty and Haman come to the feast which I will prepare for them; and tomorrow I will do Your Majesty's bidding." (5:5-8)

Esther now had the opportunity to speak her heart for a second time, but in the moment of truth she chooses to do the same thing again – to host another banquet for the king. She was given two successive opportunities. On two separate occasions, Ahashverosh said to her, "And what is your request? Even up to half the kingdom, it shall be fulfilled." Esther's answer: To host another banquet.

It is not surprising that Esther's course of action raised the eyebrows of the Sages of the Talmud, who wonder about the first encounter in the king's courtyard and about the extension of an invitation to Haman:

> [On the third day, Esther put on royal apparel] and stood in the inner court of the king's palace, [facing the king's palace, while the king was sitting on his royal throne in the throne room facing the entrance of the palace] – R. Levi said: When she reached the room of the idols – the Divine presence departed her; she said "'My God, my God why have You forsaken me [my salvation is far away from the words that I cry]' (Tehilim 22)? Do You judge an unwitting sin like an intentional sin? A compelled sin like a volitional one? Or perhaps on account of my calling him a dog, as it is written 'Deliver my life from the sword, my only one from the power of the dog.'" She therefore returned and called him a lion, as it is written "Save me from the lion's mouth [for you have answered me from the horns of the wild oxen]" (Tehilim 22). (BT *Megilah* 15b)

R. Levi maintains that Esther would have pleaded for her life at the first audience in the king's chamber, but God left her ("the Divine presence departed her"). At the moment she entered the chamber of her idolatrous husband, God abandoned her. She therefore had no choice but to revert to Persian custom and invite the king to a banquet.

The Mishnaic and Talmudic sages attempt to address a second question: Why did the queen invite Haman?

> The Sages taught: What did Esther see to invite Haman to the banquet?
>
> R. Eliezer says: She hid a snare for him, as it is stated: "Let their table become a snare before them" (Tehilim 69:23).
>
> R. Yehoshua says: She learned this from her father's house, as it is stated: "If your enemy be hungry, give him bread to eat" (Mishlei 25:21).
>
> R. Meir says: so that he would not take counsel and rebel.

> R. Yehuda says: so that it would not be found out that she was a Jew.
> R. Nehemiah says: so that the Jewish people would not say, "We have a sister in the king's palace," and consequently take their minds off of [prayers for God's] mercy.
> R. Yosi says: so that [Haman] would always be near her.
> R. Shimon b. Menasyah said: Esther said to herself: "Perhaps the Omnipresent will take notice and perform a miracle for us.
> R. Yehoshua b. Korha says: [She reasoned:] I will show him a pleasant countenance so that he and she (= Haman and Esther) are both killed.
> Rabban Gamliel says: Ahashverosh was a fickle king.
> Rabban Gamliel said: We still need the Modi'inite, as we learned: R. Elazar of Modi'in says: She made the king jealous of him and she made the other ministers jealous of him.
> Rabbah said: "Pride goes before destruction" (Mishlei 16:18)
> Abaye and Rava both say: "When they are heated, I will make feasts for them [and I will make them drunk, that they may rejoice, and sleep a perpetual sleep]" (Yirmiyahu 51:39). (BT *Megilah* 15b)

The Talmud offers no less than ten (!) different answers to this troubling question and then draws a conclusion that, at first glance, seems odd:

> Rabbah b. Abahu found Eliyahu [Elijah the prophet] and said to him: In accordance with whose understanding did Esther see fit to act in this manner? [Eliyahu] said to him: in accordance with all of the Mishnaic and Talmudic sages. (BT *Megilah* 15b)

Rabbah b. Abahu, a second generation Babylonian Talmudic sage, meets Eliyahu the prophet, who tells him that all of the motives mentioned by all of these sages factored into Esther's invitation of Haman to her private banquet. It seems that Eliyahu's answer to Rabbah b. Abahu has a broader historical meaning. When Jews live under foreign rule, they must develop a wide variety of tactics, tools, and strategies in order to confront threats they face.

All of the sages of the Mishna and Talmud who debate this issue lived under foreign rule, after the destruction of the Second Temple. They represent hundreds of years of Jewish history in exile, beginning with the first century CE sage R. Yehoshua, who likely saw the Second Temple with his own eyes, and culminating with Rava, the fourth century Babylonian sage.

It is interesting to plot these answers on a continuum. The first two answers – those of R. Eliezer ("She hid a snare for him") and R. Yehoshua ("She learned this from her father's house") – in addition to the answer of R. Yosi ("so that [Haman] would always be near her"), are variations of the same basic tactic: Keep your enemies close.

The answers of R. Yehuda and of R. Nehemiah are strange. R. Yehuda maintains that inviting Haman to the party was an attempt to conceal Esther's Jewish identity ("so that it would not be found out that she was a Jew"). R. Nehemiah makes a similar point, but from the opposite angle: to ensure that the Jews never forget that they are sustained by the grace of God, not by the benevolence of a human king ("so that the Jewish people would not say, 'We have a sister in the king's palace'").

R. Yehuda's position is quite logical. An invitation from Esther to a Persian-style banquet – to which Haman is also invited – is an effective way for her to conceal her Jewish identity.

This was a misstep on Esther's part. Had she asked for her life to be spared immediately after her fast, and if her repentance was in fact genuine, she could have been confident, as Ezra the Scribe was, that God would answer her prayer.[2] Conversely, the banquet and the ploy both

2 Compare to Yosef, who said, both in prison when he explained the ministers'

indicate that Esther did not feel comfortable with her Jewish identity. In the view of the Megilah's author, this is an expression of her weak faith. Esther has been granted the fleeting opportunity to tear off her Persian clothing, in the words of R. Benny Lau, but at this moment of truth, she returns to her Persian clothing and to her Persian banquets, while her Jewish identity fades back into obscurity.

Dr. Yonatan Grossman understands that these invitations, including the invitation of Haman, are rooted in conventional Persian practice. His opinion is certainly valid here, but the question remains. The Megilah's author is not writing a story or chronicle; Megilat Esther, like every book in Tanakh, has a distinct reason and meaning. The author did not have to record Esther's observance of Persian manners; he **chose** to.

The author describes Esther entering the king's chambers, dressed in "royal apparel." It is quite obvious that Esther sought to impress the king and request something important. She would not have risked her life – if Ahashverosh does not extend his scepter, she incurs the death penalty – just to invite Haman and the king to a banquet she planned. Worse, the king might find it infuriating that one would squander the king's special offer to grant a request on an invitation to just another of the hundreds of banquets he attends.

Clearly, Esther's initial plan was entirely different. However, at the moment of truth, she simply could not utter the words. Perhaps because she was anxious and afraid, and perhaps because she was still wary of revealing her identity, she instead requested the presence of Ahashverosh and Haman at a banquet she would host in their honor "today." In other words, like so many people, in times of great stress, Esther reverted to old habits, 'Persian customs and practice.'

Later that day, the king and Haman attended the "wine feast," where

---

dreams and when he interpreted Pharaoh's dream: "Do not interpretations belong to God?" and "It is not me, God shall give Pharaoh a favorable answer."

the drunken king repeated his offer and his promise: “What is your wish? It shall be granted you. And what is your request? Even up to half the kingdom, it shall be fulfilled.” Esther, once again, was unable to verbalize her request. Aware that time is of the essence and that she could not simply invite the king and Haman to nightly banquets *ad infinitum*, she still could not stand up in defense of her people and petition the king on their behalf. All that she was able to say is:

> “My wish,” replied Esther, “my request – if Your Majesty will do me the favor, if it please Your Majesty to grant my wish and accede to my request – let Your Majesty and Haman come to the feast which I will prepare for them; and tomorrow I will do Your Majesty’s bidding.” (5:7-8)

In other words: I will tell you tomorrow.

Rashi and the Talmudic Sages (BT *Megilah* 15) address Ahashverosh’s growing concern that Esther insisted on inviting Haman to both the first and the second party. After the first invitation, the king pressed Haman into service as Esther had requested when he ordered: “Tell Haman to hurry and do Esther’s bidding.” It is clear that when Esther invited Haman and the king to a second party, she was going off-script. This was not the original plan. This indicates that she feared that she still had to prove her Persian-ness.

Despite having fasted in a time of distress, in time-honored Jewish tradition, Esther the Jew was attempting to defeat Haman by demonstrating how unquestionably Persian she was. Esther, as we saw in chapter 2, did not feel comfortable participating in the competition to become queen of Persia; she was taken to the palace on Mordechai’s orders. But her time in the palace had made its mark. When she approached the king, she wore Persian royal attire and invited the king to a Persian-style banquet. These actions put the king at ease, and he extended his gracious offer of “even up to half the kingdom." He was convinced that his partner is thoroughly Persian.

It is hard to miss the irony here. Vashti, the gentile queen, functioned as the conscience of the Jews during the first banquet when she refused to present herself at the lewd, Persian-style drinking party. As a result, she lost her status and a decree was issued that "every man should wield authority in his home and speak the language of his own people." Esther, on the other hand, clothed herself in the Persian royal attire and invited the Persian king to a Persian-style banquet. She even influenced the king to order that Haman be brought hastily to the banquet, even though the initial decree specified that husbands shall not follow their wives' orders.[3]

I am inclined to go even further. In chapter 4, Esther said: "Now I have not been summoned to visit the king for the last thirty days." In chapter 2, the description of the royal pageant of virgins states that each girl "would go in the evening and leave in the morning." It stands to reason that these virgins did not go to the king for a discussion of current events. The Megilah tells us that these virgins would return after one night to "a second harem" and from then on:

> She would not go again to the king unless the king wanted her, when she would be summoned by name. (2:14)

After her first encounter with the king, a woman was not called for a second visit unless he called for her by name. Esther had not been summoned to the king for thirty days. The author reminds us that Vashti was invited to the king's party "wearing a royal diadem." There is a rabbinic

---

3 Note the stark contrast between Esther's promise that "tomorrow I will do your Majesty's bidding" ("e'eseh *ke*-devar *ha*-melekh") with Vashti, who ("refused to come at the king's command" ("*vatema'en...la-vo be*-devar *ha*-melekh" and was punished "for failing to obey the king's command" ("*al asher lo* aseta *et ma'amar ha*-melekh").

opinion that Vashti was invited to appear before the king wearing **only** a royal diadem, in order "to display her beauty to the peoples and the officials." Here, when Esther approached the king, she submitted to Persian custom and appeared before him in "royal" garb – clothing that would be to the king's liking. Perhaps this does not even include the diadem.... She then invited the king to a banquet with wine. The author again refers back to the events of chapter 1, suggesting that Esther's assimilation process was now complete. The process began when she was forcibly taken to the king's palace and culminates with her appearance before the king in "royal" clothing.

When Haman left the king's presence, he was happy and light of heart, and not because of the wine he had been drinking. He had always suspected that Esther would be the greatest obstacle to his increased power, but after she hosted a proper Persian banquet, Haman was convinced that Esther is truly Persian. Neither her suspected Jewishness nor her alleged ties to Mordechai could threaten him or his plans.

But then the following episode occurred:

> That day Haman went out happy and lighthearted. But when Haman saw Mordechai in the palace gate, and Mordechai did not rise or even stir on his account, Haman was filled with rage at him. (5:9)

We last saw Mordechai at the end of the previous chapter, receiving Esther's instructions to assemble the Jews of Shushan for a three-day fast. Mordechai could not enter the king's gate during those days, as he was demonstrating in sackcloth, an outfit that violated the palace's dress code. But when Haman departed the banquet "happy and lighthearted," there was his old nemesis, sitting in the palace gate. The fast, the crying, and the mourning had ended for Mordechai.

Haman immediately remembered his great humiliation. This same

Mordechai, who had been out of sight and out of mind for several days, was again sitting at the palace gate, and still he "did not rise or even stir on his account"! Haman was now convinced that his grip on the palace was unquestioned and that even the queen was on his side. The only threat left was Mordechai. His passionate hatred of Mordechai, equal parts greed and anti-Semitism, consumed Haman once more.

> Nevertheless, Haman controlled himself and went home. He sent for his friends and his wife Zeresh, and Haman told them about his great wealth and his many sons, and all about how the king had promoted him and advanced him above the officials and the king's courtiers. "What is more," said Haman, "Queen Esther gave a feast, and besides the king she did not have anyone but me. And tomorrow too I am invited by her along with the king. Yet all this is worth nothing to me every time I see that Jew Mordechai sitting in the palace gate." (5:10-13)

Haman affirmed to his confidants that profit is his primary motivation. All of his honor, his children and their political status, has no **value** for him: "Yet all this is **worth** (*shoveh)* nothing to me every time I see that Jew Mordechai sitting in the palace gate." This term appears on two other occasions in the Megilah: when Haman persuaded the king to kill the Jews ("It is not **worth** it [*shoveh*] for Your Majesty to tolerate them"), and when Esther pleads with the king ("for the adversary is not **worthy** (*shoveh*) of the king's trouble"). In both these contexts, "*shoveh*" denotes monetary value.[4]

Haman's lament about Mordechai to his wife Zeresh reflects his psychological and emotional priorities: He listed "his great wealth" first,

---

4 Thus, Rashi on 3:8 comments: "'It is not worth it' – there is no concern, that is, there is no profit."

then everything else. This order is not incidental, because in fact this is the main subject of the Megilah as well as the source of hostility between Mordechai and Haman. Haman was proud of his great wealth, pointing out that the king had promoted him and advanced him beyond the other officers and servants.

But Haman could see dark clouds gathering on the horizon. His grand plans for achieving dominion were endangered by "Mordechai the Jew" to the point that all the other honors and status symbols were not much compensation. The Jews who were close to the empire's feeding trough knocked him off-balance and shook him out of his complacency. All of his success would be worthless unless he could get rid of Mordechai, too.

Perhaps Haman thought that Mordechai's absence from the king's gate was permanent and allowed himself a "happy and light-hearted" moment as he left the party. But as soon as he noticed Mordechai, his hatred resurfaced with greater intensity.

> Then his wife Zeresh and all his friends said to him, "Let a beam be put up, fifty cubits high, and in the morning ask the king to have Mordechai hanged on it. Then you can go gaily with the king to the feast." The proposal pleased Haman, and he had the beam put up. (5:14)

This verse raises several logical questions. Why didn't Haman just kill Mordechai immediately, then and there? Why was Zeresh's suggestion so appealing? Why did this suggestion suddenly enable him to kill Mordechai, as if he couldn't have done so earlier?

Scholars who read the Megilah as a work of literature – and the Megilah is, of course, a literary work as well – suggest that the Megilah's author intends to deepen the eventual irony. Haman felt that his power was at its peak, that his clout with the king could not be undermined, thus setting the stage for his rapid downfall the next time he encountered the king, less than a day later. The verse cited by Rabbah in the passage of the Talmud cited above indeed sums up this sentiment nicely: "Pride goes before destruction and haughtiness of spirit before a fall" (Mishlei 16:18).

While all of this is true, it is still not the full picture.

Dr. Yonatan Grossman connects Zeresh's suggestion that Mordechai be hanged with the sedition of Bigtan and Teresh, who were likewise put to death by hanging. That is, Zeresh suggested that Haman fabricate a case against Mordechai and then hang him for "treason." According to Grossman, the three narrative cycles of Megilat Esther all turn on the theme of treason and sedition against the king.[5]

This literary analysis is quite convincing, but a key element is missing: Bigtan and Teresh's mutiny is clearly delineated by the Megilah – they "plotted to do away with King Ahashverosh." But how did Haman intend to fictitiously incriminate Mordechai? What evidence would he have been able to bring to support this libel? Is it possible that Haman, the foremost of Ahashverosh's ministers and certainly no slouch, did not think of this possibility until it was suggested to him by Zeresh? If it was so easy to solve the problem of the stubborn Jew sitting in the palace gate, was it really necessary to go through the complicated process of eradicating all of the Jews throughout the empire? Finally, it is hard to ignore the situational irony here: Haman returned home and started griping about Mordechai the Jew, and specifically his wife – the person who he is supposed to rule over absolutely, according to the king's edict – started giving him instructions.

It seems that the key to understanding this is the description of Haman as leaving Esther's party "happy and light-hearted." The author of the Megilah lived in Jerusalem at a time when the Second Temple has been mostly or completely rebuilt, though it is far from being a magnificent

5 Grossman, *Esther: The Outer Narrative and the Hidden Reading*, pp. 135-140, 172.

and glorious structure. He returns us to the glory days of the First Temple, hundreds of years earlier, under the reign of King Shlomo:

> On the eighth day he sent the people away and they blessed the king and went to their tents **happy and light-hearted** for all of the goodness that God had done for David His servant and for Israel His people. When Shlomo had finished building the house of God, the royal palace, and everything Shlomo had set his heart on building… (1 Melakhim 8:66-9:1)

The people in Shlomo's time were happy and expansive because the Temple has been completed and their prayers have been accepted, while Haman's heart was happy because his control over the empire was all but complete. He was finally convinced that his concerns about Esther's Jewishness were unfounded; Esther is completely Persian. But then as he left the palace and saw Mordechai sitting in the palace gate, he remembered that there is still a Jew with political clout, and this ignited his fury.

When Haman arrived at home, it seems that there was no one there. He was alone. He had to send for "his friends and his wife Zeresh." Here we have a description of a ruler and minister at home, among his "friends" ("*ohavav*," literally "those who love him"), but even here there was not much love. At his kitchen table, he sat and boasted about his "great wealth" and how "the king had promoted him" and "advanced him above the officials and the king's courtiers." We can only imagine the faces of Zeresh and "his friends," his flatterers and yes-men as they listened to the story of his wealth and greatness, a story that they must have heard hundreds, if not thousands, of times.

Haman's titles and honors were, of course, quite impressive to Persian ears, but the author of this description was a believing Jew living in Eretz Yisrael. From his perspective, these titles are not reasons to be proud, but reasons to be ashamed, for they are not of a spiritual or ethical nature.

Haman told them that he alone was invited along with the king to the queen's party, and that he would partake of the lewd and drunken festivities the next night as well. It might be true that in his house there was no one to listen to his stories, but he could take comfort in the thought that he would soon be partying with the queen at her table, perhaps even in her bed.

Zeresh advised Haman to erect a gallows that is fifty cubits tall. Given that a cubit (*amah*) is about 18 inches, this gallows reached a towering height of 75 feet.[6] As a point of comparison, the height of the First Temple was 30 cubits. The reader can almost hear Zeresh ingratiating herself to Haman: If you, my dear, great, and exalted husband, who has so much wealth and so many sons, intend to hang someone, your status mandates a gallows that is no less great and exalted.

This is why Haman liked the plan so much. The beam itself would be an impressive testament of his wealth and power, taller even than the palace, a billboard that advertises his status. In other words, it is Haman's inflated ego that persuaded him to build this gallows.

It is worth noting that Haman did not tell Ahashverosh, who must approve the hanging, about his plan to construct the gallows. The precise height of the gallows was not noted in the case of Bigtan and Teresh, and for good reason. Sedition is punished quietly, on regular-sized gallows, in part to keep others from getting similar thoughts of mutiny. Haman's gallows had a different purpose, though. He wished to demonstrate his status and publicly show what happens to a man who crosses Haman.

The Sages felt that Haman's boasting was purposefully exaggerated:

> "Haman told them about his great wealth and his many sons."
> How many sons? Rav said: Thirty. Ten died, ten were hanged,

---

6 In the Persian Empire, it was common to hoist the person being hanged by the neck to the top of the gallows. Therefore, practically speaking, a 15-20 foot high beam would have certainly been sufficient.

> and ten were reduced to panhandling. The Rabbis said: There were seventy who panhandled, as it is written: "The satiated have hired themselves out for bread" (1 Shmuel 2). Do not read it as: "The satiated" ("*seve'im*"), but as "seventy" ("*shiv'im*"). Rami b. Abba said: There were 208 altogether, as it says: "And his many (*verov*) sons." The numerical value of "*verov*" is 208. (BT *Megilah* 15)

After this episode, the Megilah picks up the pace. The time that lapses between events shortens considerably, and the story approaches its climax.

Sleep Deserted the King

At the precise moment that Haman eagerly prepared the gallows:

> That night, sleep deserted the king, and he ordered the book of records, the annals, to be brought; and it was read to the king. (6:1)

These two events are both simultaneous and in complete contrast to one another: At the precise moment that Haman plotted Mordechai's downfall, the web that will trap Haman is being spun.[1]

> "That night sleep deserted the king."[2] Rabbi Tanhum said: Sleep deserted the King of the universe. The Sages say: Sleep deserted the higher ones (= the angels), and sleep deserted the lower ones

1 This fits well with Dr. Grossman's theory that attempted overthrows are a primary literary theme of the Megilah, and that hanging is always the punishment for sedition. See p. 93 above.

2 According to some customs, these words are chanted to the tune that is used for the word "*Ha-Melekh*" ("the King") on the High Holidays, in order to illustrate the idea of this *midrash*, namely, that God Himself was the King Who was not sleeping that fateful night, and that He was behind the Jews' salvation. When I learned to read the Megilah, my teacher, Rabbi Wermuth, was adamant that I not use this chant.

> (= the Jewish people). Rava said: It was actually the sleep of King Ahashverosh. A thought occurred to him, and he said [to himself]: Why did Esther invite Haman? Maybe they are conspiring to kill me.... Right away, "he ordered the book of records, the annals, to be brought." (BT *Megilah* 15)

The Sages are acutely aware of God's absence from Megilat Esther and try to import the King of Kings into the story. But the Megilah – and the Jews of Shushan, in our understanding – leaves God out of the story. More precisely, God is removed from the story.

> That night, sleep deserted the king, and he ordered the book of records, the annals, to be brought; and it was read to the king. There it was found written that Mordechai had denounced Bigtana and Teresh, two of the king's eunuchs who guarded the threshold, who had plotted to do away with King Ahashverosh. "What glory (*yekar*) or advancement has been conferred on Mordechai for this?" the king inquired. "Nothing at all has been done for him," replied the king's servants who were in attendance on him. (6:1-3)

On the night of Esther's party, the king, lying in bed, drunk from the party, could not sleep. He asked that they read to him from the annals. Perhaps there is truth in Rava's statement ("Why did Esther invite Haman?") that Ahashverosh was preoccupied by the fact that Esther invited Haman, but it seems that he was motivated primarily by the wish to remember the good old days. His wish to remember sends us back to the story of Yosef in Bereishit 40:

> Yosef said to him, "This is its interpretation: The three branches are three days. In three days Pharaoh will pardon you and restore

> you to your post; you shall deliver Pharaoh's cup into his hand, as was your custom formerly when you were his butler. But think of me when all is well with you again, and do me the kindness of mentioning me to Pharaoh, so as to free me from this place. (Bereishit 40:12-14)

This exchange is not at all helpful to Yosef. He places his trust in a human being, and the plan fails. His successful dream interpretation does not get him out of prison, for "the chief butler did not think of Yosef; he forgot him." Yosef is punished with two additional years in prison because he places his trust in the human chief butler and not in God.[3] In Persia, at least according to Megilat Esther, God was completely forgotten.

Dr. Aaron Koller's reading is plausible here. He asserts that the author of the Megilah emphasizes that for the Jews of Persia, this exile had become a political, rather than religious, exile. They therefore had to depend on themselves rather than on the grace of God. This is the position of the Persian Jews according to the author: They did not return to Jerusalem, opting instead to remain in Persia and continue their lives as Jews without God. They chose to replace Him with political machinations.

The beginning of chapter 6 again draws our attention to the king's advisers. The king asked someone – it is not clear exactly who – to bring "the book of records, the annals" and read it before him. When he learned from this record book about the story of Mordechai and Bigtan and Teresh, he wondered aloud, to no one in particular: "What glory (*yekar*) or advancement has been conferred on Mordechai for this?" Then, out of nowhere, "the king's servants (*na'arei ha-melekh*) who were in attendance

---

3 According to the Torah, Yosef was imprisoned in the dungeon for two additional years ("After two years' time, Pharaoh dreamed...") The *Midrash* links these two years with punishment for placing his fate in the hands of the chief butler and not in the hands of God. See Rashi to Bereishit 40:23.

on him" jumped in – these being the same Jewish servants (*ne'arim*) of the king's court who had worked in the past on Mordechai's behalf. They answered the king: "Nothing at all has been done for him."

These junior advisers, these court Jews, had eluded Haman's detection for years, even as they operated right under his nose. Now, in the middle of the night, when the king could not sleep, they filled the void and took advantage of the opportunity to bring Mordechai back to center stage. It was not God but political guile that assured that the right passage of the chronicles be read to the king and lead him to the correct conclusion.

This approach is diametrically opposed to Rava's opinion in the Talmud. Rava does not even consider that Mordechai may have true allies close to the king:

> "Nothing at all has been done for him." Rava said: "This is not because they love Mordechai, but rather because they hate Haman." (BT *Megilah* 15a)

Rava's approach is somewhat surprising, and perhaps telling in light of his life circumstances: He lived in close proximity to the seat of power of the Sasanian Persian Empire and even enjoyed positive relations with the emperor of his day, Shapur II (the Talmud's "Shevur Malka"), who was benevolent toward his Jewish subjects. Rava is therefore saying that an alliance against a common enemy should not be mistaken for friendship. If a particular faction was promoting Mordechai at a given time, it was due to *realpolitik*, not because they loved the Jews.

In either case, it is logical to assume that Ahashverosh's royal court was indeed similar to the courts of most absolute rulers through the years: an arena in which different interest groups and rival forces were constantly competing for the king's good graces, with no one group achieving absolute dominance, and in which ever-shifting alliances and coalitions were formed against the dominant faction of the day. The king's "*ne'arim*," like other elements that make up the royal court, remained part of the bureaucracy even when a particular person or group gained dominance. My contention, based on what we already learned about them, is that these *ne'arim* worked to maximize the influence of their patron, Mordechai, and were not merely trying to minimize the power of Haman.

The words "glory (*yekar*) or advancement" are quite important in this context. This is not the first time that these words appear in the Megilah: "Advancement" ("*gedulah*") connotes economic leadership in the Persian Empire, just as the king "promoted" ("*gidal*") Haman. The "advancement" now promised to Mordechai refers to reward, tit for tat, for turning in Bigtan and Teresh, who sought to replace the king who had depleted the empire's treasury. "Glory" (*yekar*) is different than "advancement," of course, and it might be the most important term in this episode, since it appears seven times at this key juncture.

Dr. Grossman offers an insightful explanation when he points out that the king's insomnia is the pivot, the axis, on which the entire Megilah turns. However, the key word here is "*yekar*." It appears, in various forms, a total of ten times in the Megilah, seven of which[4] are in the first part of chapter 7, along with two instances in chapter 1 and a final time in the description of the Jewish reaction to the king's second edict. However, it is only in the context of chapter 1 that we can understand its significance:

> In the third year of his reign, he gave a banquet for all the officials and courtiers – the soldiers of Persia and Media, the nobles and the governors of the provinces in his service. For no fewer than a hundred and eighty days he displayed the vast

4 Martin Buber was the first modern exegete to note that the repetition of a key word, or *leitwort* ("*mila manhah*" in Hebrew), is a significant literary feature of many Biblical passages. Modern Bible scholars and commentators have further refined this insight and noted that a term that appears seven times in a single passage is its *leitwort*.

> riches of his kingdom and the magnificent prestige (*yekar*) of his majesty... Then will the judgment executed by Your Majesty resound throughout your realm, vast though it is; and all wives will pay tribute (*yekar*) to their husbands, high and low alike. (1:2-3, 20)

In this context, "*yekar*" here refers to wealth or monetary compensation, not to an abstract or intangible reward or glory. The king displays his great wealth to his servants and officers; wives are required to give everything of value to their husbands. "*Yekar*" does not refer to status; that is indicated by the word "advancement" ("*gedulah*"). Ahashverosh sought to give Mordechai a valuable monetary reward, remuneration for saving the king. The same is true later on in the Megilah, where it states that "The Jews enjoyed light and gladness, happiness and glory (*yekar*)." This indicates that they enjoyed things of spiritual value, such as light, gladness, and happiness, as well as things of material value – "*yekar*."

The word "deserted" (*nadedah*) likewise alludes to an earlier incident with a strong financial dimension. Most Biblical instances of this grammatical root (*NDD*) refer not to sleeplessness, but to the physical migration of a person or a bird (for example, "Madmenah ran away [*nadedah*]; the dwellers of Gebim sought refuge" [Yeshayahu 10:31]) or the inability of a person to defend himself ("Nothing so much as flapped [*nodad*] a wing, or opened a mouth to peep." (Yeshayahu 10:14)). The only Biblical incidence in which this root is linked to sleep is in the mouth of the patriarch Yaakov:

> Often, scorching heat ravaged me by day and frost by night; and sleep deserted (*va-tidad*) my eyes. (Bereishit 31:40)

Yaakov lashes out furiously at Lavan the Aramean, the manipulative father of Leah and Rachel, who chases after him as though he were a criminal, when in fact "of the twenty years that I spent in your household, I served you fourteen years for your two daughters, and six years for your flocks; and you changed my wages time and again." Yaakov earned his wages fairly, and Lavan also benefited from his work. Yaakov loses sleep because of his financial worries and while working hard in the fields and pasture land.

At this point in the Megilah, Ahashverosh was still distressed about the empire's deteriorating economic condition. He recalled that the last time he spent a great deal of money on a banquet was when he celebrated Esther's appointment as queen. Now, Esther herself was expending exorbitant sums on parties. The party was certainly not celebrated with only three people – Esther, Haman and Ahashverosh – in attendance; that was simply not the Persian way. Ahashverosh and Haman were simply the guests of honor. The banquet was presumably a proper banquet, with many invitees. Furthermore, the celebration would continue for an additional day. This is why sleep deserted the king. When the episode of Bigtan and Teresh was read to him from the annals, it was in context of this financial stress. The king remembered that Bigtan and Teresh had tried to kill him because of the financial state of the empire and decided that he will grant Mordechai the proper reward for saving his life.

This episode has clear parallels to chapter 2 of the Megilah. In chapter 2, the king chose Esther as queen ("she won his grace and favor"), hosted a lavish and ostentatious banquet,[5] and "distributed gifts as befits a king." Then Bigtan and Teresh "plotted to do away with King Ahashverosh," Mordechai exposed the conspiracy, and Haman was promoted to power. In chapters 5 and 6, Esther again won the king over, a party was held, Ahashverosh was reminded of the episode of Bigtan and Teresh, and in the end Mordechai was promoted to power.

5 Albeit less lavish and ostentatious than the parties of chapter 1, as the empire was in dire economic straits.

The story of the king's sleepless night was carefully chosen by the Megilah's author as the turning point of the Megilah, the pivotal moment of the plot. At face value, the Megilah starts over and the Jews of Persia are given another chance to decide: Will they again prefer political and economic power, or, alternatively, will they return to their ancestral faith in God and their ancestral homeland in Eretz Yisrael? If not for the episode of Ahashverosh's insomnia, one could make the claim that the message of the Megilah is that God operated behind the scenes on behalf of the Jews of Shushan. As we will see, this is far from the Megilah's message.

Haman arrived at the palace:

> "Nothing at all has been done for him," replied the king's servants who were in attendance on him. "Who is in the court?" the king asked. For Haman had just entered the outer courtyard of the royal palace, to speak to the king about having Mordechai impaled on the stake he had prepared for him. "It is Haman standing in the court," the king's servants answered him. "Let him enter," said the king. (6:3-5)

This passage is somewhat confusing. We learned from Esther's words in chapter 4 that in order to be seen by the king, one must enter the inner courtyard. Here, Haman entered the outer courtyard, and the king nonetheless saw him, or at the very least became aware that someone had entered. Additionally, it is clear that Haman did not just appear in the outer court on the off chance that he would perhaps get lucky and the king would ask, "Who is in the court?"

As per Rava's understanding (BT *Megilah* 15; see below), the king's could not sleep because he had become suspicious. History was repeating itself; the sedition of Bigtan and Teresh was caused, in our reading, by the profligate spending on Esther's inaugural Ball while the empire was in the throes of a deep economic recession, and now Esther was again spending liberally and ostentatiously while the economy remained mired in a slump. The king was therefore wide awake, consulting with his advisors, the *ne'arim*, in the middle of the night to review how he was saved from the last coup. When he learned that his allies during the last coup were never rewarded, his suspicion turned into alarm. At that very moment (at least in the Megilah's description of the conversation), the king becomes aware that someone has entered the courtyard, perhaps because his dawning realization has put him on high alert.

> Haman entered, and the king asked him, "What should be done for a man to whom the king desires to show glory?" Haman said to himself (*be-libo*, lit. 'in his heart'), "Whom would the king desire to show glory more than me?" (6:6)

This is the dramatic turning point. The words "Haman entered" ("*vayavo Haman*") are chanted with the notes for *zarka* and *segol*, which dramatically rise to a trill. Haman's arrogance, which led him to believe that only he is worthy of "glory" (*yekar*), will lead to his demise. But before Haman could even open his mouth to request permission to hang Mordechai, the king has already begun consulting with him about something else, in his capacity as a senior minister and treasurer: What reward should be bestowed upon "a man to whom the king desires to show glory (*yekar*)."

Ibn Ezra (*ad loc.*) points out yet another parallel to Bereishit. "Haman said to himself" reminds us of Esav:

> Now Esav harbored a grudge against Jacob because of the blessing which his father had given him, and Esav said to himself, "Let but the mourning period of my father come, and I will kill my brother Yaakov." (Bereishit 27:41)

Earlier, Mordechai was compared to Esav, who likewise cried out "loudly and bitterly." Now Haman draws comparison to Esav, who likewise made secret plans to kill a rival. In both of these instances, there is significance that lurks beneath the surface: Though he plotted, Esav did not actually kill Yaakov in the end, and Haman, too, will not kill Mordechai. Mordechai may have cried out like Esav about his bitter economic fate, but, like Esav's cry, his outburst was not motivated by an abiding sense of faith. When Yaakov was threatened by Esav, he turned to God and vowed allegiance ("if I return safe to my father's house – the Lord shall be my God" – Bereishit 28:20). Mordechai, though relentlessly pursued by Haman, did not turn to God.

Perhaps this episode is really about political maneuverings and temporary alliances. This is how the Talmud understands it (in the continuation of the discussion whose first part appears above):

> Rava said: It was actually the sleep of King Ahashverosh. A thought occurred to him, and he said [to himself]: Why did Esther invite Haman? Maybe they are conspiring to kill me. He then considered further: If so, wouldn't someone tell me? Then he said to himself again: Perhaps there is someone who has done a favor for me and who I have not properly rewarded, so people withhold such reports from me. Right away, "he ordered the book of records, the annals, to be brought." (BT *Megilah* 15)

According to Rava, the king feared that Esther and Haman were conspiring to overthrow him. Something was rotten in Shushan. He could not fall asleep because he was worried about a coup, and so he thought to himself: Who can I count on? Who will tip me off? Who is a true friend, if not the very man who saved me from the last conspiracy? Ahashverosh was disturbed and suspicious, and so when, as if on cue, Haman arrived in the courtyard, the king decided to trap him by exploiting Haman's lust for honor and distinction, and directing it against him.

It seems that there is another way to explain this point. The king was still worried about the kingdom's economic depression on account of Esther's various parties and celebrations. But he was particularly disturbed that Haman, his minister of finance, appeared unconcerned. He noticed that Haman did not refuse Esther's invitation and did not even bother to warn him, as was his duty, about the potential effects of Esther's wasteful policy.

Contra Rava, I do not think that Ahashverosh was worried that Haman would stage a coup (though he was concerned that, as in the case of Bigtan and Teresh, continued profligacy in a time of austerity would indeed lead to another attempted coup). Rather, he was responding to what he saw clearly. The Megilah does not tell us that Ahashverosh decided to reward Mordechai; we are told only that "nothing at all has been done for him," after which we immediately hear of Haman's arrival in the king's court,[6] having worked the entire night to construct the gallows. Haman entered the outer courtyard with great fanfare, presumably telling anyone willing to listen, and even those who would not, about his big plans.

In the meantime, the king was pacing his chambers, bleary-eyed from a sleepless night. The tumult in the courtyard bothered him, and he asked, perhaps even somewhat angrily: "Who is making all that noise in the outer courtyard?"

Haman answered the summons with alacrity, so excited to ask the king for permission to hang Mordechai that he did not notice the king's mood. Ahashverosh presumably had not heard the scuttlebutt from the courtyard

---

6 The text does not indicate that morning had arrived, so it is possible that this all happened in the middle of the night. But it is more reasonable to assume though that Haman waited until morning's first light (as Zeresh had advised) and did not dare to wake the king. I want to thank my wife for this text-based comment.

about the acrimony between Haman and Mordechai. However, on the morning between Esther's first party and second party, when Ahashverosh was preoccupied by his apprehensions about Haman's ability to function as the minister of finance, he decided to test Haman.

> So Haman said to the king, "For the man whom the king desires to show glory let royal garb which the king has worn be brought, and a horse on which the king has ridden and on whose head a royal diadem has been set; and let the attire and the horse be put in the charge of one of the king's noble courtiers. And let the man whom the king desires to honor be attired and paraded on the horse through the city square, while they proclaim before him: This is what is done for the man whom the king desires to show glory!" (6:7-9)

Haman suggested a low-cost plan, thereby passing the test of fiscal restraint. But Ahashverosh had set a trap for the braggart who constructed a stake fifty cubits high – a stake that had become the talk of the entire royal court: While accepting Haman's suggestion for the thrifty reward of a ride on a horse, he also placed him in a humiliating position vis-à-vis Mordechai. Haman himself will lead the horse through the streets.

Haman's reaction is understandable. Due to budgetary constraints, instead of a monetary reward, "glory" (*yekar*), he suggested holding a celebratory procession. All the "glory" (*yekar*) that had filled the empire's treasury at the beginning of the Megilah was gone. He therefore proposed symbolic displays of royalty, but nothing of real value. The reader can detect that Haman was well aware of the empire's financial distress, but also that he was enamored of symbolic honors – seeing as he was convinced that he would be the honoree. Haman's suggestion made sense to Ahashverosh; there was plenty of royal apparel, plenty of officers, and no lack of royal horses:

> "Quick, then!" said the king to Haman. "Get the garb and the horse, as you have said, and do this to Mordechai the Jew, who sits in the king's gate. Omit nothing of all you have proposed." (6:10)

The reader senses biting sarcasm in the words of Ahashverosh: "Quick," he said to Haman in a tone of barely-concealed *schadenfreude*, hurry up and do this yourself – for Mordechai the Jew who sits in the palace gate. He even warns him harshly: "Omit nothing of all you have proposed."

> So Haman took the garb and the horse and arrayed Mordechai and paraded him through the city square; and he proclaimed before him: This is what is done for the man whom the king desires to show glory (*yekar*)! (6:11)

There are several interesting questions that can be raised here. Firstly, there is a literary question: Haman fulfilled the king's instructions to the letter, neither adding to it nor detracting from it. But what does this dutiful execution add for the reader? Wouldn't we expect that Haman routinely follows the king's orders? So what does the description add to the story?

Another question emerges as well: What sort of encounter transpired when Haman arrived to honor Mordechai? The author of the Megilah records many conversations between different characters of the Megilah, even giving us an interior view of Haman's thought process; yet it tells us nothing of the any conversation between Mordechai and Haman. Two bitter enemies were in the midst of a life and death battle, when suddenly the notorious anti-Semite comes to collect Mordechai, at the king's order. Wasn't Mordechai afraid that it was a trick?

One final question: the Megilah repeats the phrase "This is what is done for the man whom the king desires to show glory (*yekar*)!"

several times – which makes it quite certain that this phraseology is not incidental. What, then, is the role of this phrase? What does it contribute to the plot?

The Talmud attempts to fill this lacuna with an imagined conversation between Mordechai and Haman. In its telling, Mordechai had begun to save the Jewish people with prayer and Torah study. Thanks to the merit of sacrifices, Torah, and prayer, the star of Mordechai began to shine, and the Jewish revival of Shushan had commenced:

> "So Haman took the garb and the horse." He left and found [Mordechai] with the Sages sitting before him. He was demonstrating to them the laws of *kemitzah*.[7] Once Mordechai saw him coming toward him with his horse's reins in his hands, he became frightened, and he said to the Sages: "This evil man has come to kill me. Get away from him so that you are not burnt by his coals. At that moment, Mordechai wrapped himself [in his prayer shawl] and stood up to pray. Haman came over, sat down before [the Sages], and waited for Mordechai to finish his prayer. He said to them: "What occupies you?" They said to him: "When the Temple stands, one who pledges a meal-offering would bring a handful of fine flour and achieve atonement with it." He said to them: "Your handful of fine flour has come and overridden my ten thousand talents of silver." Mordechai then said to Haman: "Wicked man, when a slave buys property, to whom belongs the slave and to whom belongs the property? [I.e., since you are my slave, everything that belongs to you really belongs to me.] [Haman] said to [Mordechai]: "Get up, put on these garments and ride on this horse, for the king wishes to show you favor." [Mordechai] said to him: "I can't until I go up to the bathhouse

7 Taking a precise handful of flour as part of the sacrificial service.

> and get a haircut, for it is not proper to use the king's garments in my present state." Esther had sent word to lock away all the bath attendants and all the barbers. [Haman] himself brought [Mordechai] to the bathhouse and washed him. Then he went and brought scissors from his house and gave him a haircut. While he was trimming his hair, he injured himself and groaned. [Mordecai] said to him: "Why do you groan?" [Haman] replied to him: "Have I now become a bathhouse attendant and a barber?" [Mordechai] said to him: "Wicked man! Weren't you once the barber of the village of Kartzum?" (It was taught: Haman was the barber of the village of Kartzum for twenty-two years.) After he cut hair, he dressed him in the garments and said to him: "Mount the horse and ride." He replied: "I can't. I am weak from days of fasting." He bent over so [Mordechai] could [step on him and] mount. As he was ascending, he kicked [Haman]. [Haman] said to him: "Don't your Scriptures say: 'Do not rejoice at your enemy's downfall'(Mishlei 24)?" [Mordecai] said to him: "That applies only to Jews. With regard to you, it is written: 'And you shall tread upon their high places.'" (Devarim 33). (BT *Megilah* 16a)

The Talmud's discomfort and displeasure all but scream from the page in this lengthy description of the conversation between Haman and Mordechai. The Talmud invents a lecture on the on the laws of the priestly service and Temple sacrifices, and places it in Mordechai's mouth. Let us remember that Ezra the Scribe, a priest – a *kohen* – whose family had served in the Temple for generations, was living in Jerusalem and working to rebuild its Temple and its people. Mordechai was living in Shushan, moving seamlessly from distinctions of honor in the Persian Empire to a lecture about sacrificial service.[8] The Talmud, one might say, attempts to

8 There are a large number of halakhic and Biblical allusions in this Talmudic

hide the plain meaning of the text by means of this narrative. Moreover, the Talmud's narrative is such a stretch of the plain meaning and the imagination that one suspects that its very baselessness simply highlights how far it deviates.

From the plain meaning of the text, it seems that Mordechai was not surprised when Haman arrived. Presumably he was tipped off by the king's *ne'arim* that Haman was on his way to take him for a ride on the horse. He was not afraid because he had no reason to be anxious, and he certainly had no reason to refuse the king's order. He also had no reason to speak to Haman. It was clear to both of them that their battle had ended – with a victory for Mordechai.

Once again, we are reminded of the parallel story of Yosef. Just as Yosef gallops "in the second chariot which he had, and they called before him, 'On your knees!'" so too, Mordechai rode on a horse as they called out before him, "This is what is done for the man whom the king desires to show glory (*yekar*)!" The author of the Megilah indicates that Mordechai was rising to a position of power, just as the next verse in Bereishit states that Yosef was put in charge of all of Egypt. He would attain stature as the man in charge of the fleshpot, together with his Jewish allies.

Royal apparel does not merely function as a distinction of honor. Recall that Esther, too, put on "royal apparel" when she arose from her fast. She returned to her Persianness, and only one day later, Mordechai too abandoned his sackcloth, ashes, and Jewish mourning customs to don Persian royal apparel. He neglected his Judaism in order to reintegrate into the corridors of power in Persia.

When Mordechai mounted the horse he effectively ensured that the Jews would remain in exile and continue to assimilate. They had hoped

---

passage, which mentions the laws of sacrifices, the laws of slavery, several Biblical quotes, and a reference to Mordechai's fast. All of the stories about Mordechai's Jewishness are designed to play up his status as a Jew.

that "relief and deliverance will come to the Jews from another quarter," and not from God, confident that their plans and schemes in exile would never run out of luck. This is what shall be done to the man, the Megilah alludes, who turns his back to Jerusalem. This is what shall be done to the man – Mordechai – who does not build the Temple with his brothers.[9]

How do we know all of this? Very simply:

> Then Mordechai returned to the king's gate, while Haman was hurried home, his head covered in mourning. (6:12)

Rashi, following the Talmud, comments that when the procession ended, Mordechai returned to his sackcloth and fasting! Could it really be so? Earlier, the Megilah specifically tells us that Mordechai abstained from going to the palace gate, "for one could not enter the palace gate wearing sackcloth." That was the law. However, when Haman left Esther's party in good spirits, he noticed "Mordechai in the palace gate, and Mordechai did not rise or even stir on his account." We can derive from here that Mordechai sat at the palace gate, and consequently he had already jettisoned his sackcloth. Additionally, when Ahashverosh directed Haman to escort Mordechai on the horse, he said specifically: "do this to Mordechai the Jew, who sits in the king's gate."

A straightforward reading of the text makes it clear that Mordechai had already stopped his mourning practices while Esther was hosting her party. That is, he knew that Esther's plan has succeeded – in his opinion, at the very least – and he returned to the palace gate as though he had never left. It is as if he knew something that Haman did not know, as if he had

---

9 There is a clear biblical parallel here to the verses that discuss a man who refuses to perform levirate marriage by marrying the wife of his childless, deceased brother. The author is essentially saying that when Mordechai rode on the horse, dressed in the royal apparel of Persia, he decided once and for all not to join his brothers in building the Temple in Jerusalem.

no reason to be worried, as if the *ne'arim* in the king's court had already informed him of his change in status.

The Megilah's author again employs a good deal of irony. Haman returned to his house "his head covered in mourning," while Mordechai jubilantly returned "to the king's gate."

> There Haman told his wife Zeresh and all his friends all that had happened to him. His advisers and his wife Zeresh said to him, "If Mordechai, before whom you have begun to fall, is of Jewish stock, you will not overcome him; you will fall before him to your ruin." While they were still speaking with him, the king's eunuchs arrived and hurriedly brought Haman to the banquet which Esther had prepared. (6:13-14)

The Megilah's author uses Zeresh, like Vashti before her, to emphasize the singularity of the Jewish people. Haman's advisers and his wife Zeresh – as opposed to Mordechai and Esther – believed in the God of Israel and in His might. They understood, and told Haman, that just as "you have begun to fall," so too "you will fall before him to your ruin." Mordechai on the other hand, placed his trust in the king and in the king's gate, and did not mention God.

Haman "was hurried (*nidhaf*) home, his head covered in mourning." It is unclear as to who is hurrying (literally "pushing") him and why, but it is clear that whatever was done – was done in a panic. One can easily imagine the following scenario: Haman could not refuse the king's command, but the procession was extremely humiliating to him. Perhaps after the procession he wanted to chase after Mordechai, yelling at him and verbally taunting him, but his people – or other officers who saw what was unfolding – restrained him and hurried him home. [10]

---

10 Another explanation of the word hurried (*nidhaf*) is that Haman simply went

Back at home, after the spectacle has ended, Haman told "his wife Zeresh and all his friends" – those who had advised him to construct the gallows for Mordechai – "all that had happened to him." Haman addressed Zeresh first, and only then addressed his friends, but his "wise men" responded first, pushing Zeresh aside.

At first glance, nothing had happened that would justify the harsh statement of Zeresh and the advisers ("you will fall before him"). After all, he had been ordered to lead Mordechai on horseback. It was not the end of the world – certainly not from the point of view of Zeresh, who knew nothing of Ahashverosh's sleepless night. Yet everyone in attendance – from Haman to his advisers – understood that there had been a dramatic change in his status. Everyone sensed where the wind was blowing.[11]

The key to understanding this passage might be the phrase "all that had happened to him (*karahu*)." These words have appeared once previously in the Megilah. In Mordechai's speech to Hatakh, he told of "all that had happened to him (*karahu*), and all about the money that Haman had offered to pay into the royal treasury." Namely, we can understand exactly what Haman said perhaps from the parallel verse that relates to Mordechai: He was losing control of the empire's finances and being ousted from his position as minister of finance. Simply said, either the king was no longer distressed about his economic situation or he felt less dependent on Haman's assistance.

---

quickly (the translation we use reflects this approach), similar to what is written with respect to the couriers in chapter 3 ("The couriers went out posthaste [*dehufim*] on the royal mission") and what is written with respect to the leprosy of King Uziyahu in 2 Divrei Hayamim 26 ("his forehead was leprous, so they rushed him out of there; he too made haste [*nidhaf*] to get out, for the Lord had struck him with a plague.")

11 This recalls the reaction of the magicians of Egypt in the aftermath of the plague of lice ("It is the finger of God"). Sometimes the advisers know and understand things that their superiors still do not admit to themselves.

Even if the phrase "everything that had befallen him (*karahu*)" simply refers to a recapitulation of the recent events in Haman's life, we can assume that the meaning of these events did not escape him. The same paranoia that led him to declare a war of annihilation against Mordechai now led him to understand that the king had changed his mind and that Haman's political and financial position was in serious danger. The good days, when "all the king's courtiers in the palace gate knelt and bowed low" to him, were long gone. Worst of all, the king knew that Mordechai was a Jew (seeing as he had specifically instructed Haman: "and do this to Mordechai the Jew"). Not only had Haman's plan to hang Mordechai gone up in smoke, but it was likely that the king would not now be inclined to follow through on the money-for-murdering-Jews deal that Haman had proffered. You wanted to destroy the Jews and Mordechai, Zeresh said to him, but now the lots have been cast, and you will fall before that same Mordechai, who "is of Jewish stock."

Haman did not have much time to think. The king's eunuchs arrived to hasten Haman to Esther's second party. He was led there, rushed and frightened. God's salvation is as quick as the blink of an eye. Things happen quickly; Haman's advisers and Zeresh understood this. Perhaps even Haman understood it. There were only two people who did not perceive what was going on exactly: Esther and Mordechai.

They Hanged Haman on the Beam

So the king and Haman came to drink with Queen Esther (7:1)

There is an obvious difference between the phrase "to drink with Queen Esther," which appears here, and "to the feast that Esther had prepared," used with respect to Esther's first banquet. These two banquets clearly parallel the first two celebrations, described in chapter 1.[1] During the second party in chapter 1, Ahashverosh asked Vashti to join his celebration and play a major part in it. When she failed to arrive, she was deposed. Esther understood the lesson well. At the first party, she played the role of hostess and did not actively participate in the festivities. At the second party, though, she assumed an active role: Haman and Ahashverosh drank **with** Esther, while she reclined on her couch. Esther passed the test that Vashti failed, thereby securing her status as queen and as part of the Persian ruling class. Her integration symbolizes the integration of the Jews in the Persian Empire, and it was this status that enabled her to beg for her life and the life of her people from the king.

---

1 Even though one of these banquets, as we discussed earlier, was a marketing campaign to promote the war against Greece and a celebration of the arrival of tax monies in the capital, not a proper Persian banquet.

> On the second day, the king again asked Esther at the wine feast, "What is your wish, Queen Esther? It shall be granted you. And what is your request? Even up to half the kingdom, it shall be fulfilled." Queen Esther replied: "If Your Majesty will do me the favor, and if it pleases Your Majesty, let my life be granted me as my wish, and my people as my request. For we have been sold, my people and I, to be destroyed, massacred, and exterminated. Had we only been sold as bondmen and bondwomen, I would have kept silent; for no such distress is worthy of the king's trouble." (7:2-4)

Esther's argument is purely economic. "Your Highness," she began, "You were tempted by Haman's offer because of a fiscal crisis, but Haman in fact seeks to kill your loyal subjects, law-abiding taxpayers who bring revenue into your royal treasury. Had he sought merely to sell my people into slavery, I would have held my tongue, because the money from that sale would have flooded the king's reserves." She continued, "My personal pain and anguish about my people's fate would not justify causing great damage to your balanced budget. However, now that I have proven that I am a loyal Persian, right here on this couch, you can see, Your Majesty, that we Jews are loyal subjects of the Persian Empire. You need to save us – for my sake, for my people's sake, but first and foremost for the sake of the kingdom's treasury."

As Yonatan Grossman and others[2] have written, the word "*nimkarnu*" ("have been sold") can refer to both monetary sales and the delivery into the hands of a rival (as in "selling out") – that is, enslavement. Either meaning can make sense in this instance, so the word choice of the Megilah's author is especially apt. It is made clear to the reader that one

---

2 Grossman, Esther: The Outer Narrative and the Hidden Reading, p. 159.

who elects to stay in exile for the sake of profit will ultimately be sold into slavery to his enemies.

The story proceeds apace:

> Thereupon King Ahashverosh demanded of Queen Esther, "Who is he? Who dared to do this?" "The man is an adversary and enemy," replied Esther, "it is this evil Haman!" And Haman cringed in terror before the king and the queen. (7:5-6)

The king could not believe his ears. Horrified, he inquired: "Who is responsible for threatening the queen's life? Who wants to murder taxpayers and hurt the imperial economy?" Esther's response was carefully worded: "The man" ("*ish*") – he is someone of high socioeconomic standing; "adversary" ("*tzar*") is a synonym for "enemy," but it also alludes to the dire economic straits ("*tzarah*") that this man has caused; and finally, she repeated that he is an "enemy" ("*oyev*").

It seems that the author is alluding to another biblical passage where this pair of words appears:

> When you are at war in your land against an adversary who attacks you (*tzar ha-tzorer*), you shall sound short blasts on the trumpets, that you may be remembered before the Lord your God and be delivered from your enemies (*oyveikhem*). And on your joyous occasions – your fixed festivals and new moon days – you shall sound the trumpets over your burnt offerings and your sacrifices of well-being. They shall be a reminder of you before your God: I, the Lord, am your God. (Bamidbar 10:9-10)

The author of the Megilah intimates that the enemy has come to attack you because you did not return to Eretz Yisrael, opting instead for assimilation. The trumpets will not remember you to your God, and the army of Israel will not come to save you from your enemy. (The author may also be indicating that ultimately you will not be spared from the adversary and enemy). This verse, which appears at the beginning of Bamidbar, was given to Israel on the eve of their entry into their land.[3] Esther, in her very own words, reminds readers where she should have been in order to find true deliverance.[4] Instead of trying to appeal to the mercy of King Ahashverosh, she should have sounded the trumpets and prayed to the King of kings.

Haman "cringed in terror" before the king and the queen. His fear was well-founded: He had just been exposed by Esther as the chief architect of the plan to kill the queen of Persia and her people. It is not clear whether the king had internalized the fact that Esther was Jewish, but Haman understood this quite well; according to our approach, he had suspected this previously.

This leads to the next strange scene:

> The king, in his fury, left the wine feast for the palace garden,
> while Haman remained to plead with Queen Esther for his life;
> for he saw that the king had resolved to destroy him. (7:7)

The moment that the queen told him that "this evil Haman" wanted to kill her, the king stormed angrily out of the banquet and went to the palace garden. He was enraged and needed a few minutes alone to work out what had just happened. Esther had not explicitly announced her Jewishness, so the king needed to connect the power he had vested in Haman – without Haman ever clearly identifying the Jews as the group

---

3 This passage appears just before the account of the sin of the spies (Bamidbar 13), who slandered Eretz Yisrael and thus condemned Israel to remain in the desert for forty years.

4 That is, the author places the incriminating words in Esther's mouth.

he sought to annihilate – with Esther's accusations.[5] Ahasheverosh had assumed that Esther was Persian, or at least completely assimilated, and now she had set herself apart and announced that she and her people are at risk of extermination.[6] More than anything, though, he was furious with Haman, who sought to kill his queen – at once a personal betrayal and an act of treason against the kingdom.

Haman was well aware of Esther's Jewishness, and so he tried what he could to beg the queen – not the king – to spare his life, for he saw clearly that "the king had resolved to destroy him." His dreams of greatness and power and his desire to see Mordechai hanged were gone; he asked only for his life to be spared.

The next verse explains further why Haman begged only Esther, not the king, for his life, though several *midrashim* try to soften the implications:

> When the king returned from the palace garden to the banquet room, Haman was falling on the couch on which Esther reclined. "Does he also mean," cried the king, "to conquer the queen in my own palace?" No sooner did these words leave the king's lips than Haman's face was covered. (7:8)

We can imagine the scene. Esther was lying on her couch in the style of a Persian noblewoman at a banquet. That her desire to assimilate into the Persian ruling class resulted in her becoming queen had agitated Haman greatly. That she invited him and the king to a banquet indicated, to his mind, that her assimilation was complete. He then fell upon Esther's

---

5 "There is a certain people, scattered and dispersed among the other peoples in all the provinces of your realm, whose laws are different from those of any other people and who do not obey the king's laws; and it is not in Your Majesty's interest to tolerate them."

6 Here we see again that anti-Semitism actually highlights one's Jewishness more than normal.

couch – a literal fall that signifies his fall from power, as predicted by his advisers and Zeresh. Yonatan Grossman explains, "The verb NPL ('to fall') is one of the key verbs in the description of Haman's demise."[7] Haman was falling on the couch, perhaps even lying atop the queen, thinking that perhaps he could persuade her to have mercy on him by making seductive propositions.

We do not know what Haman said to Esther, and, surprisingly, we likewise do not know how Esther reacted. Even a lack of protest would have been a telling reaction – as in the case where "the girl did not cry for help in the town" (Devarim 22). Only the king's reaction is recorded. Upon returning from the palace garden, he saw what was going on and cried out: "Does he also mean to conquer the queen in my own palace?"

The word "also" attests that there was another cause for the king's ire, and it seems that this does not refer to Haman's desire to annihilate the Jews. Rather, the king was angry about Haman's attempt to seize control of the palace. The king had gone out to the "courtyard of the king's palace garden" that had been the site of the seven-day banquet described in chapter 1. There, he remembered the good old days of wealth and bounty, of "silver rods and alabaster columns, couches of gold and silver." He filled with rage against Haman, his appetite for power, and his desire to ride through Shushan in royal clothing and on the back of the king's horse. It was at this party, years earlier, when he summoned Vashti to appear before him, that the kingdom began its downturn. In Ahashverosh's mind, this event merged with his desire to protect Esther and his fury against Haman's manipulations into a single essence. "Do you also" wish to take over the royal court, harm my queen, and even conquer her in bed?[8]

---

7 Grossman, Esther: The Outer Narrative and the Hidden Reading, pp. 151-154.

8 As we have seen, there are three symbols of royal status listed in Devarim: money, wives, and horses. It seems that Ahashverosh saw the apparent attempt to conquer the queen as the final element, the "also," after Haman had already expressed his lust for the king's wealth and the king's horse. See also 2 Shmuel 16:20-22, where

"No sooner did these words leave the king's lips than Haman's face was covered" – the Megilah's author does not explain exactly which of the king's words caused the covering of Haman's face. It is obvious though, that these "words"[9] made it clear to Haman that things were moving quickly in the wrong direction. Haman was not alone in understanding where the wind blows:

> Then Harvona, one of the eunuchs in attendance on the king, said, "What is more, a beam is standing at Haman's house, fifty cubits high, which Haman made for Mordechai – the man whose words saved the king." "Hang him on it!" the king ordered. So they hanged Haman on the beam which he had put up for Mordechai, and the king's fury abated. (7:9-10)

It is possible that the king did not intend to kill Haman at this stage, but merely to demote him and remove him from the royal court. But Harvona, one of the "the seven eunuchs in attendance on King Ahashverosh" mentioned in chapter 1, took full advantage of the fortuitous circumstances. Haman had been demoted, the king was furious with him; he was 'on the ropes.' Harvona then stepped forward and subtly, matter-of-factly drew the king's attention to the full depth of Haman's treachery: Look, this impudent Haman constructed a fifty-cubit gallows in his own backyard, in the hopes of hanging Mordechai on it. Harvona then tactfully

---

Avshalom demonstrates his claim to the throne by setting up a tent publicly and consorting in it with his father's concubines.

9 We note here our earlier explanation of "for it was the royal practice [to turn] to all who were versed in law and precedent," regarding deposing Vashti as queen (see p.36). At that point, the king hesitated and did not express himself, not really wanting to dethrone Vashti. He loved his queen – Vashti as well as Esther – and desired her. This time around, he did not hesitate or stammer. He uttered the words that would save his queen.

clarified that this was the very same Mordechai "whose words saved the king." Harvona did not counsel the king to hang Mordechai. He reported 'just the facts,' with some relevant background for the king to consider, but there was no doubt how it would end. The king ordered Harvona and the other servants: "Hang him on it!" When it comes to palace intrigue, a rapid loss of status is commensurate with the depth of the treachery in the eyes of the king.

In this context, R. Benny Lau notes that Harvona is the subject of discussion in the Talmud and *midrashim*. Some view him as an enemy of Mordechai, a co-conspirator of Bigtan and Teresh, while others invoke the view of R. Pinhas, enshrined for all time in the Purim liturgy: "Harvona, too, is remembered for the good" (*Bereishit Rabba* 49). Although Harvona did not necessarily mean to do good, his words, "What is more, a beam is standing at Haman's house, fifty cubits high, which Haman made for Mordechai," place him on the positive side of the ledger in our collective memory.

Aside from these brief references, the author of the Megilah does not tell us much about Harvona. We do not learn whether the king already knew about the gallows and what else Harvona may have whispered into the king's ear before saying "what is more." Perhaps Harvona was a soldier (his name bears resemblance to the word for "sword" – "*herev*"), or perhaps the king's executioner. The fact that he was mentioned in the Vashti episode indicates that he was a veteran member of the royal court: He had survived for at least nine years[10] in the service of a fickle king and through difficult times.

The expression "in attendance on the king" (*pnei ha'melekh*) that is

10 Since the Megilah begins in year three of Ahashverosh's rule, it has been nine years since we last encountered Harvona. However, it would appear that he was not a rookie advisor in chapter 1; he was among those who "saw the face of the king." It is therefore reasonable to conclude that he has been around for all twelve years of Xerxes rule.

used to describe Harvona and the officers of Persia and Media appears in only one other biblical story: the episode of Avshalom's rebellion.

> But the king said, "Let him go directly to his house and not present himself to me." So Avshalom went directly to his house and did not present himself to the king (*pnei ha'melekh*)... Avshalom lived in Jerusalem two years without appearing before the king (*pnei ha'melekh*). (2 Shmuel 14:24, 28)

In order to again appear before the king, Avshalom sets Yoav's field on fire:

> Avshalom replied to Yoav, "I sent for you to come here; I wanted to send you to the king to say [on my behalf]. Why did I leave Geshur? I would be better off if I were still there. Now let me appear before the king (*pnei ha'melekh*); and if I am guilty of anything, let him put me to death!"

Additional parallels between the Megilah and the story of Avshalom are present in the word "*hafu*" ("was covered"), which corresponds to the description of the David's grief when he finds out about Avshalom's coup ("David meanwhile went up the slope of the [Mount of] Olives, weeping as he went; his head was covered [*hafuy*], and he walked barefoot. And all the people who were with him covered their heads and wept as they went up"); in the appearance of Shimi the son of Gera, who is linked to the family tree of "Mordechai, son of Yair son of Shimi son of Kish, a Benjaminite" (see page 48); and, of course, in Avshalom's demise:

> Avshalom encountered some of David's followers. Avshalom was riding on a mule, and as the mule passed under the tangled branches of a great terebinth, his hair got caught in the terebinth;

> he was held between heaven and earth as the mule under him kept going. One of the men saw it and told Yoav, "I have just seen Avshalom hanging from a terebinth." Yoav said to the man who told him, "You saw it! Why didn't you kill him then and there? I would have owed you ten shekels of silver and a belt." But the man answered Yoav, "Even if I had a thousand shekels of silver in my hands, I would not raise a hand against the king's son. For the king charged you and Abishai and Ittai in our hearing, 'Watch over my boy Avshalom, for my sake.' If I betrayed myself – and nothing is hidden from the king – you would have stood aloof." Yoav replied, "Then I will not wait for you." He took three darts in his hand and drove them into Avshalom's chest. [Avshalom] was still alive in the thick growth of the terebinth, when ten of Yoav's young arms-bearers closed in and struck at Avshalom until he died. (2 Shmuel 18:9-15)

The abundance of imagery and terminology in the Megilah that recalls Avshalom's coup are not incidental.[11] Avshalom rebelled against his father, King David, caused a schism in the kingdom, and ultimately met his death. Perhaps the Megilah's author seeks to compare Haman and Avshalom: They are both hanged by an act of God as a rebuke against their pride and hubris: Avshalom by his magnificent locks of hair, and Haman from the gallows he arrogantly built in his yard. In both cases, power was restored to those who rightfully possessed it: Mordechai and Esther in the Megilah, and King David in the Avshalom episode.[12] The traitors were hanged.

---

11 Perhaps even the "ten shekels of silver" that Yoav offers to his servant ("*na'ar*") to kill Avshalom, and the latter's refusal to do so even for "a thousand shekels of silver," tie in to Haman's ten thousand talents of silver.

12 There are similarities between the death of Avshalom and the death of Xerxes I, who was murdered by the head of his honor guard, Artabanus, with the assistance of his eunuch Aspamitres. Artabanus also killed the king's son Darius and

The parallels abound. The expression "*p'nei hamelekh*" has a positive connotation in connection with Avshalom and a negative connotation in connection with Haman. The word "*hafu*" applies to King David in context of Avshalom's coup and to Haman in the Megilah. As noted, both Haman and Avshalom were hanged. There is such a wide range of characters and comparisons here that it is difficult to classify them in one comprehensive parallel analysis. Perhaps the author of the Megilah views the events of the royal court of Shushan as a rebellion against the real kingdom that was then taking shape in Jerusalem. Mordechai and Esther are thus presented as traitors who support Shushan and subvert the monarchy of Judah and the kingdom of God.

Either way, this episode conceals more than it reveals. The plain meaning of the text indicates that the king knew nothing about the gallows that Haman had constructed in the past thirty-six hours. Someone had decided to construct a gallows near the palace – and the king had not been notified. This type of thing would not just happen unless the royal bureaucracy was dysfunctional or the king himself was on shaky ground.

When Ahashverosh learned that Haman had secretly constructed a gallows, he began to understand that many things had been concealed from him. Most importantly, he understood that his closest and ostensibly his most loyal minister had been concealing more than anyone else. That is why he ordered that Haman be hanged from the gallows. The text gives no indication that Haman was hanged in punishment for his plot against the Jews. In fact, the edict against the Jews remained in force, even after Haman's demise. Rather, the text tells us that he was hanged on account of several crimes, including his construction of the gallows: "**What is more** (*gam*), a beam is standing which Haman made."

Harvona's words allude to Haman's other crimes against the king.

---

crowned his third son, Artaxerxes, king in his stead. Artabanus was eventually murdered by Artaxerxes.

Haman was condemned to hang not **only** on account of his apparent attempt to conquer the queen, but **also** because of his desire to conquer the queen ("Does he **also** [*gam*] mean to conquer the queen"), and **also** on account of the gallows that he constructed in order to settle a score, and **also** on account of his attempt to control the royal treasury, and **also** on account of his attempt to oust Mordechai, the king's loyal confidant.

In other words, the Megilah's author is telling us that Haman was not hanged because he threatened the Jewish people, but because he threatened the rule of Ahashverosh.

At first glance, the king saved the Jews when his servants reminded him that he had not yet rewarded Mordechai for his role in putting down the coup of Bigtan and Teresh; he saved them again when Esther incriminated Haman and the king returned from the palace garden to find Haman on Esther's couch. This is all just on the surface. The text itself tells of palace intrigue, of loyalty to the king, and of sedition. These were the real motives of Ahashverosh. Love for the Jewish people and the desire to save them were not on his agenda.[13]

It is worth noting that immediately after Esther identified Haman as "an adversary and an enemy," the king rose in a fury and headed outside. He did not get up to stop the scheme against Esther and the Jews right away, nor did he sentence Haman to death immediately. His decision to put Haman to death was made only after he returned to the party, witnessed Haman's attempt to conquer the queen, and listened as Harvona delineated Haman's other crimes, culminating in the construction of a gallows without the king's knowledge, and right under his nose.

Moreover, it is important to remember that the king did not reward Mordechai right away, in the middle of the night, when he was sleepless and the book of records was read before him. The decision to reward Mordechai only took shape in the morning, when he woke up and

---

13 In this sense, too, there are parallels to Avshalom's coup.

encountered Haman. Esther and Mordechai – like Harvona – understood that the king was not taking initiative but was responding to events; he was reactive, not proactive. They grasped that in such an environment, it is easy to fall out of the king's good graces and easy to win them back. Such was the nature of the power struggles in the royal court of Ahashverosh.

Finally, just like in the Vashti episode, "the king's fury abated." The localized problem that had so exercised the king was resolved, and calm was restored. However, the Jews still faced a threat of annihilation. Nothing had changed except that Haman had been removed from the royal court while Esther and Mordechai had regained the king's good graces and were once again influential within the corridors of power.

Mordechai Left the King's Presence

> That very day King Ahashverosh gave the property of Haman, the enemy of the Jews, to Queen Esther. Mordechai presented himself to the king, for Esther had revealed how he was related to her. The king slipped off his ring, which he had taken back from Haman, and gave it to Mordechai; and Esther put Mordechai in charge of Haman's property. (8:1-2)

The Megilah continues at a breathless pace. Haman was indeed hanged on the gallows, but the threat of annihilation still loomed over the Jews. "That very day" – meaning on the very same day that Ahashverosh sentenced Haman to be hanged – Haman's estate was given to Queen Esther, and Mordechai immediately presented himself to the king. The king transferred his ring from Haman to Mordechai, and Esther put Mordechai in charge of Haman's estate.

The narrative does not give us a dated sequence of events after the thirteenth of Nisan, when Haman's decree was issued. According to the Sages – and this is a reasonable assumption, since "the couriers went out posthaste on the royal mission" – the couriers departed with the edict of annihilation on that very day. Right away, Mordechai rent his clothes, donned sackcloth, and went out to the main square, where he conducted a conversation with Esther via Hatakh. At the end of this conversation, Esther pronounced a three-day fast, which began immediately. She appeared before the king on the third day, which we may thus presume was the sixteenth of Nisan. That very night, Esther hosted her first party, after which the king could not sleep. The next day, the seventeenth of Nisan, Esther hosted her second party, after which Haman was hanged from the gallows. "That very day," Ahashverosh gave Haman's estate to Esther , and she appointed Mordechai over it.

This sequence of events illustrates, first and foremost, that God's salvation indeed comes in the blink of an eye. The threat of complete destruction hung over the heads of the Jewish people for several days only, and it is extremely doubtful that the entire empire had even received Haman's edict of annihilation by then. The threat to Mordechai's life was quickly eliminated. The protests and the political maneuverings worked out well, at least from his and Esther's perspective.

The first verse of this chapter only hints that Mordechai and Esther had told the king that they are Jews.[1] We learn that Esther told the king that Mordechai is her relative ("how he was related to her"), but it is not clear from the text whether she told the king that she is, in fact, a Jew. It seems that the fact of her Jewishness was simply not all that important her. When she reclined on the couch at the party she said, "we have been sold, my people and I, to be destroyed, massacred, and exterminated," but the king did not bother to clarify which people she referred to, and he killed Haman as a traitor. In other words, before Esther and Mordechai did anything for the Jews, they first took care of themselves: Esther announced to the king that Mordechai is her relative, the king in turn appointed Mordechai as the chief minister in place of Haman (meaning, he handed Mordechai the signet ring that indicated his authority as chief minister), and Esther put Mordechai in charge of Haman's estate. Mordechai had

1 This is despite the fact that the king called Mordechai "Mordechai the Jew, who sits in the king's gate" when he commanded Haman to lead Mordechai on the horse. That is, Judaism was not an essential part of Mordechai's (or Esther's) identity, but an epithet that was attached to him on account of his ancestry.

achieved the status that he coveted before Haman complicated his plans for a few days.

Then things fell quiet for two entire months. Mordechai and Esther had grown complacent and comfortable with their new power. They awakened only a while later, in the month of Sivan:

> Esther spoke to the king again, falling at his feet and weeping, and beseeching him to avert the evil plotted by Haman the Agagite against the Jews. The king extended the golden scepter to Esther, and Esther arose and stood before the king. "If it please Your Majesty," she said, "and if I have won your favor and the proposal seems right to Your Majesty, and if I am pleasing to you – let dispatches be written countermanding those which were written by Haman son of Hammedata the Agagite, embodying his plot to annihilate the Jews throughout the king's provinces. For how can I bear to see the disaster which will befall my people! And how can I bear to see the destruction of my kindred!" (8:3-6)

These words are a harsh indictment of Mordechai and Esther. A continuous reading of the Megilah and the explicit link to the previous conversation ("Esther spoke to the king **again**") make it seem like not much time had elapsed, but this was not the case. The word "again" does not indicate that the second conversation transpired soon after the first, but the opposite, as though Esther remembered, a while later, that there was something else she wanted to discuss with the king – her people and her homeland. This second conversation took place long after the seventeenth of Nisan: "on the twenty-third day of the third month, that is, the month of Sivan."

By this time, Esther and Mordechai were regularly in the king's presence. Mordechai had won the plum appointment he had so coveted, and Esther was once again in the king's good graces. He had fallen back in love with her, and she was his preferred consort, never far away. For two months, she had come and gone from the king's chambers, and suddenly she remembered to present herself before him, bow low, and beg on behalf of her people.

Esther did not come and beg for her own life. She did not beg the king to abolish Haman's decree against her or Mordechai; they were well taken care of. What bothered Esther is that she did not want to **see** the implementation of the terrible decree against her people. Maybe desperate cries for help had reached her from distant parts of the empire when Haman's letter finally arrived. Maybe pangs of conscience had awakened Queen Esther from her deep slumber. Maybe.

The author of the Megilah is very cynical here. Esther was nestled in Ahashverosh's lap. Mordechai was strutting around with Haman's ring on his finger. Then, two months later, they vaguely remember something.... What was it again? Oh, yeah. Haman's desire to destroy all of the Jews. Esther and Mordechai then petitioned the king on behalf of the Jews, but as their patrons, not as a part of the nation. This was long after the couriers were sent posthaste to spread word of the impending elimination of the Jews. We learn about the real situation from the questions that Ahashverosh asked:

> Then King Ahashverosh said to Queen Esther and Mordechai the Jew, "I have given Haman's property to Esther, and he has been hanged on the beam for doing violence to the Jews.[2] And you

---

2 It is worth noting that, contrary to the king's statement here, Haman did not actually do violence to the Jews. Moreover, as we noted in the previous chapter, Haman was not punished for what he did or sought to do to the Jews, and in fact, Haman's edict remained in force. The expression used here, "*shalah yado*" (lit. "sent out his hand), is the same expression used to describe what Bigtan and Teresh **sought** to do to the king ("*vayevakshu lishlo'ah yad*"; 2:21) and what the Jews assembled to do to their enemies ("*lishlo'ah yad*"; 9:2).

> may further write with regard to the Jews as you see fit. [Write it] in the king's name and seal it with the king's signet, for an edict that has been written in the king's name and sealed with the king's signet may not be revoked." (8:7-8)

The king's questions are very much in place; he could not understand why they were suddenly so upset. Your personal needs have been taken care of, correct? "I have given Haman's property to Esther," and Haman himself "has been hanged on the beam." What exactly bothers you now? I don't want to concern myself with the Jews, and even if I wanted to, I can't, for administrative reasons. From my perspective, this affair ended when I hanged the man who threatened my sovereignty and transferred the king's ring to Mordechai. Saving the Jews is your business. I have no part in it. If you want to do something, do it on your own.

What was already done could not be undone. Haman's directives, signed and sealed with the king's signet ring, could not be annulled. It was therefore necessary to issue a new emergency directive as quickly as possible:

> So the king's scribes were summoned at that time, on the twenty-third day of the third month, that is, the month of Sivan; and letters were written, at Mordechai's dictation, to the Jews and to the satraps, the governors and the officials of the one hundred and twenty-seven provinces from India to Ethiopia: to every province in its own script and to every people in its own language, and to the Jews in their own script and language. He had them written in the name of King Ahashverosh and sealed with the king's signet. Letters were dispatched by mounted couriers, riding steeds used in the king's service, bred of the royal stud, to this effect: The king has permitted the Jews of every city to assemble and fight for their lives; if any people or province

> attacks them, they may destroy, massacre, and exterminate its armed force together with women and children, and plunder their possessions – on a single day in all the provinces of King Ahashverosh, namely, on the thirteenth day of the twelfth month, that is, the month of Adar. The text of the document was to be issued as a law in every single province: it was to be publicly displayed to all the peoples, so that the Jews should be ready for that day to avenge themselves on their enemies. The couriers, mounted on royal steeds, went out in urgent haste at the king's command; and the decree was proclaimed in Shushan the capital. (8:9-14)

On the twenty-third of Sivan, more than two months after Haman's edict had been issued, he had been hanged, and his estate had been placed under Mordechai's charge, the new edict, sponsored by senior minister Mordechai was issued: "The king has permitted the Jews of every city to assemble and fight for their lives; if any people or province attacks them, they may destroy, massacre, and exterminate its armed force together with women and children, and plunder their possessions."

The Persian Empire had two different methods for disseminating messages. Standard procedure involved sending couriers who traveled in regular caravans. It generally took three to four months to reach the extremities of the empire by this method, and even then, they only reached regions along or near the Royal Road. This explains why Haman scheduled the annihilation of the Jews for almost a year after the edict was issued (from Nisan, the first month, to Adar, the twelfth). In contrast, Mordechai's couriers were mounted. Herodotus comments on the remarkable speed of this method. These "mounted couriers, riding steeds used in the king's service, bred of the royal stud" switched daily at stations, so that very urgent messages dispatched from or sent to Shushan would reach their destination in two weeks or less.

The motives for Esther's and Mordechai's urgent actions must be explained. There are several differences between Haman's edict of destruction and Mordechai's dispatch. Firstly, the Jews receive the letter "in its own script and its own language"; secondly, the number of provinces is mentioned ("one hundred and twenty-seven provinces"), as are the addressees ("to the satraps, the governors, and the officials"); finally, the "the couriers, mounted on royal steeds," are dispatched not only "posthaste" ("*dehufim*") but also "in urgent haste" ("*mevohalim u-dehufim*").

It seems to me that these changes make several important points. Mordechai was searching for people who are loyal to him, and the Jews, obviously, represented a sort of extended family. He could correspond with them in a language only the sender and recipients could understand, namely, Hebrew. In other words, the Hebrew epistles constituted a private message of sorts. A close reading of the passage above allows us to speculate that Mordechai sent two separate messages: one "to the Jews," and the other "to the satraps, the governors, and the officials."

It is thus quite possible that Mordechai wrote one letter to the governors of the provinces, in which he announced that Haman's decree has been abolished and the Jews have been granted the right to defend themselves – "fight for their lives if any people or province attacks them, they may destroy, massacre, and exterminate its armed force together with women and children, and plunder their possessions" – and a second, more assertive letter to the Jews, "so that the Jews should be ready for that day to avenge themselves on their enemies." In other words, get ready for the big day when you will be able to square off with your enemies.

It is worth noting that Ahashverosh granted Mordechai and Esther permission to annul the decree against the Jewish people ("and you may further write with regard to the Jews as you see fit"), which would include self-defense against attackers. However, Ahashverosh did not grant Mordechai and Esther permission to expand the scope of operations by settling accounts ("to avenge themselves on their enemies"), especially since the Megilah has not previously mentioned these outstanding accounts or these enemies.

Furthermore, the natural question is why Mordechai and Esther instructed the Jews, of all things, to prepare themselves for a day of vengeance and retribution to their enemies? They could have, for example, ordered them to leave Persia and move to Eretz Yisrael, or directed them to tithe their earnings (or even just the spoils of their war against their enemies) and donate the tithes to the rebuilding of Jerusalem and the Temple. Yet their instructions were to establish a militia, prepare for vengeance, kill, and plunder.

Thirdly, there is plenty of time between Sivan and Adar. Why did the Jews have to wait until their enemies attacked? Why didn't they strike preemptively?

Fourthly, the parallels between this edict and Haman's edict are uncanny. Haman dispatched couriers with an order:

> To destroy, massacre, and exterminate all the Jews, young and old, children and women, on a single day, on the thirteenth day of the twelfth month – that is, the month of Adar – and to plunder their possessions. (3:13)

Mordechai and Esther dispatched messengers with an order:

> To assemble and fight for their lives; if any people or province attacks them, they may destroy, massacre, and exterminate its armed force together with women and children, and plunder their possessions. (8:11)

Nowhere else in Tanakh, with the exception of the commandment to eradicate Amalek, were the Jews instructed to destroy, massacre, and exterminate an enemy.[3] This was precisely Mordechai and Esther's message though; it was not self-defense, but vengeance and destruction. This begs for an explanation: could it be that anyone who stood against them was Amalek, from their perspective?[4]

Finally, the king used the plural "you" ("*atem*") when saying, "you may further write with regard to the Jews," apparently addressing both Esther and Mordechai, but only Mordechai is mentioned as the one who authored, signed, and dispatched the edict. Where did Esther go?

This last question is the key to understanding these events. Mordechai aspired to become enmeshed in the ruling echelons of Shushan and to establish his economic and political stature in Persia. Haman's demise was not only gratifying, but also sobering; it caused him to realize that political power that is not backed by military might tends to dissipate rapidly. No officer, adviser, prime minister, or even viceroy with close personal ties to the queen has a stable grasp on power without a military force that is not a dependent of the king.[5]

The political situation in Persia was somewhat tenuous. It was not just a

---

3 "Now go, attack Amalek, and proscribe all that belongs to him. Spare no one, but kill alike men and women, infants and sucklings, oxen and sheep, camels and donkeys!" (1 Shmuel 15:3)

4 The Sages infer that "Haman the Agagite" was a descendant of King Agag of Amalek (mentioned in 1 Shmuel 15). This distant familial connection seems a bit farfetched as a justification for extermination, as the Sages would presumably acknowledge. And even so, it is not conceivable that all of the enemies of the Persian Jews rose to the level of the ancient and eternal enemy from the seed of Amalek. However, it is possible that the enemies of the Jews were considered Amalek-like in some fashion.

5 Mordechai's conclusion is strengthened by the following historical examples: the victory of the privately operated militias in the struggles that led to the collapse of the Roman Republic, the rise of the Praetorian Guard as the kingmakers of the Roman Empire in the first century CE, the rise of the Carolingian dynasty after Charlemagne in the eighth century CE, at the expense of the Merovingians, who had lost control of the armed forces, etc.

province or a tribe, but a tremendous empire of "one hundred and twenty-seven provinces from India to Ethiopia," where one day the premier official in all the empire was "Haman son of Hammedata the Agagite," and the next day it was "Mordechai the Jew." No one could rely on loyalty, unless it was someone from his own people or tribe.

Mordechai, the author of the Megilah teaches us, adopted a clear strategy for establishing a loyal militia that would support his political power with military might. He enjoyed an exalted status among the Jews who had first arrived in Babylonia in the exile of "the artisan and the locksmith" – and, correspondingly, he enjoyed a very prominent status in the royal court of Ahashverosh. This was true earlier in the story, when he sat in the palace gate, and it was certainly true now that he held the king's ring and wrote "in the king's name" while retaining a staunch ally in the palace.

Mordechai wrote "to the satraps, the governors, and the officials," telling them that a new militia under Mordechai's command would be established in their provinces. He wrote to "the Jews of every city" separately, telling them "to assemble and fight for their lives" and to prepare for the day they would have to "avenge themselves on their enemies." Mordechai was minister of finance, but in order to bolster his position and the positions of his supporters in a significant fashion, he needs an independent military force that is not at all reliant on Ahashverosh.

The critique of the Megilah's author stems from that which Mordechai did **not** do: take advantage of his political stature to bring the Jews back to Eretz Yisrael, as Ezra and Nehemiah did. Nor did he establish an army to assist the returnees. Nehemiah, the cupbearer of King Artaxerxes, capitalized on his relationship with the king – the son of Xerxes/Ahashverosh – to request one thing, and one thing only: "Send me to Judah, to the city of my fathers' burial place, so that I may rebuild it." Mordechai, on the other hand, sought to build a Jewish militia to reinforce his political stature in Persia.

The author of the Megilah is cynical in his treatment of Mordechai. Dr. Grossman notes that lot-casting (such as Haman's "*pur*") was an important part of Persian mystical practice. Therefore, the "the decree (*dat*, a term that denotes both law and religion) was proclaimed in Shushan the capital (*bira*)," and not in Jerusalem the capital (*bira*). The source of instruction was Persian law from the Persian capital rather than Torah from Jerusalem's Temple ("For instruction/Torah shall go forth from Zion, the word of God from Jerusalem").[6] Yet Mordechai nevertheless waited until the thirteenth of Adar to launch his strike. He wanted to demonstrate that Persian magic was also under his control and that he governed the entire apparatus of Persian rule, in all its worldly and otherworldly manifestations. Haman cast a lot in order to determine the day that the gods deemed most auspicious for the destruction of the Jews. Mordechai took this *pur* and completely flipped the script.

Mordechai sent his message to "one hundred and twenty-seven provinces from India to Ethiopia" because that was his objective: full control over all the provinces of the kingdom. The use of horses was a display of imperial power,[7] as was the use of "mounted couriers, riding steeds used in the king's service," who were used sparingly, and only for

6 "King David uses the word "*bira*" to describe the Temple when he commands his son Shlomo to build the Temple using the materials that he had prepared (see 1 Divrei Hayamim 29:1,19). Before the period of Megilat Esther, the Hebrew word "*bira*" had a different meaning in Tanakh [in the tractate of *Midot*, the Temple is called "*bira*"]. See Menachem Leibtag's study at http://www.tanach.org/special/purim/purims1.htm.

7 As in the commandment concerning kings of Israel: "He shall not keep many horses" (Devarim 17:16). Avshalom demonstrated that he was king by providing himself with "a chariot, horses, and fifty runners."Adoniyahu the son of Hagit, who likewise claimed Davidic succession, "provided himself with chariots and horses, and an escort of fifty runners." Of course, the horses pulling Yosef's chariot come to mind as well. Even today, the basic unit of measure for physical power remains the horse, as in "horsepower."

urgent royal needs. Haman was not allowed to make use of these horses; Mordechai was. This high level of urgency that mandated that the couriers be sent "in urgent haste" was Mordechai's doing. His desire to rule the empire was very urgent.

Mordechai's primary objective was obtained:

> Mordechai left the king's presence in royal robes of blue wool and fine white linen, with a magnificent crown of gold and a mantle of fine linen and purple wool. And the city of Shushan rang with joyous cries. The Jews enjoyed light and gladness, happiness and honor. And in every province and in every city, when the king's command and decree arrived, there was gladness and joy among the Jews, a feast and a holiday. And many of the people of the land professed to be Jews, for the fear of the Jews had fallen upon them. (8:15-17)

These verses unsettle me to no end. Mordechai left the king's presence "in royal robes of blue wool and fine white linen" and the city of Shushan "rang with joyous cries." Two different things receive their stamp of approval here. First, Mordechai had become completely integrated into the power structure of Shushan and fully assimilated into Persia, much like Yosef when he rode the second chariot to the pharaoh.

Second, however, Mordechai engaged in a disturbing act of self-worship. Our teacher Moshe was an ideal leader; he did not seek a leadership role and was shocked when leadership was foisted upon him. When people came to praise and salute him, he deflected the limelight elsewhere – toward God or toward his brother Aharon. This was also the manner of the prophet Shmuel, King David, and even initially to King Shaul, Mordechai's ancestor.

Not Mordechai, though. He strutted out of the palace in full regalia, thirsting for public adulation – and getting it. He was now the most senior official in the kingdom, enjoying a close relationship with the king and the power brokers of the kingdom. Everyone wanted to be his friend, or a friend of his friends.

The Jews were happy, or so it seems. Haman's edict was annulled before it could be carried out, and the Jews received "honor" (*yekar*) – the monetary prize granted to those closest to the king. The Jews had not yet been saved, but they were already celebrating "a feast and a holiday." The reason for this is quite clear: They had assimilated. From their perspective, the ultimate goal had been reached. Despite the threats to their power and status in Persian society, they were closer than ever to the government and had become a secure and popular bloc within the empire. It is worth noting again that the Jews had not yet been saved from the evil decree, but Mordechai emerged as a hero, and they could celebrate. The greatest goal had been realized; the Jews again enjoyed governmental power in Persia.

This was no mere "holiday" for the Jews, but rather "a feast and a holiday" ("*mishteh ve-yom tov*) – a phrase that will reappear in various forms ("a day of feasting and merrymaking"; "a day of merrymaking and feasting, and as a holiday," etc.). The author of the Megilah intimates that even these ostensibly Jewish celebrations were really Persian banquets (as indicated by the word "*mishteh*"). These were hardly rabbinically-sanctioned holidays. They were Shushan-style parties.

Because the Fear of Mordechai had Fallen upon Them

Chapter 9 continues the focus on Mordechai:

> And so, on the thirteenth day of the twelfth month – that is, the month of Adar – when the king's command and decree were to be executed, the very day on which the enemies of the Jews had expected to get them in their power, the opposite happened, and the Jews got their enemies in their power. Throughout the provinces of King Ahashverosh, the Jews assembled in their cities to attack those who sought their hurt; and no one stood in their way, for the fear of them had fallen upon all the peoples. Indeed, all the officials of the provinces – the satraps, the governors, and the king's stewards – championed the Jews, because the fear of Mordechai had fallen upon them. For Mordechai was now powerful in the royal palace, and his fame was spreading through all the provinces; the man Mordechai was growing ever more powerful. (9:1-4)

Ten months had passed since Mordechai issued his letter in the name of the king. Mordechai and the Jews seem to have used their time well, organizing for the decisive day – the very same day on which the king's previous orders were to be carried out. What did Persia's Jew-haters do in the meantime? Nothing at all. They wanted to harm the Jewish people, but in reality they did nothing.

R. Benny Lau notes that although Mordechai's edict gave the Jews the right to plunder their enemies ("and plunder their possessions") – the same right granted by Haman to the enemies of the Jews – the Jews desisted. The text emphasizes this, stating on three separate occasions: "But they did not lay hands on the spoil." According to R. Lau:

> This is the difference between an unruly mob that operates without discipline and without direction and a nation that assembles in self-defense. Jew-haters attempt to besmirch and criminalize the Jews by describing the battle in the cities of the Persian Empire in terms of lack of restraint and primal dissolution. However, Scripture bears witness to their restraint in battle, even as they added another day of fighting so they could complete their triumph over their enemies.

These events, R. Lau emphasizes, drew the attention of many exegetes and scholars. Some developed theories about Jewish bloodlust, and others engaged in apologetics. I am inclined to think that this episode can be understood if we begin our reading from the last verse in chapter 8.

Firstly, it is important to consider this issue from a demographic perspective. In the time period under discussion – the fifth century BCE – it is estimated that there were 100 million people in the world, 15 million in South America, and the remaining 85 million in the Mediterranean basin, Africa, Europe and Asia. The Megilah tells us that on the thirteenth of Adar, the Jews killed 75,000 people. In other words, about one per mil of the world's population was wiped out on the thirteenth of Adar of the twelfth year of Ahashverosh's reign. For comparative purposes, this would be the equivalent of eight million deaths given the global population today.[1] This is the plain meaning of the Megilah's text, but I cannot imagine that this massacre actually happened, or at the very least, that it happened in the way presented by those who seek to tarnish the image of the Jews. The author of the Megilah is presenting us with a more symbolic message – which begins in the final verse of Chapter 8:

> And in every province and in every city, when the king's command and decree arrived, there was gladness and joy among the Jews, a feast and a holiday. And many of the people of the land professed to be Jews, for the fear of the Jews had fallen upon them. (8:17)

The Jewish people hosted feasts and a holiday – a fusion of Persian custom and a Jewish festival. Mordechai's power and Jewish might influenced those who surround them and bought them closer to Judaism. It is not known whether they actually converted or merely allied themselves with the Jews of Persia. Either way, according to the author, on the thirteenth of Adar, many non-Jews joined the fight on the side of the Jews.

Here is where things spun out of control. Mordechai issued an edict for the Jews to gather together and fight for their lives, but many other people, who were not "of holy seed"[2] joined the initiative, leading to a full-fledged war with many causalities. Many open accounts were settled on that day – including those of Jews defending themselves from their enemies, but not limited to that alone.

The number of people killed is not important. The author's intent is to

1 Today, we know that the civil war in Syria has left half a million dead and the conflict far from resolved.

2 Bear in mind that the author of the Megilah was "of holy seed" living in the land of Israel.

point to a phenomenon in the assimilated city of Shushan. Mordechai's rise to power encouraged many non-Jews to mix in with the Jewish population, dramatically changing its character and nature.[3] The nation defending itself in Jerusalem had become an assimilated nation of murderers in Shushan:

> Indeed, all the officials of the provinces – the satraps, the governors, and the king's stewards – championed to the Jews, because the fear of Mordechai had fallen upon them. For Mordechai was now powerful in the royal palace, and his fame was spreading through all the provinces; the man Mordechai was growing ever more powerful. (9:3-4)

All of the officials of the provinces "championed (*menase'im*) the Jews" – that is, assisted them in war. The author does not mean to say that the nations of the land showed honor to the Jews; we have already seen that they were afraid, not respectful, of Mordechai, and consequently the Jews. Rather, they became the Jews' arms-bearers (*nos'ei kelim*).[4]

Likewise, the term "assembled" ("*nik'halu*") is not accidental. Aside from Megilat Esther, this expression appears one other time in Tanakh, and it is linked to Jerusalem and the Temple. In 2 Divrei Hayamim 20:1

---

3 In Shemot we encounter a similar phenomenon when the hordes (*erev-rav*) and the mob (*asafsuf*) join the Jewish people as they leave exile (Shemot 12:38: "Moreover, a mixed horde went up with them"). According to many biblical commentators, it is this horde that incites and stimulates complaints and disputes with Moshe in the Sinai desert.

4 In Scripture, the term "arms-bearer" ("*nosei kelim*") generally refers to the person who bears the weapons of a leader or describes the act of bearing weapons for oneself or others. See, for example, 1 Shmuel 14, which describes Yonatan and his young "arms-bearer" (*nosei keilav*); 2 Shmuel 18, which discusses "ten young arms-bearers of Yoav," King David's general; etc.

the "Moabites, Ammonites, together with some Ammonim, came against Yehoshafat to wage war." Yehoshafat stands in the new courtyard of the Temple and prays to God for help: "Truly You are the God in heaven and You rule over the kingdoms of the nations." He urges the nation: "Listen to me, O Judah and inhabitants of Jerusalem. Trust firmly in the Lord your God and you will stand firm; trust firmly in His prophets and you will succeed" (*ibid.* 20). Immediately thereafter:

> As they began their joyous shouts and hymns, the Lord set ambushes for the men of Amon, Moab, and the hill country of Seir, who were marching against Judah, and they were routed.... And when Yehoshafat and his people came to take away their spoils, they found among them abundance of riches with the dead bodies and precious jewels, which they stripped off for themselves, more than they could carry away. And they were there for three days gathering the spoils, it was so much.[5] On the fourth day **they assembled (*nik'halu*)** in the Valley of Blessing – for there they blessed the Lord; that is why that place is called the Valley of Blessing to this day. All the men of Judah and Jerusalem with Jehoshaphat at their head returned joyfully to Jerusalem, for the Lord had given them cause for rejoicing over their enemies. They came to Jerusalem to the House of the Lord, to the accompaniment of harps, lyres, and trumpets. The terror of God seized all the kingdoms of the lands when they heard that the Lord had fought the enemies of Israel. The kingdom of

5 From here it seems that an organized army may take spoils of war. The Jews of Yehoshafat's army plundered the spoils, whereas the Jews of Shushan desisted from doing so. It is possible that the author of the Megilah is communicating a veiled message: When a war is fought in accordance with God's will, the spoils can be taken, because the plunderers have pure motives. In contrast, in a privately sponsored war, it is forbidden to take spoils.

> Yehoshafat was untroubled, and his God granted him respite on all sides. (*ibid.* 22, 25-30)

The use of the word "*nik'halu*" in this context by author of Megilat Esther, living in Jerusalem, is a deliberate contrast. In Jerusalem, a few hundred years earlier, Yehoshafat assembles the nation in order to bless God and petition Him to fight on behalf of the Jewish people. That is, God protects the people, making it unnecessary for the Jews in Jerusalem to assemble in order to kill and destroy, as they did in Shushan. In both cases, enemies cower in fear of the Jews; in the case of Yehoshafat though, it was "fear of God" ("when they heard that the Lord had fought the enemies of Israel"), while in Shushan it was "fear of Mordechai" and "fear of the Jews."

With this one word, the author demonstrates the extent to which Persia's Jews, with Mordechai at their helm, had distanced themselves from God, His people, and His city. They did not assemble in prayer to beseech God for help; they assemble for the purpose of murder. They had become a cult of the "fear of Mordechai," not a God-fearing people. Mordechai's fame was spreading and his clout was increasing.[6] The author criticizes this state of affairs: this was not the worship of God, but the worship of man. Mordechai had learned the lesson of self-deification and self-glorification from his boss Ahashverosh.

> So the Jews struck at their enemies with the sword, slaying and destroying; they wreaked their will upon their enemies. In Shushan the capital the Jews killed a total of five hundred men.

---

6 A similar observation could have been made about Moshe: "Moshe himself was much esteemed in the land of Egypt, among Pharaoh's courtiers and among the people" (Shemot 11:3). However, the very next verses states: "Moshe said, "Thus says the Lord: Toward midnight I will go forth among the Egyptians." Here, in Megilat Esther, God is not mentioned either before or after.

> They also killed Parshandata, Dalphon, Aspata, Porata, Adalia, Aridata, Parmashta, Arisai, Aridai, and Vayzata, the ten sons of Haman son of Hammedata, the foe of the Jews. But they did not lay hands on the spoil. (9:5-10)

There are several puzzling elements here: The Jews "wreaked their will upon their enemies" and struck them "with the sword, slaying and destroying." Five hundred people were killed in the carnage in Shushan. This figure sounds rather low considering the total number of people who were killed (75,000). Was this the proper reaction to Haman's aspiration to destroy all of the Jewish people, old and young alike? Was this all the "slaying and destroying" that the Jews could muster?"

The author again seems to be using irony. The letters were sent to all of the provinces, and the edict was issued in the capital city of Shushan – but Mordechai was only interested in a show of power in Shushan, the seat of power and the city of his residence. They killed "five hundred men" – not children, not women, not the elderly. As we have seen, the term "men" ("*ish*") implies important personages, potential threats to Mordechai's status. Most importantly, they killed, and then hanged, Haman's ten sons, who are mentioned by name.

Rashi explains that these "ten sons of Haman" were:

> The ten sons who wrote an accusation against Judah and Jerusalem, as stated in the book of Ezra: "And in the reign of Ahashverosh, at the start of his reign, they drew up an accusation against the inhabitants of Judah and Jerusalem" (Ezra 4:6). What was the accusation? To cancel the immigration of exiles from the time of Cyrus, who had begun rebuilding the Temple. The Kuthites slandered them and stopped their progress. When Cyrus died and Ahashverosh became king, Haman was promoted and made sure that the people in Jerusalem did not build. They sent

> a letter in the name of Ahashverosh instructing the officers of Trans-Euphrates to stop them.

According to Rashi the sons of Haman were part of the conspiracy to thwart the rebuilding of Jerusalem and its ramparts. By killing the sons of Haman, Mordechai did the work of the Jews in Eretz Yisrael by settling the score on their behalf. As a global Jewish leader, he protected the Jews of Jerusalem as well.

However, I believe that the Megilah's author meant something else entirely. The Babylonian Talmud discusses how the names of Haman's sons appear in the Megilah:

> Rabbi Hanina b. Papa said: Rabbi Shila of the village of Tamarta expounded: All songs (in Tanakh) are written in the form of a half brick arranged upon a whole brick and a whole brick arranged upon a half brick, aside from this song (= the list of the sons of Haman) and the song listing the kings of Canaan who were defeated by Yehoshua, which are written as half bricks atop half bricks and whole bricks atop whole bricks. Why? Such that they should never rise from their downfall. (*Megilah* 16b)

Rabbi Hanina contrasts the list of Haman's ten sons to other songs in Tanakh, stating that this song is written in the Megilah as a column, one partial line ("half brick") of text directly over another, so that they cannot climb the bricks as a ladder. Likewise, the names of the kings of Canaan are written in a column.

The comparison of Haman's sons to the kings of Canaan is quite apt, but the reason offered in the Talmud demands an explanation. In the song of Devora and the song at the sea, the author certainly did not wish that Sisera, the Canaanites, or the Egyptians would resurge. Yet these songs that celebrated Jewish victories were written in alternating lines of two half bricks and one whole brick, namely, in the form of a ladder. It seems that the Talmud expects these enemies to have a revival.

Perhaps the author is using the unique textual format to indicate that the Jews of Persia were trying to establish their presence in Persia in the same way that the Israelites established their presence in Eretz Yisrael. It is as though they were saying: Shushan is our home. Just as the kings of Canaan were killed in order for Israel to take possession of its land, so too, Haman and his sons were killed to enable the Jews to take possession of Shushan. In the words of *Meshekh Hokhmah*: "Berlin is Jerusalem."[7]

Mordechai fortified his position by eliminating a limited number of people and hanging Haman's sons. He neutralized potential adversaries,

---

7 R. Meir Simha of Dvinsk, *Meshekh Hokhmah* on Vayikra 26:44, s.v. "*ve-af gam zot*":

This has been the pattern of the nation. When it entered a foreign land, it would be with people not steeped in Torah, as they would have become weakened by the troubles, decrees, and expulsions. Then a Divine spirit would awaken within them and seek to return them to their holy source. They would study and spread Torah. They would perform wonders, to the point that the Torah achieves its fullest expression. That generation will have nothing to improve and perfect upon from previous generations. What is man, who is meant to improve and innovate, to do? He will criticize that which he received from his fathers, replacing their ideas with false ideas. He innovates new ideas and forgets what his nation experienced as they wandered through the sea of tribulations, no matter what. Soon he will say, "Our fathers bequeathed to us lies." The Jew will forget his origins and fancy himself a full citizen. He will abandon the study of his religion in order to learn foreign languages; he will learn from their failures and not their good ideas. **He will think that Berlin is Jerusalem** and act like the debased among the nations, not like those among the nations who act properly. "Rejoice not, O Israel, unto exultation, like the peoples" (Hoshea 9:1). Then a storm wind will come and uproot the nation from its trunk, carrying it to a distant nation whose language they do not know. They will then know that they are sojourners; that their language is the holy tongue and that foreign languages can be changed as clothing; that their source is their Jewish roots; and that their comfort is from the prophets of God, who prophesied about the scion of Yishai at the end of days.

used force to deter opposition, and signaled to all of Shushan that there was a new sheriff in town. The author of the Megilah draws a parallel between Mordechai's war and the war of Yehoshua to demonstrate that Mordechai and Esther sought to settle permanently in Shushan, not in Jerusalem.

The parallel to the book of Yehoshua is not limited to the similar format of Canaanite king list. It extends to the general description of events:

> Throughout the provinces of King Ahashverosh, the Jews assembled in their cities to attack those who sought their hurt; and no one stood in their way, for the fear of them had fallen upon all the peoples. (9:2)

And in the book of Yehoshua:

> The Lord gave to Israel the whole country which He had sworn to their fathers that He would assign to them; they took possession of it and settled in it. The Lord gave them rest on all sides, just as He had promised to their fathers on oath. **Not one man of all their enemies stood in their way**; the Lord delivered all their enemies into their hands. Not one of the good things which the Lord had promised to the House of Israel was lacking. Everything was fulfilled. (Yehoshua 21:41-43)

The parallel is striking. In the book of Yehoshua, we are told "not one of the good things which the Lord had promised to the House of Israel was lacking" and therefore nobody stood in the way of the Jewish people when they captured the land. In the Megilah though, God is absent – we are only told "for the fear of them had fallen upon all the peoples."

The number of people killed is not necessarily exact; it is quite possible that Dr. Grossman is right that these numbers are not especially large in context of Tanakh.[8] Whether more or fewer people were killed, the message is clear: Shushan's Jews viewed the war as a way to reinforce their presence and status in a foreign land, just as the defeat of the Canaanite kings established a Jewish presence in Eretz Yisrael.

They Did Not Lay Hands on the Spoil

There is an obvious discrepancy between Mordechai's directive, "and plunder their possessions," and the actual events; the author tells us on three different occasions that "they did not lay their hands on the spoil."

> The king said to Queen Esther, "In Shushan the capital alone the Jews have killed a total of five hundred men, as well as the ten sons of Haman. What then must they have done in the provinces of the realm! What is your wish now? It shall be granted you. And what else is your request? It shall be fulfilled." "If it please Your Majesty," Esther replied, "let the Jews in Shushan be permitted to act tomorrow also as they did today; and let Haman's ten sons be impaled on the stake." The king ordered that this should be done, and the decree was proclaimed in Shushan. Haman's ten sons were impaled: and the Jews in Shushan assembled again on the fourteenth day of Adar and slew three hundred men in Shushan. But they did not lay hands on the spoil. The rest of the Jews, those in the king's provinces, likewise assembled and fought for their lives. They disposed of their enemies, killing

---

8 Grossman, *Esther: The Outer Narrative and the Hidden Reading* , p. 227. It is difficult for me to accept his theory that the Jews killed their enemies because Mordechai was placed in charge of Haman's estate, and Haman, in his capacity as chief security officer of the capital city, had left among his personal effects all of the battle plans that had been formulated against the Jews. It would seem that Haman did not have enough time to devise such plans, seeing as only several days passed from his request to Ahashverosh until his drastic change of fate.

> seventy-five thousand of their foes; but they did not lay hands on the spoil. (9:12-16)

R. Lau understands their desistance as a sign of the discipline of Mordechai's militia. There are two other possible explanations, though. One possibility is that the discrepancy between Mordechai's edict and the nation's refusal to act on it reflects a disagreement between Mordechai and the nation regarding the degree to which the Jews had established themselves in the Persian exile.

Another possible explanation of the discrepancy has to do with attitudes toward money and property. Mordechai strove for a strong economic foundation, "and plunder their possessions." This was his motive for waging war. However, the Jews refused to partake in this. Perhaps this reflects the author's hope that the people had not yet been completely caught up in the spell of Shushan's riches. Perhaps they would still return and join their brothers in Eretz Yisrael. The author hopes that the Jewish masses will reject the symbol of Mordechai the Jew, the assimilated government minister.

Rashi demonstrates this point:

> **They did not lay their hands on the spoil** so that the king would not be jealous of their wealth.

That is, the simple Jewish folk understood intuitively what Mordechai did not grasp: Those who enrich themselves by plundering their neighbors will become targets for plundering when the wheel of fortune turns again. The phenomenon of "A new king arises in Egypt who did not know Yosef" is enduring; a basic sense of self-preservation life demanded caution and restraint in preparation for the post-Mordechai era in Persia.

Mordechai wanted the spoils. In this defensive war, he commanded the Jews to loot, because it would enrich him, too. He pursued the benefits of power and close proximity to the king, "royal robes of blue and white, with a magnificent crown of gold and a mantle of fine linen and purple wool," plus treasures of gold and silver that were plundered from those vanquished in battle. The people, though, considered the day after as well.

Miracles and Deep Processes

It is hard not to be impressed by the rapid turnabout, the Purim marvel in which "the opposite happened." It was truly a reversal. An upheaval. Mordechai had been rising steadily for years until Haman came along and reshuffled the deck. Mordechai fell from the heights to the depths and then rose higher than ever, all in the span of a few days. But therein lies the problem of quick transformations: they do not leave enough time for the various factors and motivations to seep into the spirit, souls, and consciousness of those who experience them.

Reversal is not a deep process. The endless, Sisyphean process that began with the first *aliyah* of returnees to Zion, Zerubavel, Ezra, and Nehemiah, and spanned a century, contrasts starkly with the Purim turnabout, which all happened over the course of a week. When someone undergoes a lightning quick transformation, the hand of God and the power of survival in the face of a clear and present danger are not engraved in his mind and consciousness. The deeper meanings of identity and values do not penetrate. The Sages tell us that what a maidservant saw at the sea, neither the prophet Yirmiyahu nor the prophet Yehezkel ever saw – in other words, the moment of prophecy, when a prophet hears the word of God, is inferior to the miracles and the prophecies that a Jewish maidservant saw at the time of the splitting of the sea.

The plagues in Egypt and the extraordinary, yet fleeting, revelation of God at the sea did not endure. Those same maidservants, along with all of Israel, began to complain about God and their leader, Moshe, almost immediately after the spectacular signs, wonders, the plague of the firstborn, the splitting of the sea, and the drowning of the Egyptians:

> In the wilderness, the whole Israelite community grumbled against Moshe and Aharon. The Israelites said to them, "If only we had died by the hand of the Lord in the land of Egypt, when we sat by the fleshpots, when we ate our fill of bread! For you have brought us out into this wilderness to starve this whole congregation to death." (Shemot 16:2-3)

The splitting of the sea was a miracle, not a deep, internal process. The immense first impression that it generated therefore quickly dissipated.[9] Wandering through the desert for forty years was the deep, internal process. The same is true of Shushan: Everything happened too quickly. The hand of God was not recognized in the events of the story, especially in the eyes of a nation in exile that had pushed God out of its consciousness and therefore struggled to see anything but happenstance in the four-day turnabout.

The suffering was also too quick. It is doubtful that word of Haman's edict even reached the Jews at the frontiers of the empire. In chapter 4 we are told: "Also, in every province that the king's command and decree reached, there was great mourning among the Jews." But there were provinces where news did not reach, and their Jews knew nothing about the edict; the mourning was limited to those who lived in Shushan and its environs. This is why Mordechai assembled only "the Jews who live in Shushan" for the emergency gathering. On the other hand, Mordechai's letters and the relief they brought reached all 127 provinces of the Persian Empire with the royal stallions, well before the couriers who trailed slowly behind, in caravans. The reversal in the palace, by which Haman rose to

---

9 In Tanakh, the classic example of this phenomenon is the story of the prophet Eliyahu (1 Melakhim 18-19). Despite a massive miraculous display, Israel does not turn away from Baal worship. He is then shown, by God Himself, that He is not heard in storms, fires, or earthquakes, but in a still, small voice.

power, was a secret that relatively few knew about, but the power vested in the Jews, under Mordechai's patronage, was open for all to see.

Everything happened quickly and ended quickly. Some Jews experienced only the victory, without even a moment of fear or dread. This is not a recipe for perceiving God's intervention or for building a strong Jewish identity – certainly not in a culture that was inundated with idolatry and self-worship.

Popular with the Multitude of his Brethren

This interpretation of Megilat Esther opened with a straight-forward question: Why did the author of the Megilah begin his narrative with the story of the banquets and the description of the splendor of the royal court in chapter 1? This was followed by a related question: Why does the author conclude the Megilah's narrative with a discussion of the tax that Ahashverosh levied in chapter 10?

The answer should be clear by now. The Megilah's real subject is the prioritization of money over values and morals, and of proximity to power in Shushan over the fledgling Jewish commonwealth in Jerusalem. The story informs us about the assimilation of the Jews who have remained behind in Shushan and the growing gap between them and the Jews of Jerusalem.

The power to tax and the monopoly on legitimate use of physical force are two fundamental properties of government. It follows that the two basic functions of government are the protection of its subjects and the delivery of services by expenditure of taxes collected. In chapter 9, Mordechai protected citizen-subjects of King Ahashverosh as a sign of his closeness to the regime and as an indication by the Megilah's author that the main subject of the story is not the king's military campaigns but Mordechai's monetary concerns. Therefore, in chapter 10, Mordechai levied a tax on the empire, on behalf of King Ahashverosh:

> King Ahashverosh imposed tribute on the mainland and the islands. All his mighty and powerful acts, and a full account of the

> greatness to which the king advanced Mordechai, are recorded in the Annals of the Kings of Media and Persia. (10:1-2)

Herein lies the significance of the first verse and its connection to the second verse: Mordechai, like Yosef before him, was second in command to the king. Even the islands – the mighty Greek islands – had surrendered to the Persian Empire and were now under the control of Mordechai the Jew.[1] After he removed Haman from the stage, Mordechai could resume his climb from third-generation immigrant to the king's second in command, ruler of half of the civilized world. He had come as close as possible to the very source of power.[2]

The Megilah's author describes Mordechai as someone who gained prominence under the patronage of the king, in contrast to Yehoshua, whose rise to prominence was under God's patronage, and Moshe, whose fame spread throughout Egypt. Mordechai did not advance; rather, "the king advanced Mordechai." In this, he was similar to Haman, who told "Zeresh and all of his friends" about "how the king advanced him." The

---

1 Yisrael Rozenson (*Hadassah Hi Esther*, p. 226) points out that when Ahashverosh and Mordechai levied this tax on the islands, Greece had already been liberated from the Persian Empire. This intensifies the author's irony and sharpens his ironic approach to Mordechai. It is instructive to note that in the period of Darius II, the grandson of Xerxes I, Persia regained control of the Greek islands that it had controlled prior to the Greco-Persian Wars.

2 It is possible that this tax was burdensome to the nation. It is interesting that in the book of Nehemiah, the eponymous character says about himself: "Furthermore, from the day I was commissioned to be governor in the land of Judah – from the twentieth year of King Artaxerxes until his thirty-second year, twelve years in all – neither I nor my brothers ever ate of the governor's food allowance." In other words, Nehemiah did not pocket any of the taxes that comprised a heavy economic burden on the Jews of Eretz Yisrael. In this way, he actually worked to ease their tax burden, against the prevalent Persian custom for profiting from tax monies.

author of the Megilah is intimating that things are business as usual in the world. Mordechai was enjoying the benefits of high stature, but it, too, would pass. His power was derived from the king, who also would eventually be replaced. Mordechai will not be mentioned in the Annals of the Kings of Judah, the Biblical book of Divrei Hayamim, which was being authored at just about the same time. His name appears only in the Annals of the kings of Persia and Media. This was where he arrived, there he stayed, there he achieved greatness, there he assimilated, and there he left his mark.

The author emphasizes the size of the Ahashverosh's empire, which extends all the way to the islands of the Mediterranean, in complete contrast to the tiny, fragile kingdom of Judah, centered in Jerusalem and living under constant threat. Yet some kingdoms, physically small as they are, exhibit a great deal of inner strength. "For they dealt faithfully" (2 Melakhim 12:16) And some great empires erode and collapse.

In this how the story ends:

> For (*ki*) Mordechai the Jew ranked next to King Ahashverosh and was highly regarded by the Jews and popular with the multitude of his brethren; he sought the good of his people and interceded for the welfare of all his descendants. (10:3)

The word "for" (*ki*) indicates that the last verse explains the first two verses of the chapter. Why did King Ahashverosh impose "tribute on the mainland and the islands"? Because Mordechai ranked second to the king. Why were "All his mighty and powerful acts, and a full account of the greatness to which the king advanced Mordechai" written in the Annals of the Kings of Persia and Media? Because Mordechai the Jew ranked second to King Ahashverosh.

Mordechai was dictating the economic policies of Ahashverosh's kingdom because of his status in the kingdom. He was responsible for imposing and collecting taxes throughout the empire. This was his aim from the beginning, when he aspired to become part of the Persian nation, to become connected to the dynastic family, and influence Ahashverosh's kingdom and its revenues. Mordechai was held in high regard by the Jews who remained in Shushan, and was a source of inspiration to all those who wished to remain in exile, to flourish there, and to become familiar in the corridors of power. The author therefore tells us that Mordechai was popular with "the multitude of his brethren" – the majority who are centered on Shushan, as opposed to the minority who returned to Eretz Yisrael. "The king" of Israel was among his brethren; King Ahashverosh was not.[3]

Mordechai "sought the good of his people," but the source of his power, like that of any politician or leader who must cultivate a power-base, was mainly in that he "interceded for the welfare of all his kindred." Nepotism begins at home. Mordechai was trying to cultivate a Jewish dynasty within the Persian Empire, a dynasty of seconds in command, of assimilated Jews who would rule Persia. These are "his descendants."

The final words of the Megilah, "[Mordechai] interceded for the welfare (*shalom*) of all his descendants," remind us of the brothers of Yosef, who "could not speak a friendly word (*shalom*) to him." So, too, Mordechai, the son of Yair, the son of Shimi, the son of Kish, was able to intercede for the welfare of all of his kindred, but his brothers in Eretz Yisrael "could not speak a friendly word to him." His aspirations, his status, and his lifestyle disconnect the Jews who would remain in Shushan and be swallowed up there from the Jewish people that had returned to Jerusalem.

The Megilah is ultimately a Jewish tragedy. God was sidelined; His name is not mentioned. The nation assimilated, under the direction of

---

3 Devarim 17:15 "You shall be free to set a king over yourself, one chosen by the Lord your God. Be sure to set as king over yourself one of your own people; you must not set a foreigner over you, one who is not your brethren."

their leaders. The powerful Jews remained in exile; they did not come to the aid of their brothers, who were rebuilding the kingdom of Judah and Eretz Yisrael. "The opposite happened" too quickly. It was not taken to heart by the Jews. It was not absorbed in a manner befitting of an act of God. Instead, it was viewed as intervention and court intrigue of the typical variety, the result of well-placed Jews in the Persian court.[4] The Jews were not exterminated through Haman's decree, but their eventual disappearance through assimilation had become all but certain. This is the real tragedy; some Jews are wiped out violently, but far more simply assimilate and disappear without a trace.

The tragedy of the Megilah ends only with the emergence of the next senior Jewish official, Nehemiah, who works to repair the mistakes of Mordechai and Esther.

4 In his book on Megilat Esther, *The Dawn*, Yoram Hazony explains that the purpose of the Megilah is to teach Jews how to wield political power in the post-prophetic era.

Until One is Unable to Distinguish: Why Do We Celebrate the Holiday of Purim?

Every Purim, my wife scrutinizes the drunk yeshiva students and comments: "I do not know what the Sages had in mind for this holiday, but I am quite certain that this is not it."

In the Babylonian Talmud, we learn:

> Rava said: A person is obligated to become intoxicated on Purim that he will not be able to distinguish between "Mordechai is blessed" and "Haman is cursed" (BT *Megilah* 7b)

Rava lived in Mehoza, in the Sasanian Persian Empire and wanted to see people get so drunk that they could not differentiate between "Haman is cursed" and "Mordechai is blessed." The real reason for this: There is no difference between them. The former sought to destroy the Jewish people by the sword.[1] The latter actually led the Jewish people to destruction by means of assimilation into Persia.

Rava fought against the rampant assimilation of Jews in Mehoza, a quarter of Ctesiphon, the capital of the new Persian Empire. He tried to

---

1 Lest I be misunderstood, I am not suggesting that there is no difference between killing people by sword and their assimilation. I am suggesting that, from Rava's perspective and that of Jewish peoplehood, the result is the same.

explain why assimilation is so dangerous to the future of the Jewish people. From Rava's perspective, the insight of Purim is that, over the long term, there is no real difference between "Mordechai is blessed" and "Haman is cursed": They will both bring devastation to Jewish peoplehood. Rava was concerned that celebrating Purim is liable to give the Jewish people the mistaken impression that they have it good in the exile and that when the chips are down, the Persian king will change his tune and come through for them. Rava understood that this is delusional; he knew that the danger imposed by one type of annihilation is in fact no worse than the other.[2]

* * *

The holiday of Purim developed in stages. In the Book of the Maccabees, Purim is mentioned as "The Day of Mordechai,"[3] and it seems that the masses, or at least some of them, celebrated this holiday. As we know from the Megilah itself, where much of chapter 9 is devoted to the specific celebratory practices of Purim, the celebration emerged from the grass roots:

> But the Jews in Shushan gathered on both the thirteenth and fourteenth days, and so rested on the fifteenth, and made it a day of feasting and merrymaking. (9:14)

These feasts and celebrations broke out spontaneously after the Jews of Shushan assembled and defeated their enemies. However, the attempt to establish Purim as an official holiday met with varying degrees

2 It is instructive to note Rava's explanation for why we do not recite Hallel (psalms of praise and thanksgiving) on Purim: "We are still slaves of Ahashverosh" (BT *Megilah* 14a).

3 The 2 Maccabees 15:42. The Second Book of Maccabees was written in Greek, the *lingua franca* at the time of its composition, and was most likely composed in the diaspora, in Alexandria, Egypt.

of resistance through the generations. It also seems that the text of the Megilah itself reveals the roots of this resistance and their ramifications for the character of the holiday.

A careful reading of the Megilah shows that the second half of chapter 9 is quite different from the rest of the Megilah; it is stylistically awkward and repetitive. It summarizes earlier portions of the Megilah. The reader gets the sense that it was written in several stages and in several different historical settings, as the holiday developed.

> The king ordered that this should be done, and the decree was proclaimed in Shushan. Haman's ten sons were hanged: and the Jews in Shushan assembled again on the fourteenth day of Adar and slew three hundred men in Shushan. But they did not lay hands on the spoil. The rest of the Jews, those in the king's provinces, likewise assembled and fought for their lives. They disposed of their enemies, killing seventy-five thousand of their foes; but they did not lay hands on the spoil. That was on the thirteenth day of the month of Adar; and they rested on the fourteenth day and made it a day of feasting and merrymaking. (But the Jews in Shushan gathered on both the thirteenth and fourteenth days, and so rested on the fifteenth, and made it a day of feasting and merrymaking.) (9:14-18)

This description of the establishment of the holiday appears immediately after the account of the war's end in Shushan on the fourteenth of Adar. The text then returns to "the rest of the Jews, those in the king's provinces" and gives an account of how they killed their enemies "on the thirteenth day of the month of Adar" and spontaneously celebrated with feasting and rejoicing on the fourteenth. The Jews of Shushan celebrated on the fifteenth of Adar, since "in Shushan [they] gathered on both the thirteenth and fourteenth days."

These celebrations prompt Mordechai to seek to establish these days as celebratory days for generations to come:

> That is why village Jews, who live in unwalled towns, observe the fourteenth day of the month of Adar and make it a day of merrymaking and feasting, and as a holiday and an occasion for sending gifts to one another. (9:19)

Given the way that the words are phrased, it would seem that Mordechai is trying to take an existing custom – the observance of the fourteenth of Adar as a day of rest, feasting, and rejoicing – and establish it as a holiday. The Jews in the exile that resided in unwalled towns – sprawling, secure towns in the Persian Empire that were not under threat of conquest by foreign forces – already celebrated Adar 14 as a festival, and Mordechai attempted to give it a permanent place in the consciousness of Persia's Jews and link it to himself and his deeds.[4]

The main practical mitzvah that Mordechai ordained, according to the Megilah's author, is "sending gifts to one another" (*mishlo'ah manot*). This practice demands an explanation, because immediately thereafter, additional customs and practices are added to the holiday. In its first iteration, the holiday was intended for the Jews who lived in the unwalled towns, and its goal was to strengthen, by means of the symbolic gesture of

---

4 R. Yoel Bin-Nun asserts that the words "Jews of the villages" (*perazim*) alludes to the author's criticism of Jews in exile, who brazenly established holidays according to celebrations taking place in their environs. These words reverberate even louder when we recall that the walls of Jerusalem were still in ruins at that time, as it is written in Zekhariah: "Jerusalem shall be peopled as a city without walls (*perazot*), so many shall be the men and cattle it contains. And I Myself – declares the Lord – will be a wall of fire all around it, and I will be a glory inside it" (Zekhariah2:8-9). It is as if the people of the unfortified cities of the Babylonian exile exult in Jerusalem's ruin.

sending gifts to one another, their sense of shared fate and brotherhood-in-arms.

This concludes the first stage of the establishment of the holiday of Purim, according to the Megilah. It is not possible to know what motivated Mordechai to issue a new edict for the next stage of the holiday's development, which establishes the fourteenth and fifteenth of Adar as holidays for the Jews who lived "near and far":

> Mordechai recorded these events. And he sent dispatches to all the Jews throughout the provinces of King Ahashverosh, near and far, charging them to observe the fourteenth and fifteenth days of Adar, every year – the same days on which the Jews enjoyed relief from their foes and the same month which had been transformed for them from one of grief and mourning to one of festive joy. They were to observe them as days of feasting and merrymaking, and as an occasion for sending gifts to one another and presents to the needy. (9:19-22)

Here Mordechai authoritatively instructed all of the Jews in the Persian Empire ("charging them to observe") to institutionalize the holiday. It was at this point that he first fixed the fifteenth of Adar as a holiday. As Grossman explains in great detail, Mordechai actually seeks to have the Jews celebrate both days.[5]

This was an unprecedented innovation. At that time, there was no Jewish holiday that had not been ordained by the Torah, and there was no holiday that lasted for two days. Moreover, there were no holidays that were established in exile. It was nothing less than a complete transformation of the Jewish religious worldview during the time of the return to Zion.

The way that Mordechai attempted to implement his revolutionary

5 Grossman, *Esther: The Outer Narrative and the Hidden Reading*, p. 199.

decision, according to the author, was monetary, that is, through gifts to the needy (*matanot le-evyonim*). In order to understand this mitzvah, its impact on the institutionalization of the holiday, and its singular name, it is instructive to delve somewhat into the word used to describe the poor, "*evyon*," which was meticulously chosen by the author of the Megilah. In several contexts, the Torah defines who is an *evyon* and what the term signifies. Thus, it is written with regard to the sabbatical year:

> Every seventh year you shall practice remission of debts. This shall be the nature of the remission: every creditor shall remit the due that he claims from his fellow; he shall not extract from his fellow or kinsman, for the remission proclaimed is of the Lord. You may extract from the foreigner; but you must remit whatever is due you from your kinsmen. There shall be no **needy** (*evyon*) among you – since the Lord your God will bless you in the land that the Lord your God is giving you as a hereditary portion. (Devarim 15:1-4)

In other words, if you observe the sabbatical year, there will not be any needy (*evyon*) among you. In my view, the primary difference between a pauper ("*ani*") and an *evyon* is that an *evyon* is a landowner who has difficulty producing revenue and profit from his property. An *evyon* is no poorer than an *ani*, but he is in a different predicament. Both are "kinsmen," but they face in dissimilar situations. This is clarified in the subsequent verses:

> If, however, there is a **needy person** (*evyon*) among you, one of your kinsmen in any of your settlements in the land that the Lord your God is giving you, do not harden your heart and shut your hand against your **needy** (*evyon*) kinsman. Rather, you must open your hand and lend him sufficient for whatever he needs.

> Beware lest you harbor the base thought, "The seventh year, the year of remission, is approaching," so that you are mean to your needy kinsman and give him nothing. He will cry out to the Lord against you, and you will incur guilt. Give to him readily and have no regrets when you do so, for in return the Lord your God will bless you in all your efforts and in all your undertakings. For there will never cease to be needy (*evyon*) in your land, for that reason I command you: open your hand to the poor (*ani*) and needy (*evyon*) kinsman in your land. (Devarim 15:7-11)

When there is an *evyon* "in any of your settlements" (lit. "in one of your gates"; a city or dense settlement) or "in the land" (in Eretz Yisrael or in your ancestral lot), you are obligated to "lend him sufficient for whatever he needs." That is, you must give him a loan so that he can provide for his needs.

The Torah emphasizes giving an *evyon* a loan, not a handout, to cover his costs of living and supply him with whatever he lacks. The *evyon* is not a charity case. He owns real estate but lacks liquidity. He needs working capital to buy seeds, tools, or beasts of burden for the upcoming planting season. It is therefore incumbent on every Jew who has the financial means to lend him money, so that he can continue to support himself from his own land.[6]

It therefore emerges that Mordechai intended for the wealthy Jews

---

6 Rashi on Amos 2:6. "'Because they have sold for silver those whose cause was just' – the judges would sell out the person who was innocent in judgment for bribe money that they received from his opponent in judgment. 'And the needy (*evyon*) for a pair of sandals' – Targum Yonatan explains on two separate occasions (Amos 5:12) 'in order that they should inherit the land.' But I maintain that this is the explanation: **They would bias the judgment of the** evyon **to force him to sell his field**, which was located among the judges' fields. He would indirectly force him to sell his field for a paltry sum."

living in exile to send money in honor of the holiday to *evyonim*, the Jewish communities that were trying to establish themselves – in Jerusalem and Eretz Yisrael, where landowners did not have capital to invest in producing crops and generating revenue.

This is in complete contrast to the Book of Nehemiah (Chapters 7-8). On Rosh Hashana ("the seventh month"), the nation gathers together and reads the "book of the Torah of Moshe," and when the nation erupts in tears upon hearing the words of Torah, Ezra and Nehemiah implore them: "You must not mourn or weep… Go, eat choice foods and drink sweet drinks, and send portions (*shilhu manot*) to whoever has nothing prepared." In other words, Ezra and Nehemiah call on the people to combine their holiday joy with charity and with concern for sending portions (*mishlo'ah manot*) to those who have nothing prepared. Here, help is offered even to those who will never have the possibility of making a feast on his own. In contrast, the second mitzvah ordained by Mordechai, *matanot le-evyonim*, is the equivalent of putting a coin in the blue JNF box – a generous gift from the rich uncle in the Diaspora to the impoverished kinfolk in Jerusalem.

There is another novel aspect of Mordechai's enactment: the holiday he instituted was not on the same day that the miracle occurred. Every other Jewish holiday was set on the date of a specific event. Mordechai sought to create a festival on the day that the people rested, **after** their miraculous victory.

Perhaps the addition of this day was one of the reasons that the holiday was not as accepted among Jews who lived in the various provinces. The text gives no indication as to when Mordechai sent these letters. Was it that same year? The next year? After several years? Regardless, the extra day was clearly not immediately accepted by the Jewish people.

> The Jews accordingly assumed as an obligation that which they had begun to practice and which Mordechai prescribed for them. (9:23)

It was only after the addition of *matanot le-evyonim* that the Jews adopted that "which Mordechai prescribed to them" to "that which they had begun to practice." A holiday tradition began to take form – apparently over the course of many years – wherein the first day was celebrated as a local holiday for the Jews residing in exile, and the second day was celebrated as a holiday for the benefit of the Jews of Jerusalem, to whom they would send donations.[7]

> For Haman son of Hammedata the Agagite, the foe of all the Jews, had plotted to destroy the Jews, and had cast *pur* – that is, the lot – with intent to crush and exterminate them. But when [Esther] came before the king, he commanded: "With the promulgation of this decree, let the evil plot, which he devised against the Jews, recoil on his own head!" So they hanged him and his sons on the stake. (9:24-25)

These verses mark the first time that a "revisionist" (and more accurate) view of the reasons for the holiday is offered. The great threat posed by Haman is that he "plotted to destroy the Jews." In other words, the threat was not actually implemented or even properly prepared for. As we explained – it was merely Haman's plot or evil thought and it lasted only four days.

---

7 Jerusalem, like Shushan, was walled, and is in fact the only city with a clear tradition of having been walled in the days of Yehoshua bin Nun. The Talmud's precise formulation with regard to establishing the additional holiday on the fifteenth of Adar relates to Eretz Yisrael in its entirety, and not only to Jerusalem: "R. Simon said in the name of R. Yehoshua: They showed respect to Eretz Yisrael, which was in a state of destruction in those days, in that they made [the status of the city] dependent [on the presence of a wall] from the days of Yehoshua bin Nun." This clearly shows us the rift between the Jews of Eretz Yisrael and the Jews of the Diaspora vis-à-vis this holiday.

The strength of Haman's threat resided in the fact that a lot – *pur* was cast before Haman. He used the prevalent Persian custom to test fate and determine which day would be most favorably disposed to carry out his plot. From here we can see that not only Haman and the Persians believed in the power of the *pur*, but also the Jews believed in its ability to choose an inauspicious time when it would be possible to wreak havoc upon them and destroy them – and, after the reversal, their enemies.

To their minds, the event that reversed the lot, in contrast to what is written in the Megilah, was not the actions of Mordechai and Esther and certainly not Divine intervention. Rather, it was the king who said "let the evil plot, which he devised against the Jews, recoil on his own head!" Accordingly, King Ahashverosh's change of heart was the cause for the entire holiday. Not a war, not a miracle, and not Divine intervention; the king thought one thing at first, and he later changed his mind, "so they hanged him and his sons from a beam." In contrast to all the other Jewish festivals – such as Pesach, which celebrates God's rescue of His nation from Egypt, and Sukkot, which commemorates how God sheltered Israel in huts in the desert – when it comes to Purim, there is no mention of God's name.

The Sages were aware of the problematic nature of these things. This awareness can be discerned by means of a comparison of the texts of the "*Al Ha-nisim*" ("For the Miracles") prayer addition for Hanukkah and Purim. [8] The Hanukkah version of the prayer reads as follows (according to the Ashkenazic custom):

> In the days of Matityahu, the son of Yohanan, the High Priest, the Hasmonean, and his sons – when the wicked Greek kingdom rose

8 The origins of this prayer are murky. As early as the Mishnaic period, we find references to the invocation of Hanukkah and Purim in the prayers. The first work that contains *Al Ha-nisim* in its current form, more or less, is the prayer book of R. Amram Gaon of the Geonic period, which postdated the Talmud's compilation.

> up against Your nation Israel to make them forget Your Torah and compel them to stray from your laws – You in Your great mercy came to their aid in the time of their distress. You took up their grievance, You judged their claim, You avenged their wrong. You delivered the strong into the hands of the weak, the many into the hands of the few, the impure ones into the hands of the pure ones, the wicked into the hands of righteous, and the sinners into the hands of the diligent students of Your Torah. For Yourself You made a great and holy name in the world and for Your nation Israel you brought a great victory and salvation as this very day. Afterwards, Your children came to Your Temple, Your house, cleaned Your Temple, purified Your Temple, and lit candles in the courtyard of Your Temple, and they established these eight days of Hanukkah to express thanks and praise to Your great name.

By Purim it says (again, according to the Ashkenazic custom):

> In the days of Mordechai and Esther, in Shushan the capital, when Haman the wicked rose up against them and sought to destroy, massacre and exterminate all the Jews, young and old, children and women, on a single day, on the thirteenth day of the twelfth month – that is, the month of Adar – and to plunder their possessions. But You in Your abundant mercy, nullified his counsel and frustrated his intention and returned him his due on his head and hanged him and his sons from the gallows.

In the case of Hanukkah, the prayer tells of a spiritual decree ("to make them forget Your Torah"), while the Purim prayer recounts a physical edict ("Haman the wicked sought to destroy"). With respect to Hanukkah, God plays an active role: "You came to their aid… You took up… You judged… You avenged…You delivered." The purpose of this response was also primarily spiritual: to deliver the impure ones into the hands of the pure ones, the wicked into the hands of righteous, and the sinners into the hands of the diligent students of Your Torah. On Purim, the role ascribed to God is simply that he induced Ahashverosh to change his mind, such that Haman's evil plan was reversed.[9]

The results were also entirely different. In the instance of Hanukkah, God's deeds glorify His name and save His people – the nation of Israel rises from the dust and restores its monarchy in its land. More importantly, the Jewish people return to the Temple and purify it – again, a spiritual accomplishment. The holiday itself was established as an outgrowth of this: "To express thanks and praise to Your great name." On Purim, the text of the prayer is much more austere. It ends with, "[they] hanged him and his sons from the gallows." There is no mention of any subsequent response from the Jews or God, and no account of how the holiday was established, as there is in connection with Hanukkah.

In the text composed by the Sages for Purim, the Sages' discomfort with the holiday is almost palpable. Their laconic formulation, "[they] hanged him and his sons at the stake," does not even tell us, nor do they wish to tell us, who hanged him. It goes without saying that they had no interest in explaining the reason for the institution of this holiday. In contrast to Hanukkah, they do not speak of "a great victory and salvation

9 This reflects the story of the Megilah, of course. However, when the Sages composed these prayers, they tended to present the Jewish people as being dependent on God and His salvation. With regard to Hanukkah, the main reason for the holiday, as reflected in the prayer, is the military victory. Yet, the prayer ascribes God a major role in acting on behalf of His people, as do the Maccabees in the non-canonized accounts of that period. Rambam, in explaining the reason for establishing the holiday of Hanukkah says: "**The monarchy returned to Israel for more than two hundred years.**" This is true with regard to Israel's Independence Day (*Yom Ha'atzmaut*) as well. In contrast, on Purim the monarchy was not restored to Israel.

as this very day," because there was none. Indeed, those Jews who "made it a day of feasting and merrymaking" – what were they in fact celebrating? A theoretical edict that was rescinded after four days? And who were these Jews? Were they not the Jews of Shushan, who assimilated and faded away?

Let us return to the Megilah:

> For that reason they called these days Purim, after the *pur*. For that reason, of all the instructions in the said letter and of what they had experienced in that matter and what had befallen them – the Jews undertook and obligated themselves and their descendants and all who had joined themselves to them, that it cannot be abrogated, and all who might join them, to observe these two days in the manner prescribed and at the proper time each year. (9:26-27)

This passage is somewhat opaque. The expression "for that reason" ("*al ken*") appears twice in one verse to explain why the holiday is called 'Purim.' The first reason indicates that popular practice gave the holiday its name: "[The masses] called these days Purim." They saw these events as a **reversal of fortune** – an upending of Haman's lottery ("*goral*"), which altered the fate ("*goral*") of the Jewish people. Since the celebration had already been accepted, the leaders of the Jewish community in Persia and Media decided to validate it, through "the said letter," in which they institutionalized the name of the holiday and thus eternalized Persian notions of fate as the prime cause of the nation's salvation. When one compares these verses to the efforts of Ezra and Nehemiah to attribute every outcome and event to God, the basic difference in approach between the Jews of Persia and the Jews of Eretz Yisrael becomes apparent: the latter follow God, while the former follow fate.[10]

---

10 The expression "for that reason" ("*al ken*") appears hundreds of times in

If the first part of this passage raises confusion, then the latter part intensifies it. What is the meaning of the legalistic formulation that the Jews "undertook and obligated themselves" and "all who had joined themselves to them"?[11] And what is the meaning of "that it cannot be abrogated?" Must joyful celebrations be preserved by means of laws and directives that echo the expression "the laws of Persia and Media, **so that it cannot be abrogated**" that appears in connection with the edict regarding Vashti?

The following verse intensifies the questions even further:

> And these days are recalled and observed in every generation: by every family, every province, and every city. And these days of Purim shall never cease among the Jews, and the memory of them shall never perish among their descendants. (9:28)

On the surface, it seems that this verse was written several generations after the events of the Megilah; it says that Purim is "recalled and observed in every generation," in the past tense. Interestingly, it omits "all who had

---

Tanakh. Still, I cannot avoid the sense that these instances are connected to the aforementioned passages about caring for *evyonim*: "For there will never cease to be needy (*evyon*) in your land, **for that reason** (*al ken*) I command you: open your hand to the poor (*ani*) and needy (*evyon*) kinsman in your land" (Devarim 15:11).

11 We have seen that Rava frequently comments on the Megilah and have suggested that his life circumstances gave him great insight into the machinations of the court of Ahashverosh. In his well-known comments on this verse, he explains the acceptance of Purim as a second acceptance of the Torah. This commentary seems to oscillate between apology and irony: "'And they encamped at the base of the mountain' (Shemot 19): R. Avdimi bar Hama bar Hasa said: This teaches that God held the mountain over their heads like a tub and said: If you accept the Torah, that is good; and if not, your burial will take place there. R. Aha bar Ya'akov said: From here there is a great protest with regard to (the acceptance of) the Torah. Rava said: They accepted it again in the days of Ahashverosh, as it is written: 'The Jews undertook and obligated themselves' (Esther 9); they undertook what had already been obligated" (BT *Shabbat* 88a).

joined themselves to them," "in the manner prescribed and at the proper time," and any mention of the *pur* as the reason for the celebration.

This seems to indicate the changes that were made to the celebration of Purim. There was opposition to the inclusion of hangers-on, those "who had joined themselves" to the Jews, the same people who "professed to be Jews, for the fear of the Jews had fallen upon them."

For the Jews of Shushan, the inclusion of gentile allies seemed natural and obvious, a merry celebration in accordance with the best of the Persian tradition. The author, who added these verses later, does not accept this. Reality is what it is – "These days are recalled and observed in every generation." For the Jews of Eretz Yisrael, a drinking party that had been adopted by the people was acceptable, for better or worse, but only among family; the inclusion of gentiles "who had joined themselves" was a non-starter.[12]

The Final Establishment of the Holiday

The Mishna[13] makes no mention of *mishlo'ah manot* or the mitzvah to

---

12 In this context it is instructive to mention R. Leibtag's comment that compares the term "a Jewish man" used here and in the book of Zekhariah (Zekhariah 8:23) – the only two places where this phrase appears. According to R. Leibtag's approach, there is no small amount of cynicism here in comparing Mordechai who assembles communities of non-Jews and assimilating Jews in Persia and does not bring them to Jerusalem, to the prophecy of Zekhariah: "In those days, ten men from nations of every tongue will take hold – they will take hold of every Jew by a corner of his cloak and say, "Let us go with you, for we have heard that God is with you."

13 It is perhaps telling that the Mishna was compiled by R. Yehuda Ha-Nasi and put the Oral Torah into a fixed form. He was the Nasi, the political leader of the Jews in Eretz Yisrael, and a scion of the family of R. Gamliel, which traced itself, through Hillel (who had come to Eretz Yisrael from Babylonia) to the Davidic line. He was known for his wealth and his close connections with key figures in the Roman Empire.

have a feast on Purim. This omission raises several questions. There may be an allusion to this in the final verses of chapter 9.

> Then Queen Esther daughter of Avihayil wrote a second letter of Purim for the purpose of confirming with full authority the aforementioned one of Mordechai the Jew. Dispatches were sent to all the Jews in the hundred and twenty-seven provinces of the realm of Ahashverosh with an ordinance of integrity and honesty. These days of Purim shall be observed at their proper time, as Mordechai the Jew – and now Queen Esther – has obligated them to do, and just as they have assumed for themselves and their descendants the obligation of the fasts with their lamentations. And Esther's ordinance validating these observances of Purim was recorded in a scroll. (9:29-32)

In verse 28 we learned that the celebration of Purim took root amongst the Jews, even though that verse omitted the *mitzvot* that had been mentioned previously: *mishlo'ah manot* (twice) and *matanot le-evyonim* (once). Verse 29 refers to an earlier time and transitions the reader back to the story of Mordechai and Esther, which continues in chapter 10.

In these final verses of the chapter, the holiday takes on a different character. Firstly, it seems that Mordechai's letter alone did not yield the desired effect. Another letter was sent, in the name of "Queen Esther daughter of Avihayil" – bearing queen's name, title, and obvious Jewish ancestry. Secondly, the holiday practices mentioned above were omitted, replaced with "an ordinance of integrity and honesty" ("*divrei shalom ve-emet*") from Esther and Mordechai. To understand this ordinance, we return to chapter 8 of Zekhariah:

> These are the things you are to do: **Speak the truth** (*dabru emet*) **to one another** (*ish et re'ehu*), render **true** (*emet*) and

> **perfect** (*shalom*) justice in your gates. And do not contrive evil **against one another** (*ish et ra'at re'ehu*), and do not love perjury, because all those are things that I hate – declares the Lord. And the word of the Lord of Hosts came to me, saying: Thus said the Lord of Hosts: The fast of the fourth month, the fast of the fifth month, the fast of the seventh month, and the fast of the tenth month shall become occasions for joy and gladness, happy festivals for the House of Judah; but you must love **honesty and integrity** (*emet ve-shalom*). (Zekhariah 8:16-20)

The practice of "sending gifts **to one another**" (*mishloah manot* ish le-re'ehu), mentioned in verses 22 and 19 is transformed into a different sort of relationship between fellow – that of the book of Zekhariah: "true and perfect justice," "honesty and integrity," justice for the weakest elements of society – the convert, the orphan. This will transform days of fasting and mourning into "occasions for joy and gladness, happy festivals."

Esther's "second letter of Purim" marks the internalization of the message expressed by the prophet Zekhariah and validates a holiday whose observance is characterized by "integrity and honesty," that is, concern for the weaker elements of society. This corresponds to the character of the holiday as presented in the Mishna, compiled by R. Yehuda Ha-Nasi seven centuries after the events described in the Megilah: The holiday is about concern for the physical needs and security of fellow Jews. Its primary observances are the reading of the Megilah – a story that, though tragic, is about Jews' concern for one another – and *matanot le-evyonim*. The emphasis has been shifted from a day of partying and drinking to a day of collective responsibility and concern for the less fortunate, essential elements for a nation that aspires to return to Zion. These elements generate the joy, gladness, and happy festivals of the prophet Zekhariah's consolation. Thus, according to the Mishna, Purim is a holiday of collective responsibility and gifts to the needy – *mitzvot* that are most suited for Eretz Yisrael, whose community is built on the foundation of national and economic solidarity (as expressed by Zekhariah: "Thus said the Lord: I have returned to Zion, and I will dwell in Jerusalem. Jerusalem will be called the City of Faithfulness, and the mount of the Lord of Hosts the Holy Mount"). This is in contrast with Diaspora Jewry, which has no future but threats and assimilation.

This, then, is how I believe the holiday evolved: First there was a spontaneous folk celebration among Persian Jews, whose expression mirrored Persian practice: "gladness and joy among the Jews, a feast and a holiday."[14] This celebration was not popularly accepted and was certainly rejected by the Jews who had returned to Eretz Yisrael. To address this discrepancy, the Jews of Babylonia added the dimension of providing *matanot le-evyonim* to their brothers in Eretz Yisrael. This charitable element helped establish the holiday, but it stagnated again, as it wavered between being a true festival and a folk celebration (the Hasmonean "Day of Mordechai").

The sages of the Mishna established two core practices for the holiday: reading the Megilah and *matanot le-evyonim* (gifts to the needy). A close reading of the Mishna shows that its sages view *matanot le-evyonim* as the central observance of the holiday; reading the Megilah was an excuse to bestow gifts on the needy. The Mishna establishes that the Megilah need not be read on the day of Purim itself; it could be read earlier, on market days. The Sages grasped that the reading of the Megilah was not enough to tempt the villagers to make a special trip to the city just to hear the

14 The Jerusalem Talmud (*Megilah* 1:1) records a fascinating discussion among third-generation Talmudic sages about whether the term "holiday" ("*yom tov*") as used in the Megilah means that labor is prohibited on Purim, as on other Jewish holidays. R. Yehuda Nesi'ah, grandson of R. Yehuda Ha-Nasi, plants a tree on Purim to demonstrate that labor is permitted on Purim. According to his and his grandfather's tradition, this "*yom tov*" has a very different meaning than the Biblical "*hag*" ("festival").

reading of the Megilah, and they most certainly would not come just to give *matanot le-evyonim*. They therefore ordained that the Megilah is read to the villagers on market day; the masses would already be gathered, and they would be willing to listen to the reading of the Megilah. The poor could then circulate among the reveling villagers and receive gifts from them and from other sellers in the market.[15]

The holiday underwent another major change in Babylonia. Most *midrashim* and statements from which we learn their understanding and interpretation of the Megilah originate with the first and subsequent generations of Babylonian Talmudic sages. The sages of the Mishna are all but silent about the Megilah.[16] The bulk of these discussions are based

---

15 The discussion of the mitzvah of *mishlo'ah manot* took place early in the Talmudic era, in context of an ironic story about R. Oshaya and R. Yehuda Nesi'ah: "R. Yudan Nasi sent the great R. Hoshaya one flank and one pitcher of wine. He responded: You have fulfilled *matanot le-evyonim* through us. He then sent him one calf and one barrel of wine. He responded: You have fulfilled *mishlo'ah manot* through us" (JT *Megilah* 1:4; cf. BT *Megilah* 7a). R. Yosef, a third generation Babylonian Talmudic sage, established the formal requirements of *mishlo'ah manot*.

16 The most extensive discussion about the Megilah among the sages of the Mishna relates to Esther's name. Their discomfort about her name, which is derived from a pagan deity, is apparent:

"He was foster father to Hadassah – that is Esther." She is referred to as 'Hadassah' and she is referred to as 'Esther.' What was her real name? It is taught: R. Meir says: Esther was her name. Why was she called Hadassah? On account of the righteous who are called myrtles (*hadassim*), as it is stated: "He stood among the myrtles (*hadassim*)" (Zekhariah 1). R. Yehuda says: Hadassah was her name. Why was she called Esther? Because she concealed (*misateret*) matters about herself, as it is stated: "Esther did not reveal her people or her kindred." R. Nehemiah says: Hadassah was her name. Why was she called Esther? Because the gentiles named her after Ishtar. Ben Azzai says: Esther was neither tall nor short, but of average, like a myrtle (*hadassah*). R. Yehoshua ben Korha said: Esther was greenish, but a threat of grace extended upon her. (BT *Megilah* 13)

on the expositions of Rava and his peers.[17] It is easy to understand why the Jews of Babylonia living in the fourth and fifth centuries CE in the Sasanian Persian Empire find inspiration in the story of the Megilah. They feel the need to translate the story of the Megilah and the salvation of the Jews into terms that are more resonant for them. In their hands, the Megilah undergoes a 'conversion' of sorts and becomes a story of Divine salvation and providence showered by God on the Jews of the Persian Empire, who He saves from their adversary and enemy and shields from assimilation. In other words, they present the Megilah as the diametric opposite of what its author intended some eight hundred years earlier. The story of Mordechai's rise to power was "made kosher" for Babylonian Jewish public opinion as the story of God's deliverance of the oppressed Jews of Persia.

17 Including some of his teachers, namely, R. Nahman and his teacher, Rav. There are several statements at the end of the first chapter of BT *Megilah* that are attributed to Mishnaic sages, but a close analysis of most of these statements shows that they are not commentaries to the Megilah, but rather general statements of those sages that were expounded with reference to verses from the Megilah.

Afterword

One wintry day, I was asked to speak to a group of several dozen young adults visiting Tel Aviv from South America. They wanted to hear about the "Start-Up Nation." The participants came from all parts of the Jewish spectrum – secular and Orthodox, Reform and Conservative. All they had in common, aside from their geographic origin, was that they were all considered 'leaders' in the Jewish communities that had sent them. At the end of the presentation, there was time for questions. One of the participants asked me whether the financial opportunities in the Start-Up Nation were a reason to move to Israel.

"Among others," I said.

"Like what?" they asked.

I asked them to turn off the recording devices.

"How many of you think Jewish identity important?" I asked. Everyone's hands immediately shot up.

"For how many of you is Jewishness the single most important part of your identity?" A third of the hands dropped.

"I've got news for you," I continued, "Unless Jewish identity is the most important part of your identity, you will never settle in Israel; and if you don't settle in Israel, most of your descendants will not be Jewish."

Those with their hands still in the air were looking pretty smug.

"Your situation is no better," I said to them, with a smile that conveyed my concern. "For you, perhaps, it will take another generation or two or three, because you will be more successful in imbuing the importance of Jewish identity, but history proves that no inoculation endures in the Diaspora. In another generation or two, a considerable number of your descendants will be faced with an identity conflict, and their Jewish identity will be eroded. You can see the future if you look at the past. Even before the Holocaust, assimilation was rampant – and today, more Jews have been lost to assimilation than were lost in the Holocaust. It is true that assimilation is not nearly as cruel as blood libels, pogroms, and the horrific anti-Semitism of the Nazis – but quietly and consistently, assimilation exacts its price and ensures that its final results will be dramatic."

I summarized: "In the Diaspora, financial crisis unleashes anti-Semitism. Economic prosperity, which is always followed by economic downturn, generates assimilation. If Jewish identity is important to you, and if it is important to you that your children are part of the Jewish people, then move to Israel. You will also find respectable income here in the Start-Up Nation."

* * *

It was not for naught that I asked them to turn off recording devices for the duration of the lecture. This truth – the true story of assimilation and its results, of abandoning the Jewish people during the long years of exile – is the story that people dare not speak about. It is the disturbing truth that lies behind the debates and accusations between different streams of Judaism. Assimilation breaks all boundaries and affects every stream. It is linked to the choice of a primary identity and a secondary identity. It is bound to an unalterable law of nature, a raging river that has flowed in only one direction for two thousand years of exile, sweeping up masses of Jews who get lost at sea in an ongoing, inevitable process. Our national identity survives, but in exile, it will only ever survive among the very few. Jewishness, Israeliness, and the Jewish identity of individuals will not survive. Anti-Semitism, in certain instances, actually strengthens Jewish identity; it is opportunity that erodes it.

This is the disturbing truth of Megilat Esther, the Megilah of assimilation. It is not the story of a man who wants to grow close to his God, his people, and his land, but the story of an ambitious man who wants to become the second in command to the king, and sends his niece Esther to the king's bedroom to achieve his goal.

This truth is so troublesome and painful that it was even difficult for the Sages to accept. In an effort to adroitly explain Esther's years in Ahashverosh's bedroom, they employ all kinds of odd explanations. In the Babylonian Talmud, for example, it is said:

> But Esther's [ongoing sexual relationship with Ahashverosh] was public! Abaye says: Esther was passive. (BT *Sanhedrin* 74b)

The Talmud is discussing why Esther was not required to give up her life rather than sleep with Ahashverosh, the Persian king. Abaye, a contemporary of Rava, held that Esther was "mere ground," an object, utterly passive. As Rashi clarifies, Esther "did not perform an action; Ahasheverosh would perform an action upon her."

These are hard words to accept about someone who the Babylonian Talmudic sages praised for saving Persian Jewry. Abaye calls Esther "mere ground ("*karka olam*"), an inanimate surface with no feeling or emotion. She was not just passive, she was like the earth. These harsh words represent an attempt to find any excuse to avoid confronting the plain meaning of the text – that Esther, named for a pagan goddess, married a gentile and assimilated.

Another reason that I asked for the recording to be turned off is because my statement contained an unpleasant truth: that assimilation places a growing wedge between the Jews of Israel and the Jews of the Diaspora. In Israel, every stream and faction preserves Judaism and Jewishness at an immeasurably higher rate than any Diaspora movement. The annual calendar, the atmosphere, the social and cultural milieu, the language, the army, and the value system all ensure Jewish-Israeli identity.[1]

This is the troublesome reality, but it is not pleasant to tell Diaspora Jews to their faces that their descendants might not be Jewish. It is far easier to talk about terror in Paris or rising anti-Semitism in Kiev or Brooklyn. These are topics that we can all rally around and condemn.

Not long ago, I watched a YouTube video produced by two Jewish outreach organizations that promote Jewish identity among American Jews. The video features an American Jewish woman talking for three minutes about her desire to make *aliyah* – after which she adds, "But, I am doing holy work in the United States!" She continues: "I consulted leading rabbis, who told me that it will be time to move to Israel only when they start killing Jews in the US."

I could not believe my ears. A woman who works to strengthen Jewish identity in the Diaspora does not understand that the best solution for strengthening Jewish identity is *aliyah*?! With rabbinic approval, she waits for an outbreak of anti-Semitism so she can move to Israel. Doesn't she know that the most successful identity-building programs for US Jews – Birthright Israel and gap year programs, for instance – essentially outsource this vital task to Israel and the Israeli experience?

We have heard things like this before. In fact, we heard it from some European Jews and rabbis on the eve of the Holocaust. Once again, the Jews focus on the wrong threat.

It is indeed possible that both threats – anti-Semitism and assimilation – lurk simultaneously. In the winter of 2016, the executive vice chairman of the Conference of Presidents of Major Jewish Organizations in the United States remarked in an interview that 75% of Jews on university

---

1 The broadcast of the annual International Bible Quiz on the afternoon of Israel's Independence Day is a salient expression of the connection between Judaism, Israeli culture, and a family-like orientation.

campuses in the United States have experienced anti-Semitism. "It's not Europe yet," he said, "but anti-Semitism is definitely on the rise." And I ask myself: What is he waiting for? And how can you expect a Jewish kid on a college campus to identify Jewishly in the face of so much pressure? How will he define his identity? What will the implications be for his children?[2] Won't it be much easier for him to simply disappear into the American mainstream?

It is not easy to discuss the issue of identity, but it is vital. This discussion has direct ramifications for the number of Jews in the world. It has political repercussions as well, not just for local Jewish communities in various countries, but also for Israel's ties with countries that have large or influential Jewish populations. It is of the utmost importance for the future of the Jewish people in general, and for Israel specifically – for beyond Israel's borders, the Jewish people are shrinking and being swallowed up. The only place in the world today where the Jewish population is not in steep decline is Israel – just like it was 2,500 years ago.[3]

The numbers don't lie. There is a clear trend of Jews disappearing in the global village and losing their identities in the Diaspora. Jews account for 0.2% of the world's population today, and their numbers are steadily dwindling in almost every country in the world – Israel excepted.[4] If we examine the situation over time, the situation is even more ominous. In 1970, there were 12.6 million Jews in the world. In 2015, there were 14.2 million Jews in the world. In that time, the Jewish population in Israel doubled itself (from 3 million to 6.3 million), while the Jewish population

2 http://www.ynetnews.com/articles/0,7340,L-4767884,00.html .

3 For a fascinating, though empirically thin, discussion about Jewish assimilation from the middle of the Second Temple era until fifty years after the Temple's destruction, see John M. G. Barclay, *Jews in the Mediterranean Diaspora*, especially pp. 105,110, 149 and Chapter 11 in its entirety.

4 According to some researchers, during the Roman era, Jews accounted for c. 10% of the empire's total population. Other researchers place the number at about 4%.

of the rest of the world shrunk by about 2 million – a decline of more than 15 percent.

Nobody is taking dramatic action, because taking action is so uncomfortable. From a financial vantage point, immigration to Israel is not always easy. It is certainly uncomfortable from a cultural perspective; immigrants to Israel feel *déclassé* in Israeli communities. "It's just not the right time," say the world's Jews. "I feel out of step with Israeli culture." "I don't like the way they do things in Israel." "I've heard from friends that life can be tough in Israel." "I've been told that it's hard to be a Torah observant Jew there."

All of this might be true. I do not agree with these assertions, neither from a sober, historical perspective nor from personal experience, but perhaps there is something to them. The price of remaining in the Diaspora is very clear, though, even if it is not immediately apparent. Jews around the world may have good stories – just like in the Megilah – but reality will ultimately take over the plot and affect most families: in Lakewood, Brooklyn, Oklahoma, Palo Alto, Paris, and Sao Paulo. History does not repeat itself, but it rhymes.

Ironically, it is far easier to talk about anti-Semitism. It is easy to talk about how Haman wanted to exterminate us and failed. It is easy to talk about it, because when the Haman of the day rises up against the Jews, he can be blamed for all of this evil, and we are absolved from all responsibility.

Of course, these Hamans are indeed guilty. Very guilty. Hitler, Himmler, Khmelnytsky, Petliura, Torquemada, the Inquisition, the popes in the time of the Crusades, and so on and so forth – were all completely evil. We have memorial days for their victims, such as Yom Ha-Sho'ah (Holocaust Remembrance Day), and prayers like "*Av Ha-rahamim*" and "*El Malei Rahamim*," which commemorate those killed in the Crusades and the Holocaust. However, we do not have days to commemorate the missed opportunities of the return to Zion in the days of Zerubavel and early waves of *aliyah* in modern times. We do not have prayers against assimilation and the silent disappearance of Jews, even though their number far exceeds the number of Jews killed by the Haman of each generation.

The young adults with whom I spoke that day were aware that a significant percentage of their descendants will not be Jewish. They were aware, precisely the same way that Mordechai and Esther were aware. Perhaps they care and perhaps they do not care; the main thing is that it's not real to them. The threat does not confront them today. It lies somewhere in the future.

In the days of Mordechai and Esther, it was likewise unpleasant to speak about this issue. The Megilah was therefore written with sarcasm, irony, and allusions to other Biblical stories. The Jews who lived in Eretz Yisrael did not want, or perhaps did not dare, to place a mirror before the Diaspora Jews. It would have been distasteful.

The Shushan of old has been reincarnated today in New York, Buenos Aires, Berlin, Los Angeles, London, Johannesburg, and Melbourne. The dilemmas that Mordechai faced in the Persian Empire, when confronting a dominant culture and the world's first cosmopolitan empire, also confront Diaspora Jews and expat Israelis who, more than ever before, can leave home and try to conquer the world.

They certainly may seek out these opportunities; it is even valuable, but the price must be stated clearly and openly: **There is no substitute for a Jewish-Israeli identity. One who does not join the Jewish state will most likely lose both his Jewishness and his Israeliness within a few generations**. He will be cut off from the one and only eternal nation that ever entered the historical arena. The nation's ship will sail on; they will simply not be aboard.

Mordechai's end was similar to the end of Lot, Avraham's nephew, who chose the fertile cities of Sodom and Amorah. Avraham's trademark characteristics of justice and righteousness were diametrically opposed to the value system of Sodom and Amorah. Mordechai was wealthy; he enjoyed a close relationship with the important people in government, just like Naomi's husband Elimelech, whose sons intermarried with the affluent families of Moav. Mordechai was able to preserve his wealth and his political influence with the queen and in the royal court of Persia.

A hundred years after Mordechai and Esther – too far into the future to be foreseeable – the center of Jewish life returned once again to Eretz Yisrael. Nehemiah, the antithesis of Mordechai, moved to Eretz Yisrael, bringing along his vast managerial and administrative knowledge that allowed the second Jewish commonwealth to prosper economically and politically. There, in Eretz Yisrael, the Men of the Great Assembly flourished and ordained fixed prayers. They changed the script of the Torah to the Assyrian block script, so that every Jew would be able to study and understand the Torah. Jewish culture blossomed in Eretz Yisrael. The Jewish people remained there and multiplied, until the destruction of the Second Temple some 500 years later. The Diaspora, on the other hand, almost evaporated, as if it had never existed.

Then, as now, there was a need for talented Jews to come and build up the country. The State of Israel is now almost seventy years old, a venerable age for a human, but the blink of an eye in historical terms. Those who came to Eretz Yisrael in the "First Aliyah"[5] of modern times were like Zerubavel in his time: They laid the foundations of the modern State of Israel, and then the Second Aliya began to establish its institutions, culture, and credibility. They initiated the unprecedented project of the reinventing the ancient language of Tanakh as a modern, spoken language. During the Second Aliyah and subsequent *aliyot*, spiritual leaders, authors,

---

5 My editor, Elli Fischer, correctly pointed out that the "First Aliyah" was not the first of anything in any significant way except one: it was the first time that non-observant Ashkenazim made *aliyah* in any appreciable numbers. However, I think it is fair to say that it was a harbinger of the modern State of Israel and an attempt to root Jews and Judaism in the physical soil of Eretz Yisrael.

administrators, clerks, and a wide range of Jews from all over the Diaspora arrived. The state arose and was built up.

Now we need people like Nehemiah, people with experience in administration, business, and education, to keep building a modern, rejuvenated, vibrant state and economy. The time has come for people who will preserve their Jewish-Israeli identity, founded on a two thousand year old heritage, in the one and only place on Earth where they can survive and flourish for generations: the State of Israel in the land of Israel. The swamps have already been drained; the age of the little blue JNF *pushkes* is over. Israel no longer needs handouts, *matanot le-evyonim*. It has a thriving economy with global reach,[6] but within sovereign borders and rooted in its own culture, which preserve the identity of the eternal nation.

Historical Perspective

But the day will come when the ephemeral souls of the Diaspora will find their eventual rectification in our holy land:

> Upon three things will the State of Israel will stand: On justice. Which justice? The truth, the Torah of truth. Then all the different factions will make peace, and justice will be done, truth will be done, and peace will be made. We will merit that "The Lord will grant strength to His people; the Lord will bless on His people with peace."[7]

---

6 Between the publication of the Hebrew and English versions of the book, Israel passed France in GDP per capita and England is within sight.

7 This citation is from *Or Geulat Yisrael*, published in New Jersey in 1964 by my great-grandfather, R. Aharon Reuben Charney. Papa Charney, as he was called, was an avid Zionist, a friend and peer of R. Avraham Yitzhak Kook on a London rabbinical court, and a member of the Mizrahi movement, who was not privileged to make *aliyah*. At my *brit milah* I was given the name Aharon Meshulam, though everyone knows me as Michael; such are the vestiges of the Diaspora.

The twenty-first century brings new challenges for the Jewish people. A glance at the world shows that globalization is eroding the particular identity of many nations, the Jews included. On the other hand, the same globalization and pluralism are provoking reactions in which religious and ethnic identities are intensified, as in so many Islamic countries. This is nothing new – similar processes took hold in the days of the Persian kings Darius and Cyrus and throughout history – except for the intensity of the processes today.

Whether by design or by necessity, since the destruction of the Second Temple and the Roman exile two thousand years ago, Jews isolated themselves in their communities and their religion. The survival of Jewish national, religious, and communal identity through the ages is one of history's open miracles. For a millennium, ascendant Christianity expected the disintegration of Judaism and the disappearance of the Jews. It did not happen. Muslims expected the same when they downgraded Jews to second class citizens in their lands. This too did not happen. The Jews, a besieged minority incessantly exposed to the dangers of assimilation, managed to survive and preserve their religion in the various exiles, from Northern Africa and the Middle East to Europe, America, and Australia.

The Assyrians, Babylonians, Parthians, Medians, Hurrians, Phoenicians, Carthaginians, Romans, and Akkadians have exited the stage of history. Those who live in modern-day Egypt, Macedonia, Greece, or Spain share geography with their predecessors, but not ethnic or religious identity. The Jews alone continued to survive, in a set of communities that rarely, if ever, communicated with one another, stubbornly clinging to their culture, educational system, and religion, while always playing an important role in wider human arena, from Rambam to Albert Einstein.

There was a reason for their survival. Israel, or "the children of Israel," as the Torah calls them, began as a family, a clan with many wives and children. Yaakov went down to Egypt at the end of his life, accompanied by sixty-six descendants, to be reunited with his beloved son Yosef.[8] The Jewish people began to proliferate in the Goshen region of Egypt, eventually became enslaved to the Egyptians, and left Egypt in order to receive the covenant, the Ten Commandments, and the religious, cultural, moral, social, administrative, and ritual code of the nation that would one day inherit its ancestral land once again. One of the goals of the Torah is clearly the creation of a model society in the land of Canaan.

In this new society, there would be farmers who donate a portion of their yield to those who had none of their own. They would worship the one true God, not a full pantheon full of deities. They would circumcise their sons, in accordance with their ancestral tradition. They would observe a weekly Sabbath,[9] the great equalizer in which everyone, slaves and maidservants included, has a day of rest to spend with family and reconnect with the spirit. In this society, there would be respect for women and for the sanctity of marriage. They would treat workers and slaves properly. They would establish a government with limited power and ability to accumulate property, which would be responsible for its actions and the actions of its citizens, its land, and foreigners who live within its borders: "You shall not wrong a stranger or oppress him, for you were strangers in the land of Egypt."

It is hard to appreciate, after so many years, how revolutionary this was in the history of the nations. This vision was so vastly different from the one that guided other nations, religions, and cultures of the Ancient Near East. During their forty years of wandering in the desert, Israel both

---

8 "All the persons belonging to Jacob who came to Egypt – his own issue, aside from the wives of Jacob's sons – all these persons numbered sixty-six." (Bereishit 46:26). An additional four descendants of Yaakov were already in Egypt, namely: Yosef, his wife, and children.

9 Unlike months and years, which follow the natural path of the moon and sun respectively, the seven-day week, and, consequently, the idea of a weekly day of rest, is a uniquely Jewish contribution to world civilization.

crystallized its belief system and established the social cohesiveness that would be essential for life in the Promised Land and for disseminating their teachings by means of exemplary individuals, society, and state. To paraphrase David Ben-Gurion "A people builds an army that builds a people," we can say that this people built a way of life, a political entity, and a land that built a people.

Moshe's Torah and the prophets of Israel envisioned a faithful and moral society that would influence its citizens and its government, life within the society, and life in its environs. This is the ethos cultivated in Eretz Yisrael, about which one can learn from the harsh rebukes of Israel's prophets to the degenerating Israelite society at the end of the First Temple period.

The prophecies of Yeshayahu, son of Amotz, who prophesied in the days of Ahaz and Hizkiyahu, about 150 years before the destruction of the First Temple, begin with a scathing rebuke of the nation and its leadership ("Hear the word of the Lord, You chieftains of Sodom; give ear to our God's instruction, You folk of Amorah!"). He admonished: "Uphold the rights of the orphan; defend the cause of the widow.... Your princes are rebellious and companions of thieves. Everyone loves bribes and follows after rewards. They do not judge the orphans, nor does the cause of the widows reach them." Therefore, he foretold, the sinners will be punished, and the Temple and the land will be destroyed on account of their sins.

The prophet Yirmiyahu prophesied during the last days of the First Temple, about a hundred years after Yeshayahu. He stood at the Temple gate and did not mince words against pilgrims who arrived with mouths full of God's praise, but whose actions were a complete desecration of God's Holy name:

> Now, if you really mend your ways and your actions; if you execute justice between one man and another; if you do not oppress the stranger, the orphan, and the widow; if you do not

> shed the blood of the innocent in this place; if you do not follow other gods, to your own hurt – then only will I let you dwell in this place, in the land that I gave to your fathers for all time. (Yirmiyahu 7:5-7)

It is not enough to offer sacrifices and mumble words of prayer, warns Yirmiyahu. God has required of His nation only one thing: "Listen to My words and I will be for you a God and you will be for me a nation." But the nation's ears have fallen deaf, and so their fate is sealed: "Therefore, behold days are coming…and the carcasses of these people shall be food for the birds of heaven…and the land shall be desolate" (*ibid.* 33-34).

The Jewish people have undertaken to build a just society, in which weak and strong alike are treated fairly and equally before the law and the government and administration are honest, to serve as an exemplar for the surrounding nations. Faith in the one true God is not about prayer or sacrifice, but about belief in a Higher Power Who dwarfs human kings and renders every last member of Israel[10] the equal of the king. Even the king is a servant of God. He must therefore establish a just society, not a society that serves him, his belly, and his wallet.

This was not the practice of the kings living in the vicinity of Eretz Yisrael, but it was mandatory for kings of Israel as well as its officers and the people at large. The diametric opposite of the model Israelite king was Ahashverosh, as depicted in the Megilah: an absolutist, ostentatious ruler over a vast empire who cannot even control his own wife and household. The author of the Megilah mocks his outward appearance of aggressive imperialism that is hollow, lacking values, and weak on the inside.

---

10 The prophet is admonishing the Jewish people for their treatment of other Jews. However, I believe the admonition applies to the mistreatment or exploitation of any underprivileged human beings, regardless of religion, creed, or nationality. This is explicitly stated numerous times in the Torah: "and you shall love the stranger for you were strangers in the land of Egypt."

The destruction of the First Temple and the earlier exile of "the artisan and the locksmith" were not just national and political upheavals; they also constituted a formative test and a milestone for the history and identity of the Jewish people. For the first time since they entered the land about a thousand years earlier, Jewish identity – the tribal identity of Judah – was disconnected from Israelite identity, from an identity rooted in Eretz Yisrael. The Israelites were cast out of their land by God, Who guided and enabled the Babylonians to do so. In many respects, the nation returned to its desert identity. They still believed in the one true God and His commandments, but they no longer had the ability to realize them in their land. However, unlike the desert generation, the Jews were now embedded in a foreign nation and an alien culture.

Many relinquished their Israelite identity and instead adopted a Jewish identity among the nations of the region. They became Persian Jews, Babylonian Jews, and later Hellenizing Jews and Roman Jews. Some of them looked forward to when they would be able to return and rebuild an authentic Israelite identity in an exemplary state on the soil of Eretz Yisrael, but others adopted a thoroughly Jewish identity: the identity of Diaspora Jews.

Jewish identity as we know it took shape only after the destruction of the Second Temple. By that time, some 650 years after the destruction of the First Temple and the Babylonian exile, the Jews of Shushan had completely assimilated. Their Jewish identity was not strong enough to preserve them in exile.

In his book about Judaism in exile in Egypt and the "West" during the Second Temple era,[11] Barclay establishes an index for measuring assimilation and affiliation with the host society. The index ranges from low to high, both in terms of the degree of assimilation and in terms of the socio-political character of the assimilating Jew. Very few kept the

11 Barclay, *Jews in the Mediterranean Diaspora.*

flame alive; most vanished, assimilating into the religions and customs of the host nation.[12] It is possible that rivalry with their brothers who had returned to Eretz Yisrael marginalized them. Perhaps they did not set up the infrastructure or produce leaders that would suffice to preserve them. Therefore, as the Megilah foresaw, the exiles were saved from physical annihilation, only to vanish among the host nations.[13]

Things were different after the destruction of the Second Temple. When R. Yohanan b. Zakkai petitioned Vespasian, "Spare for me Yavneh and its sages," he deliberately severed Jewish custom and *mitzvot* from the capital city of Jerusalem. Yavneh was not just another town; it was a place of exile in Eretz Yisrael, where Jewish identity and the rabbinic tradition that would allow it to flourish were developed.

In hindsight, the strong Jewish identity that the Sages fashioned in the generations after the Second Temple's destruction was a great success. Five centuries after Mordechai and Esther's failed attempt to create a Diaspora Jewish identity, the Sages succeed, and the Jewish identity they forged survived two thousand years of exile. R. Yohanan b. Zakkai and his tenacious, creative students established infrastructure, practices, and *mitzvot* that reinforced Jewish identity even after it was severed from the

---

12 We do not have much knowledge or data about Diaspora Jews of the Second Temple era. Estimates of the Diaspora Jewish population are mere conjecture, like all estimates of ancient populations, and there are large discrepancies between various estimates. There is no doubt that Jewish culture blossomed in the Diaspora at that time; in Egypt there was even Jewish literature, such as the *Second Book of Maccabees* and the writings of Philo of Alexandria. The influence of the host societies and economic opportunities had a strong impact, though, and these Jews vanished. One point worth noting, in my opinion, is that there are about 120 sages of the Mishna. All but three (that we know of) lived in Eretz Yisrael: R. Natan of Babylon, Nahum the Medean, and R. Yehuda b. Beteirah. The Talmud also notes that Hillel the Elder moved to Israel from Babylonia, but his life's work and his revolution took place in Israel.

13 There were a few who even became Jew-haters.

national entity of Israel and from Eretz Yisrael. In this sense, from my perspective at least, R. Yohanan b. Zakkai was perhaps the all-time greatest shaper of Jewish identity.

Judaism developed in different centers and in various forms, but its core, its nucleus, remained intact. Judaism and Jewish identity became the greatest country club in the world;[14] a Moroccan Jew could feel at home on a business trip to France or to Poland.[15] The shapers of Jewish identity managed to build a decentralized home for the Jewish people, a home that is found wherever there are Jews, a home characterized by familiar practices, mutual trust between communities and individuals, and room for meaningful development.

Jewish identity became a portable home, like a tortoise shell. Wherever they wandered, the Jews managed to establish communities with schools, study halls, ritual baths, infirmaries, and soup kitchens. The centerpiece of the community was the synagogue, the house of meeting and prayer. The communal structure and welfare services were strikingly similar despite wide temporal and geographic variance.

The level and character of Jewish 'religiosity' underwent noticeable changes, strengthening and deteriorating in accordance with the threats and opportunities that Jews faced. Jewish law and philosophy developed continuously: Talmudic literature was produced in Babylonia, Germany, Spain, and North Africa. There, the great Jewish philosophical works were composed as well, from R. Yehuda Halevi's *Kuzari* to Rambam's *Moreh Nevukhim*, to the Talmudic and Biblical exegesis of Rashi in France, to the legal code of R. Yosef Karo in Tzefat and R. Moshe Isserles in Krakow, and many others.

---

14 I heard this apt expression from R. Shlomo Riskin, the rabbi of Efrat and, prior to his *aliyah*, rabbi of the Lincoln Square Synagogue in New York City.

15 R. Asher b. Yehiel, known as the Rosh, moved from Ashkenaz (Germany) to Sepharad (Spain) and became a leading rabbi there.

Diaspora Jewish identity, which failed in the days of Mordechai and Esther, was fleshed out under the inspiration of R. Yohanan b. Zakkai. The sages of the Mishna and Talmud, the thinkers, the exegetes, and the judges and codifiers of Jewish law continued to fuel the fire of tradition in each generation. Jewish identity became stronger and richer, but the Jewish population did not grow accordingly. Everywhere, and in every generation, the ranks of the Jewish people were depleted by assimilation into the prevailing culture.

The Jewish Sages created a wonderful solution to the question of Judaism, but it did not solve the question of the Jews. Jews with a strong identity and with sufficient religious and mental fortitude could protect themselves against assimilation into the swirl of identities surrounding them, but so many others drowned in that same sea, including many descendants of the strongest Jews. Some deliberately apostatized and jettisoned their Jewish identity: people like Heinrich Heine, Lorenzo Da Ponte, or David Ricardo did not hide their utilitarian reasons for converting out.[16] Others simply slipped away, assimilated, and were swallowed into the identity of the host country. Jewish identity in the Diaspora was only as thick as the walls of the synagogue and the home where one grew up. Like a raging current, national identity was much stronger than religious identity for so many. As R. Meir Simha wrote, an enlightened citizen suppresses his traditional identity.

Every Jew in a country other than Israel has a hybrid identity and must ask himself: Is my national identity primary, or my traditional Jewish identity?[17] When I was twenty years old, I approached Rabbi Jacob J.

16 Heinrich Heine was one of the great German poets; Lorenzo Da Ponte wrote the librettos for some of Mozart's most famous operas; and David Ricardo was one of the most important economists of the nineteenth century.

17 This is not only true for Jews, but also for Christians, Muslims, Buddhists, and any immigrant to a new country, like Koreans and Chinese who come to the United States.

Schacter[18] – then rabbi at the Jewish Center in Manhattan, and today the director of Yeshiva University's Center for the Jewish Future[19] in New York – and asked him whether, in his opinion, a Jew in America is a Jewish American or an American Jew? He told me that this is the million dollar question and that each person's capacity for survival and for maintaining a connection to the Jewish people is contained within his answer. Perhaps R. Schacter was correct then and is correct now too, but to me it seems that this very identity conflict shakes one to the core. Most of the people whose grandfathers would have identified as Jews now consider themselves to be Americans. Judaism is alive in America, but the Jews themselves are disappearing.

The Pew Research Center's comprehensive surveys clothe this paradox in statistics and data.[20] Among American Jews, only Orthodox Jews, who adhere to the view that Jewish law is the building block of their Judaism, have experienced growth. According to the Pew survey, 100% of Orthodox Jews surveyed stated that their Judaism is important to them or extremely important to them. Among respondents from all other streams of American Jews, Judaism was important to less than half, and their numbers continue to dwindle. More than 60% of Orthodox Jews in the United States attend synagogue at least once a week.[21] Their communal life still centers around the synagogue. And still, almost 15% of Jews who

---

18 Rabbi Schacter is a man I respect greatly and a longtime family friend. When I was in college, I approached him with numerous philosophical and Jewish existential questions. He officiated at my wedding.

19 One might find it ironic that an institution calling itself the "Center for the Jewish Future" is located in Washington Heights, New York.

20 See "A Portrait of Jewish Americans" and "A Portrait of American Orthodox Jews" at http://www.pewforum.org/2013/10/01/jewish-american-beliefs-attitudes-culture-survey/ and http://www.pewforum.org/2015/08/26/a-portrait-of-american-orthodox-jews/ respectively.

21 It may seem surprising that, according to the Pew report, a higher percentage of "Modern Orthodox" Jews (81%) than "Ultra-Orthodox" Jews (71%) attend

identify as Conservative or Reform responded that they grew up in an Orthodox home – which proves that nobody is immune.[22] In fact, the ranks of Conservative Jewry in the United States are populated mostly by Conservative families and formerly Orthodox families. From generation to generation, Jewish religiosity fluctuates.[23]

The meaning of these findings is that every Jewish family, from all streams of Judaism, will lose some of its descendants over time. Every denomination will lose members to assimilation. When I ask people whose grandfathers were born in the United States, "Do you have a cousin who intermarried?" the answer, about 80% of the time, is, "Yes." Members of the fourth generation are the ones that anecdotally and statistically fully assimilate. The threat is not palpable, and the existence of intermarriage is suppressed, especially within "Ultra-Orthodox" and "Modern Orthodox" communities, but the threat does exist and is only intensifying.[24] The trickle

---

synagogue at least once a month; of course, it is not too surprising once one factors in that Ultra-Orthodox women tend not to go to *shul*.

22 This statistic includes Jews raised "Ultra-Orthodox." Small Orthodox sample sizes and the vagueness of some of the survey questions make it hard to be certain about the accuracy of the statistics. It is also plausible that one of the reasons Reform and Conservative ranks are dwindling is because, unlike in earlier generations, very few Jews who grow up Orthodox join other denominations; if they give up religious observance, they either opt out of religious affiliation completely or continue to attend Orthodox synagogues on the occasions when they do come.

23 The exclusive growth of Orthodox Jewry from among all sectors of Jews derives from two different factors: One, the number of children per family; two, the gradual disappearance of Jews from other streams. Orthodox growth is thus relative.

24 In a blog post entitled "The Rise of Interfaith Marriage in the Modern Orthodox (MO) Community", the guest author, Ruvie, the father of an intermarried son, suggests that 5-20% of children raised in Modern Orthodox homes intermarry. The entire piece is worth reading and can be found at Prof. Alan Brill's blog: https://kavvanah.wordpress.com/2017/01/17/the-rise-of-interfaith-marriage-

of Jews out of Judaism in the Diaspora gains momentum with each passing year. Of course, it is always possible to play games with statistics and keep stretching the definition of 'who is a Jew' in different directions, but the trend will continue as it was. Jews who adopt the national identity of a different nation or society, by choice or by osmosis, will not return to take their place among the Jewish people; they will be swallowed up in the depth of the host nation.[25] Just like Mordechai. Exactly like Esther. It happened in Muslim Spain and again in Christian Spain, under threat of expulsion. It happened in nineteenth- and twentieth-century Europe, up until the Holocaust. It is happening today in the US, UK, Canada, and Australia.[26]

According to the Pew study, 20% of America's Jews define themselves as having no religion. That is, they are Jewish by blood relation and, in some cases, through some customs, but these ties to do not last long. The percentage of Jews who identify first and foremost as Americans has risen steadily through the years, from only 6% among those born in the early 1900s to almost a third of those born after 1980. Among these Jews, nearly 80% intermarry, just like Queen Esther. Their children are not really Jewish anymore. Their grandchildren might not know that they were once Jewish.

A similar phenomenon exists among expat Israelis. It is, perhaps, even

---

in-the-modern-orthodox-mo-community-ruvie/. It appeared just this English translation was finalized.

While it is unsupported by any evidence other than anecdotal, I think paints a picture. I would suggest that this is the obvious outcome of national identity superseding particular identity in times of cultural assimilation and successful economic integration. The trend is likely accelerating.

25 My friend Rabbi Ryan Bauer of San Francisco would say "you need to be 'all in' on Judaism today.

26 In *Sapiens: A Brief History of Humankind*, Yuval Noah Harari writes that a conquering religion must missionize or find an 'agent,' like Constantine the Great, to convert the residents of the empire. Judaism is an obvious exception in that it has no missionary component.

more pronounced in this community. I have met many of them in the Silicon Valley and amid New York's skyscrapers. Most of them proclaim, until they are blue in the face, that their Israeli identity and values are important to them. I believe them. They raise their children in Hebrew, celebrate Jewish holidays more than they did in Israel, and even establish umbrella organizations for Israeli culture; I once even visited an Israeli folk dancing class in California.

However, this effort is hard to sustain. A separate national identity, like Israeliness, cannot endure in the long term when it is embedded within different nation. National identity is the result of language, calendar, shared values, and collective experiences like military service; a people builds an army that builds a people.

When one builds an army in Persia, the results mirror those in the Megilah. Without the cohesiveness of the Israeli army and its ethos and within the nation of Israel, through the Hebrew calendar and the Hebrew language, national identity erodes and disappears, because it is too dependent on physical location and time. Israeli folk dances quickly become rave clubs in California. The first generation stammers on the foreign tongue. The second generation flees from the folkways and customs of its predecessors.

Several months ago, in a discussion of identity, a colleague asked me: "Why is Jewish identity so important to you? I grew up on a kibbutz," she said of herself. "I am Israeli, not Jewish." I asked her to explain herself. What is an Israeli identity? She does not keep Shabbat halakhically, but as an Israeli, Shabbat is her day of rest, just like Sunday is the Roman Catholic Sabbath. The Jewish holidays are her vacation days. She attends a Seder on Passover, lights candles on Chanuka, and dresses up in costume on Purim. She sings "Hatikva," invoking the two thousand year old hope of being a free people in our land. She cares deeply about social justice and the weaker elements of society. She and her family put their lives on the line for Israel. She built an army that built a people.

To the ears of someone like me who was raised in the Diaspora, it sounded very familiar. Very Jewish, very Israeli.

This is precisely the point – Israeliness, the Israeli identity that is still being developed, that is only seventy years old, is an emerging identity. It began with the tribes that came to Israel from the four corners of the globe, and slowly those tribes became a spectrum with every color of the rainbow. In time, and in fits and starts, they will become a people. It is best not to listen to journalists and politicians, who, in their effort to sell papers or collect votes, play on tribal sympathies. They are the extremes. Most people who live in Israel are somewhere on the rainbow, within the continuum, slowly but surely creating an Israeli identity.

A growing number of Israelis, including even those who identify as Haredim, serve in the army. A growing number of Israelis are studying traditional texts. Many Israelis are returning to their Jewish-Israeli roots and their Jewish-Israeli values. Societal concern for the weakest of Israel's citizens has developed significantly in recent years. Israeli-Jewish identity is being built slowly, as a result of a shared life. Moroccan Jewish identity, like American, Polish, French, Yemenite and Bulgarian Jewish identity, is merging over time into an Israeli national identity. For example, many North African Jews have returned to their roots and reinvigorated the composition and performance of *piyyut* (religious liturgical poetry) in Israel, and in turn, the *piyyut* movement has become a broader Israeli cultural phenomenon that is impacting and being adopted by Israelis of all shapes and sizes, including Ashkenazim.

I see this in my own home, with my own children, who chuckle at their American father. They are not American; they are Israeli, just like their friends who arrived here from all over the world. They are connected to one another through their Jewish-Israeli identity that is expressed through the Hebrew language, the celebration of the Israeli-Jewish Shabbat and holidays, and the Jewish-Israeli ethos of protecting Israel and Israelis. Their national Israeli identity merges with their Jewish one.

The Megilah's Lesson

The wealthy Jews left Eretz Yisrael for the Diaspora even before the destruction of the First Temple and the fall of the kingdom of Judah. In the Diaspora, they encountered Persian culture, became enthralled with its charm, and were captivated by its riches. These were among the wealthiest Jews, skilled artisans and craftsmen. When they arrived in a land of boundless opportunity, an empire of 127 provinces, they integrated well into the economic, administrative, and indeed every facet of its life. They enjoyed the empire's protection, military might, financial strength, and total control of the world's major trade routes. With the destruction of the First Temple, many other Jews were exiled from Eretz Yisrael and joined them.

These immigrants saw that things were good. They worked to hide their accents, wore their hats Persian-style, and began to integrate. Their successes merely whet their appetite for more. They strove to join the palace courtiers, to sit at the king's gate, to serve as ministers and noblemen, and even to penetrate the king's bedroom. There, in the seat of power, through which all of empire's tax revenues flowed, the greatest economic opportunities of all arose. Nepotism, protectionism, and money.

At the same time, a thousand miles from Shushan, the Jews who had returned to Eretz Yisrael in the wake of Cyrus's edict began to build rebuild the Jewish commonwealth in Eretz Yisrael. The second Jewish-Israelite kingdom was born. Poverty abounded; planting vineyards, building homes, establishing religious institutions, and recreating cultural frameworks demanded a great deal of effort. The Jewish returnees waited for more manpower, leaders, skills, administrators, and talent to arrive from the Diaspora and help with their fledgling and still-fragile project.

That courageous handful of people, with shining eyes, sunburnt skin, and labor-calloused hands, believed that God would deliver them if only they would make a wholehearted effort to raise their land and their state from neglect and ruin. They attempted to rebuild the fallen Temple, spiritually and physically. They recreated religious institutions; under the leadership of Ezra, the scribe and priest, they strengthened Jewish identity by insisting on the termination of intermarriages among the Jews who had remained in Eretz Yisrael, and begin to build a model society, founded on mutual responsibility.

That Rosh Hashana, Ezra assembled all of the poor Jews in the heart of Jerusalem:

> He further said to them, "Go, eat choice foods and drink sweet drinks and send portions to whoever has nothing prepared, for the day is holy to our Lord. Do not be sad, for your rejoicing in the Lord is the source of your strength." (Nehemiah 8:10)

Do not despair when you hear of the glorious Jewish past in Eretz Yisrael and compare it to today's poverty. Don't worry. Things are going to be great here. Just take care of one another, and provide for the weak and needy. God will take care of all of us. The prophet Zekhariah verbalized this same idea during this same era:

> Thus said the Lord of Hosts: There shall yet be old men and women in the squares of Jerusalem, each with staff in hand because of their great age. And the squares of the city shall be crowded with boys and girls playing in the squares…but what it sows shall prosper: The vine shall produce its fruit, the ground shall produce its yield, and the skies shall provide their moisture. I will bestow all these things upon the remnant of this people… The many peoples and the multitude of nations shall come to seek the Lord of Hosts in Jerusalem and to entreat the favor of the Lord. Thus said the Lord of Hosts: In those days, ten men from nations of every tongue will take hold – they will take hold of every Jew by a corner of his cloak and say, "Let us go with

> you, for we have heard that God is with you." (Zekhariah 8:4-5, 12, 22-23)

Meanwhile, back in Shushan, Mordechai sent Esther to marry the Persian king, changed her Hebrew name of Hadassah to the Persian Esther-Ishtar. Mordechai had already assimilated and taken the name of the Mesopotamian deity, Marduk.

Mordechai's plan was clear: He sought political influence, and the surest path to the palace was through the selection of his beautiful cousin as queen of Persia.

In the background to this story was a deep economic recession, exacerbated by the crowning of Esther and the king's economic populism. This led to a rise in anti-Semitism and enabled the rise of the opportunistic Haman. The consequent threat confronted all the Jews, but Mordechai was most concerned with his personal loss of rank and status in the empire and the economy.

Haman rose to power in order to stabilize or ameliorate the economic crisis. From his perspective, the Jews were an easy scapegoat, especially since killing them off dovetailed with his personal struggles against Mordechai, who refused to recognize Haman's rank and authority. Haman won the king's approval to his genocidal plan by promising an astronomical sum to the king, hoping to recoup the loss through plunder.

Haman's plan failed; the threat to the Jews was removed within four days. The Megilah's author teaches us parenthetically just how deeply assimilated Persia's Jews were. In a time of distress, they neither turned to God nor engaged in true introspection. Mordechai, their leader, did not place his trust in God, but rather in his political connections in the king's court, in Esther's relationship to Ahashverosh, in the king's natural suspicion towards Haman, and in his own ability to influence the king.

The Jews survived the ordeal, but even after they emerged victorious, they never asked themselves what happened and why. From their perspective, it was a matter of fate; the king thought one thing, and then he changed his mind. This constituted a reason for "gladness and joy among the Jews, a feast and a holiday"; four days in the shadow of danger had ended, the Megilah's author mocks, on account of the resourceful queen who managed to seduce the Persian king at precisely the right moment.

Ezra the scribe, upon arriving in Jerusalem, found a band of wretched Jews in a state of spiritual, physical, and cultural crisis. He called out to God and campaigned against the sins that brought calamity to Jerusalem and led to its destruction. He engaged in classic Biblical repentance, rending his garments, plucking the hair from his beard, and petitioning God, on behalf of the entire nation, to forgive their sins: "From the time of our fathers to this very day we have been deep in guilt. Because of our iniquities, we, our kings, and our priests have been handed over to foreign kings, to the sword, to captivity, to pillage, and to humiliation, as is now the case." (Ezra 9:7) He was shocked by the intermarriage among the nobility, the political and economic leaders of Eretz Yisrael, and he raised difficult questions about Jewish-Israelite identity and about the double assimilation that the exile wrought: the Jews on foreign soil assimilated, while the Jews who remained in Eretz Yisrael – a flock of sheep without a shepherd – assimilated in Eretz Yisrael for lack of Jewish civilization and commonwealth.

In Persia, once the danger had passed, Mordechai and Esther returned to their influential roles and intensified their ambitions. Mordechai assumed control of the Persian treasury, a position that had been dramatically vacated with the hanging of Haman.

Mordechai was quite busy. With all of the celebrations and good wishes on the occasion of his new position and his coronation ceremony "in royal robes of blue wool and fine white linen, with a magnificent crown of gold," that there was time for little else. Two entire months went by until he could attend to the unfinished business of canceling Haman's decree.

The end of the story resembles its beginning: Mordechai and Esther brought Diaspora Jewry a few steps closer to becoming Persian. Mordechai "ranked next to King Ahashverosh," restored the Persian economy to its glory days, and imposed "tribute on the mainland and the islands." Nevertheless, Mordechai disappeared. He became Marduk. Esther became Ishtar. Persian Jews became Persians. In a celebratory tone that masks the irony, the Megilah's author states: "All his mighty and powerful acts, and a full account of the greatness to which the king advanced Mordechai, are recorded in the Annals of the Kings of Media and Persia."

This is all true, except for one small detail: neither Esther nor Mordechai is mentioned in the Annals of the Kings of Media and Persia. They and their descendants faded from Jewish history, but ultimately they did not even merit a single line in the Annals of Media and Persia.

Here in Eretz Yisrael, the author indicates, we can deal with the poverty. Jewish identity and Israelite tenacity will once again make the desolation flourish and bloom. It won't be easy, there will be challenges, but ultimately the work will pay off.

Nehemiah, the Biblical character who immediately follows Mordechai, is, as his name indicates, a source of God's comfort (*nehama*). Nehemiah renounces his Persianness, resigns from his high rank at the king's court, and brought his formidable administrative skills to Eretz Yisrael. He faces the schemes of Geshem the Arab, Sanballat the Horonite and Tobiah the Ammonite, who all try to prevent the construction of the wall around Jerusalem, and overcomes them: "The wall was completed on the twenty-fifth of Elul, after fifty-two days."

R. Lau's call, in the introduction to this book, to read the first two chapters of Nehemiah on Purim is not just an acceptable custom, but also an apt one. The Jewish-Israelite national rebirth in Zion is the preferred sequel to the story of Purim. Nehemiah the son of Hakhaliah hears from Hanani about the unfortunate plight of the Jewish refugees, and he is completely shocked. He decides to take action: "The God of Heaven will grant us success, and we, His servants, will start building. But you have no share or claim or stake in Jerusalem!" This is the real lesson of the Megilah: We will arise. We will rebuild. Those who assimilate, to our great sorrow and pain, will have no share or claim or stake. The boat will sail on without them.

We must not become complacent. It is incumbent upon those of us who reside in the State of Israel to have concern for our brothers and sisters, and it is our responsibility to translate our concern into action. We have no right to sit with our arms crossed. We need to create and fashion a caring, embracing State of Israel that attracts Jews and others from around the wide world. The State of Israel in the twenty-first century need not be a refuge for persecuted Jews; it must be a magnet that attracts, accepts, and embraces new immigrants and returning Israelis. We do not want to watch our brothers and sisters of all denominations vanish into foreign cultures, for they are our flesh and blood.

We must rise up and keep building with greater determination. The era of Nahshons and Zerubavels has passed; we have entered the epoch of Nehemiah. We must build an economy here and deepen the Israeli ethos. We are on the way, as innovation and GDP per capita continues to increase. Israel could be within a decade or two of passing the United States in GDP per capita.

There is a great need for dedicated public servants who run the country efficiently, out of care and concern for all of its residents, citizens, and whomever else has entered its borders. It is the responsibility of citizens, entrepreneurs, friends, and neighbors to establish a positive, encouraging economic and cultural atmosphere in which new immigrants and old-timers alike can live well in the land of our collective heritage and shared destiny.

Those who have assimilated have dissolved into an era of unrivaled opportunity in their countries of residence even while the age of globalization allows Israel to offer Diaspora Jews more opportunities than ever before. The small country between the Jordan and the Mediterranean, which in antiquity was situated on major trade routes, has once again become a trade destination for the worlds' merchants and businessmen. Once upon a time, caravans of ancient Canaanite merchants passed through Eretz Yisrael on their way from Egypt and Africa to the Fertile Crescent and Asia Minor. Nowadays, the goods travel in packets, on high speed internet lines. We must make educational, social, cultural, and economic preparations to grant every man and woman in Israel the freedom to contribute their share to the success of others and to attract our brethren from the Diaspora. We must not sit idly by, waiting for an outbreak of anti-Semitism and for Jews to be killed in the streets. In this new era, financial opportunities will be created in Israel – but only if we are determined to build an exemplary society that is based on true mutual responsibility.

Epilogue: A Jewish Wake-Up Call: From Purim-Era Persia to the Modern United States

The 2016 election cycle in the United States, Britain, and elsewhere exposed a growing global trend toward nationalism. When I wrote the first version of this book in Hebrew in 2015, the epilogue summarized the conditions that led to the rise of Haman: a deep but ephemeral financial crisis throughout the empire of Ahasuerus; populist policies that deepened the financial crisis; an opportunist instigator who rose to power on a promise to stabilize the economy. Once in power, the opportunist instigator, now second-in-command of the Old World's first superpower, imperial Persia, worked to dispose of his personal enemies and the Jews.

This is the classic cycle of anti-Semitism. Its roots may run deep, but its fuel and fertilizer is a bad economy. It lies dormant for a while but then pushes through the surface, to the text of royal edicts and to Facebook and Twitter feeds. As has been well-documented, it never ends with the Jews; they are generally just the first victims, the canaries in the coal mine. Eventually, hate claims many victims.

When countries and societies encounter difficult economic times, it rarely leads to introspection. Unfortunately, they do not seek to identify the root causes, examine educational deficiencies, or pinpoint government inadequacies. Rarely, in real time, does the general population or government contemplate the fragility of human psychology or the behavior of *homo economicus*, who joins runs on banks, stock market mania and hysteria, and herd behavior. Instead, it seeks perpetrators, the other. Blame follows. Hate and persecution follow blame.

Economic cycles also tend to have short memories. More accurately, those who live through economic downturns and those who preside over them in the government and bureaucracy rarely learn the right lessons or apply the right policies. Blame games and conspiracy theories become fodder for cocktails and consultations in the king's palace, where the party never stops as taxes roll in.

Concomitantly, many people to whom the economy has been kind in boom times forget those who have been left behind. The fortunate are not adequately solicitous of the economically unfortunate. We are insufficiently mindful of the Biblical commandment to take care of the poor and despondent, to do business with someone who is down on his luck, as Maimonides encourages us – until the unfortunate and misfortunate rise up and revolt, that is. It is the cycle of the economy that drives history.

Generally, xenophobia finds firm footing in tough economies. Anti-Semitism in particular has reared its ugly head time and again as Jews find financial success and then the economy experiences an inevitable downturn. Even when the economy rebounds, the animosity does not disappear. It just builds momentum for the next cycle. Every time we think anti-Semitism is coming to an end – in Babylonia, Spain, Poland and the United States – we find that it has only been hibernating, even for a few centuries, the blink of an eye in historical terms.

The grotesque hate that is rearing its ugly head today is fueled by people's fear for their economic well-being. As Yoda said, "Fear leads to anger. Anger leads to hate. Hate leads to suffering." We must address this fear and hate by redoubling our efforts to understand, engage, and tolerate. The Jewish Sage Hillel's famous admonition, "That which is hateful to you, do not do to your fellow,"[1] is more relevant today than at any time I can remember.

Moreover, we must address this fear with compassion. The fast-moving tech economy of the twenty-first century and the disruption it has wrought with respect to the jobs and economic hope of hundreds of millions of people globally are here to stay. We are in the middle of the greatest disruption since the Industrial Revolution, and perhaps even earlier. Many people across the United States, Great Britain, and other countries have been, and will be, left behind by the information economy. Governments are not doing enough to bring them into this century, nor should we rely on byzantine bureaucracies to help our brethren. It is up to us, the citizenry, to show compassion and caring for our fellow man, *homo economicus*. When others suffer, when they have no jobs or income, it should trouble us and cause sleep to desert us. This is both the deepest of Jewish values and the essence of our humanity. We cannot sit behind browsers and small screens and "like" our way to economic gains. We must collectively roll up our sleeves to create jobs, upward mobility, and empathy and pull people into the twenty-first century. The Talmud tells us that "unemployment leads to boredom and boredom leads to sin."[2] This employment displacement will pass; it always has. It will take time, but jobs will come back. This time is not different. However, the scars of resentment run deep and will outlast the economic downturn.

However deplorable this hatred is, it does not constitute an existential crisis for the Jews who form the primary audience of this book. Hate is an existential crisis for humanity, but not for each culture or people. This is particularly true at the beginning of the twenty-first century, almost

---

1 BT *Shabbat* 31b.

2 BT *Ketubot* 59b. A similar phrase exists in many cultures, for instance: "Boredom is an illness for which work is the remedy" (Pierre-Marc-Gaston de Levis); "Boredom is the root of all evil" (Soren Kierkegaard); and the Arabic saying, "The bored man plays with the devil."

seventy years after the founding of the State of Israel. The snowballing hate might become a physical crisis for Diaspora Jews, as happened in Persia, Babylonia, Medieval England, France, Spain, Russia, Egypt, Syria, and Germany. However, in the collective American experience, anti-Semitism has not directly claimed many lives nor caused much discomfort on US soil, yet. Although, one can argue, as the great R. Samson Raphael Hirsch did, that hate fosters ethnic, cultural, and religious solidarity among persecuted minorities, I don't think that we should aspire for such a dangerous and lethal approach to Jewish identity.

There is a more pernicious – though less lethal – threat to the Jewish people, as I detailed throughout the book and that I am concerned with here. It is far more dangerous to Jewish peoplehood because it is both a long-term threat and is subtle. It does not stare us in the face or fill our social media feeds. It happens slowly, gradually. It is noticed only when it is too late, after the kids have flown the coop. It is an uncomfortable topic, so we don't really confront it early enough or often enough. Assimilation is the primary threat against cultures and peoples. It is a silent killer of cultures, religions, and peoples, and by the time one is alerted to it, it's too late. And it is silently killing the Jewishness of Jews in the United States and Europe. The assimilated and their progeny are no longer Jewish, neither by birth nor by choice.

As I detailed in these chapters, the numbers bear this out. The rate of assimilation is accelerating, regardless of stream or denomination. I know that many of my Orthodox friends will point to a growing Orthodox population as a counter-argument, but this is both myopic and ignorant of history. The Jewish population of the United States is shrinking – and shrinking rapidly. Orthodox growth is a historical blip that proves only that right now, fertility rates among the Orthodox are very high relative to other denominations and in absolute terms. It says nothing of the predisposition of those children to stay true to Judaism in the face of 400 million other people who determine the cultural milieu these children will grow up in or the national affiliations that will lay claim to them. Moreover, we are still early in the game. As I pointed out throughout the Megilah story, the key generation is the fourth one. Many of the Orthodox, especially the Hasidic sects with the highest birth rates, are just beginning to produce their fourth generations in America. And even if they hang on for an extra generation or two, they will assimilate, too, as surely as the sun sets.

Many Israelis who read the Hebrew edition of this book told me of friends who had moved to the United States, settled in, and were now worried about their children intermarrying and shedding generations' worth of Israeli identity or Jewishness. Statistics and anecdotal evidence alike show their worries are well-founded. The pursuit of economic opportunity caused them to look the other way while their kids lost their identity. This does not mean that everyone will assimilate; it means that the numbers are against you maintaining your Judaism.

I am not judging anyone; people are entitled to make their own choices. A key tenet of the Jewish religion is *behira hofshit,* the power of free choice. You have the power to choose whether, and to what extent, you will risk assimilation in a host culture. You have the power to choose whether to send your children to the Jewish school, the cheaper school, or the better school. However, it is important to remember that choices have consequences, even when they are not immediate. I wrote this book because I believe that this is the message that the author of the Megilah wanted to convey and because I want the choice to be an informed choice. We tend to ignore consequences when they are not clear and present; my goal is to place those uncomfortable consequences front and center.

Not long after publishing the Hebrew edition of this book, I had the opportunity to meet David Bloomberg, the Chairman of the National Library of Israel, someone who I have known for over 20 years. He asked me if I knew how many Jews moved from Russia and Poland to North and South America at the end of the nineteenth and beginning of the twentieth century. I did not. There were 3.5 million such Jews. He asked me what I think happened to those Jews, who are now five and six generations post-immigration? There was little to no lethal anti-Semitism in North and South America during those times. How many Jews would there be in the United States today, had they not assimilated? How many Americans, with no Jewish identity to speak of, have Jewish ancestors in the not-too-distant past?

For most of history, there were no "denominations" in Judaism. One either remained part of the Jewish community, which tolerated a certain degree of non-observance but closely resembled what we call "Orthodox" today, or else one left the fold, assimilated into the host culture, and lost their Jewish roots. Why? Because it is objectively difficult to hold onto two core identities. It is more difficult to hold onto both identities (Jewish and American, for example) as one becomes more successful and integrates more fully into the host society, as Mordechai did. More potently, social psychologists have argued[3] that social structures and society shape one's identity, until eventually that identity has morphed into something different from the root identity and in turn becomes the "root" identity of the next generation, which likewise undergoes change. This helps explain the fourth-generation phenomenon of assimilation that we see with respect to Mordechai in the Megilah as well as in every Diaspora.

Not everyone assimilates. Some prioritize their Jewish identity over that of their host nationality. They choose to be Jewish and not American or French. It is difficult but not impossible. This book, however, deals with the masses; the masses assimilate, and the numbers prove it. Most likely, a significant number of your descendants will be part of those masses. As I mentioned in the prologue, I have second cousins who have assimilated. Their ancestor, my great-grandfather, would never have dreamt that it

3 George Herbert Mead, *Mind, Self, and Society* (Chicago: University of Chicago Press, 1934).

could happen to him. I am sure many of you have second cousins who no longer know they are Jewish or identify as Jews.

Ezra the Scribe understood this phenomenon when he implored the Jewish people in Eretz Yisrael to learn the lessons that the Jews were failing to learn in exile. Nehemiah got his wake up call in the king's palace, and only when he arrived in Eretz Yisrael could he look back and understand that Mordechai lacked a sense of Jewish kinship. This book examines those who rise to roles of political and economic leadership, who have suppressed their Jewish identity in favor of their Persian, American, French, or British identity. However, this is not a historical examination. It is as relevant today as ever.

Just as a small number of Jews returned to Zion with Zerubavel 2500 years ago, a small number came back in the 1800s and early 1900s, in the first waves of *aliyah*. Just as a larger number returned during the times of Ezra and Nehemiah, so too, there have been great waves of *aliyah* since the 1940s. Most of these Jews came to Israel to escape persecution and hardship, from host countries that identified them as Jews, even if they themselves did not identify foremost as Jews; some, particularly the early waves, when the doors to wealthy states were still open, came out of free choice and with a strong sense of identity.

Nehemiah also saw the ills of his new society in Eretz Yisrael. No society is perfect. Politics and nation building are messy. He railed against intermarriage, idolatry, Shabbat desecration, and corruption amongst the Jews of Eretz Yisrael.[4] He recalled that the financial success of King Shlomo brought moral turpitude and religious attrition. He urged the people who were building the foundation of the second Jewish commonwealth to repent and build a model society. However, he, Nehemiah, was part of the solution. He was, in the immortal words of Teddy Roosevelt, "in the arena."[5]

4 Nehemiah ch. 13.

5 "It is not the critic who counts; not the man who points out how the strong man

Nehemiah understood that the calendar and character of the entire society was the only way to perpetuate a strong sense of identity, of Jewish identity. He and Ezra kicked off an era that lasted for centuries, during which the Jews of Eretz Yisrael laid the foundations for the post-Biblical Judaism that has survived to this day. They sculpted the contours of Jewish identity, held onto the Jewish calendar and its holidays, and formulated the ethical, moral, and interpretive covenants of our people. That is our challenge and opportunity today as well. It is insufficient to avoid doing bad things ("*sur me-ra*" – "turn away from evil," in the words of the psalmist) and just not assimilate; we must do good, "*aseh tov*," and build the future of the Jewish people. I firmly believe we have a message for humanity, a responsibility toward the people of the world, many of whom are suffering, from Syria to the heartland of America. Today, we have an opportunity to be a light unto the nations, do unto others as we wish others would do unto us. We can do it as a nation, but only if we harness all of our greatest talents. Make sure you are "in the arena," now and for generations to come.

---

stumbles, or where the doer of deeds could have done them better. The credit belongs to the man who is actually in the arena, whose face is marred by dust and sweat and blood; who strives valiantly; who errs, who comes short again and again, because there is no effort without error and shortcoming; but who does actually strive to do the deeds; who knows great enthusiasms, the great devotions; who spends himself in a worthy cause; who at the best knows in the end the triumph of high achievement, and who at the worst, if he fails, at least fails while daring greatly, so that his place shall never be with those cold and timid souls who neither know victory nor defeat." From "Citizenship in a Republic," a speech delivered at the Sorbonne in Paris, France on April 23, 1910.

English Translation of the Book of Esther

Based on the 1985 Jewish Publication Society translation

Chapter One

1 It happened in the days of Ahashverosh – that Ahashverosh who reigned
over a hundred and twenty-seven provinces from India to Ethiopia. 2 In
those days, when King Ahashverosh occupied the royal throne in Shushan
the capital, 3 in the third year of his reign, he gave a banquet for all the
officials and courtiers – the military leadership of Persia and Media, the
nobles and the governors of the provinces in his service. 4 For no fewer
than a hundred and eighty days he displayed the vast riches of his kingdom
and the magnificent prestige of his majesty. 5 At the end of this period, the
king gave a banquet for seven days in the courtyard of the king's palace
garden for all the people who lived in Shushan the capital, high and low
alike. 6 [There were hangings of] white cotton and blue wool, caught
up by cords of fine linen and purple wool to silver rods and alabaster
columns; and there were couches of gold and silver on a pavement of
marble, alabaster, mother-of-pearl, and mosaics. 7 Royal wine was served
in abundance, as befits a king, in golden beakers, beakers of varied design.
8 And the rule for the drinking was, "No restrictions!" For the king had
given orders to every palace steward to comply with each man's wishes.
9 In addition, Queen Vashti gave a banquet for women, in the royal palace
of King Ahashverosh.

10 On the seventh day, when the king was merry with wine, he ordered
Mehuman, Bizzeta, Harvona, Bigta, Avagta, Zetar, and Karkas, the seven
eunuchs in attendance on King Ahashverosh, 11 to bring Queen Vashti
before the king wearing a royal diadem, to display her beauty to the
peoples and the officials; for she was good-looking. 12 But Queen Vashti
refused to come at the king's command conveyed by the eunuchs. The king
was greatly incensed, and his fury burned within him.
13 Then the king consulted the sages learned in procedure. (For it was the
royal practice [to turn] to all who were versed in law and precedent. 14 His
closest advisors were Karshena, Shetar, Admata, Tarshish, Meres, Marsena,
and Memukhan, the seven ministers of Persia and Media who had access to
the royal presence and occupied the first place in the kingdom.) 15 "What,"
[he asked,] "shall be done, according to law, to Queen Vashti for failing to
obey the command of King Ahashverosh conveyed by the eunuchs?"
16 Thereupon Memukhan declared in the presence of the king and the
ministers: "Queen Vashti has committed an offense not only against Your
Majesty but also against all the officials and against all the peoples in all
the provinces of King Ahashverosh. 17 For the queen's behavior will make
all wives despise their husbands, as they reflect that King Ahashverosh
himself ordered Queen Vashti to be brought before him, but she would
not come. 18 This very day the ladies of Persia and Media, who have heard
of the queen's behavior, will cite it to all Your Majesty's officials, and there
will be no end of scorn and provocation!
19 "If it please Your Majesty, let a royal edict be issued by you, and let it be
written into the laws of Persia and Media, so that it cannot be abrogated,
that Vashti shall never enter the presence of King Ahashverosh. And let
Your Majesty bestow her royal state upon another who is more worthy
than she. 20 Then will the judgment executed by Your Majesty resound
throughout your realm, vast though it is; and all wives will defer to their
husbands, high and low alike."
21 The proposal was approved by the king and the ministers, and the king

did as Memukhan proposed. 22 Dispatches were sent to all the provinces of
the king, to every province in its own script and to every nation in its own
language, that every man should wield authority in his home and speak
the language of his own people.

Chapter Two

1 Sometime afterward, when the anger of King Ahashverosh subsided,
he thought of Vashti and what she had done and what had been decreed
against her. 2 The king's servants who attended him said, "Let beautiful
young virgins be sought out for Your Majesty. 3 Let Your Majesty appoint
officers in every province of your realm to assemble all the beautiful
young virgins in Shushan the capital, in the harem under the supervision
of Hege, the king's eunuch, guardian of the women. Let them be provided
with their cosmetics. 4 And let the maiden who pleases Your Majesty be
queen instead of Vashti." The proposal pleased the king, and he acted
upon it.
5 In Shushan the capital lived a Jewish man by the name of Mordechai,
son of Yair son of Shimi son of Kish, a Benjaminite. 6 Who had been
exiled from Jerusalem in the group that was carried into exile along with
King Yekhoniah of Judah, which had been driven into exile by King
Nebuchadnezzar of Babylon. – 7 He was foster father to Hadassah – that
is, Esther – his uncle's daughter, for she had neither father nor mother. The
maiden was shapely and good-looking; and when her father and mother
died, Mordechai adopted her as his own daughter.
8 When the king's order and edict was heard, and when many girls were
assembled in Shushan the capital under the supervision of Hegai, Esther
too was taken into the king's palace under the supervision of Hegai,
guardian of the women. 9 The girl pleased him and won his favor, and he
hastened to furnish her with her cosmetics and her rations, as well as with
the seven maids who were her due from the king's palace; and he treated
her and her maids with special kindness in the harem. 10 Esther did not

reveal her people or her kindred, for Mordechai had told her not to reveal
it. 11 Every single day Mordechai would walk about in front of the court of
the harem, to learn how Esther was faring and what was happening to her.
12 When each girl's turn came to go to King Ahashverosh at the end of the
twelve months' treatment prescribed for women (for that was the period
spent on beautifying them: six months with oil of myrrh and six months
with perfumes and women's cosmetics, 13 and it was after that that the
girl would go to the king), whatever she asked for would be given her to
take with her from the harem to the king's palace. 14 She would go in the
evening and leave in the morning for a second harem under the charge
of Shaashgaz, the king's eunuch, guardian of the concubines. She would
not go again to the king unless the king wanted her, when she would
be summoned by name. 15 When the turn came for Esther daughter of
Avichayil – the uncle of Mordechai, who had adopted her as his own
daughter – to go to the king, she did not ask for anything but what Hegai,
the king's eunuch, guardian of the women, advised. Yet Esther won the
admiration of all who saw her.

16 Esther was taken to King Ahashverosh, in his royal palace, in the tenth
month, which is the month of Tevet, in the seventh year of his reign. 17 The
king loved Esther more than all the other women, and she won his grace
and favor more than all the virgins. So he set a royal diadem on her head
and made her queen instead of Vashti. 18 The king gave a great banquet
for all his officials and courtiers, "the banquet of Esther." He proclaimed
a remission of taxes for the provinces and distributed gifts as befits
a king.

19 When the virgins were assembled a second time, Mordechai sat in the
palace gate. 20 But Esther still did not reveal her kindred or her people, as
Mordechai had instructed her; for Esther obeyed Mordechai's bidding, as
she had done when she was under his tutelage.

21 At that time, when Mordechai was sitting in the palace gate, Bigtan and
Teresh, two of the king's eunuchs who guarded the threshold, became

angry, and sought to do violence to King Ahashverosh. 22 Mordechai
learned of it and told it to Queen Esther, and Esther reported it to the
king in Mordechai's name. 23 The matter was investigated and found to be
so, and the two were hanged on beams. This was recorded in the book of
annals at the instance of the king.

Chapter Three

1 In the aftermath of these things, King Ahashverosh promoted Haman son
of Hammedata the Agagite; he advanced him and seated him higher than
any of his fellow officials. 2 All the king's courtiers in the palace gate knelt
and bowed low to Haman, for such was the king's order concerning him;
but Mordechai would not kneel or bow low. 3 Then the king's courtiers
who were in the palace gate said to Mordechai, "Why do you disobey
the king's order?" 4 When they spoke to him day after day and he would
not listen to them, they told Haman, in order to see whether Mordechai's
resolve would prevail; for he had explained to them that he was a Jew.
5 When Haman saw that Mordechai would not kneel or bow low to him,
Haman was filled with rage. 6 But he disdained to lay hands on Mordechai
alone; having been told who Mordechai's people were, Haman plotted to
do away with all the Jews, Mordechai's people, throughout the kingdom
of Ahashverosh.

7 In the first month, that is, the month of Nisan, in the twelfth year
of King Ahashverosh, pur – which means "the lot" – was cast before
Haman concerning every day and every month, [until it fell on] the
twelfth month, that is, the month of Adar. 8 Haman then said to King
Ahashverosh, "There is a certain people, scattered and dispersed among
the other peoples in all the provinces of your realm, whose laws are
different from those of any other people and who do not obey the king's
laws; and it is not worth it for Your Majesty to tolerate them. 9 If it please
Your Majesty, let an edict be drawn for their destruction, and I will pay
ten thousand talents of silver to the stewards for deposit in the royal

treasury." 10 Thereupon the king removed his signet ring from his hand
and gave it to Haman son of Hammedata the Agagite, the foe of the
Jews. 11 And the king said, "The money and the people are yours to do
with as you see fit."
12 On the thirteenth day of the first month, the king's scribes were
summoned and a decree was issued, as Haman directed, to the king's
satraps, to the governors of every province, and to the officials of every
people, to every province in its own script and to every people in its own
language. The orders were issued in the name of King Ahashverosh and
sealed with the king's signet. 13 Accordingly, written instructions were
dispatched by couriers to all the king's provinces to destroy, massacre, and
exterminate all the Jews, young and old, children and women, on a single
day, on the thirteenth day of the twelfth month – that is, the month of
Adar – and to plunder their possessions. 14 The text of the document was
to the effect that a law should be proclaimed in every single province; it
was to be publicly displayed to all the peoples, so that they might be ready
for that day.
15 The couriers went out posthaste on the royal mission, and the decree
was proclaimed in Shushan the capital. The king and Haman sat down to
feast, but the city of Shushan was dumfounded.

Chapter Four

1 Mordechai learned of all that had happened, Mordechai tore his clothes
and put on sackcloth and ashes. He went through the city, and he cried
out loudly and bitterly, 2 until he came in front of the palace gate; for
one could not enter the palace gate wearing sackcloth.– 3 Also, in every
province that the king's command and decree reached, there was great
mourning among the Jews, with fasting, weeping, and wailing, and
everybody lay in sackcloth and ashes.– 4 When Esther's maidens and
eunuchs came and informed her, the queen was greatly agitated. She sent

clothing for Mordechai to wear, so that he might take off his sackcloth;
but he refused.
5 Thereupon Esther summoned Hatakh, one of the eunuchs whom the
king had appointed to serve her, and sent him to Mordechai to learn the
why and wherefore of it all. 6 Hatakh went out to Mordechai in the city
square in front of the palace gate; 7 and Mordechai told him all that had
happened to him, and all about the money that Haman had offered to
pay into the royal treasury for the destruction of the Jews. 8 He also gave
him the written text of the law that had been proclaimed in Shushan for
their destruction. [He bade him] show it to Esther and inform her, and
charge her to go to the king and to appeal to him and to plead with him for
her people. 9 When Hatakh told Esther Mordechai's words, 10 Esther told
Hatakh to take back to Mordechai the following reply: 11 "All the king's
courtiers and the people of the king's provinces know that if any person,
man or woman, enters the king's presence in the inner court without
having been summoned, there is but one law for him – that he be put to
death. Only if the king extends the golden scepter to him may he live. Now
I have not been summoned to visit the king for the last thirty days."
12 They told Mordechai what Esther said, 13 Mordechai had this message
delivered to Esther: "Do not imagine that you, of all the Jews, will escape
with your life by being in the king's palace. 14 On the contrary, if you
keep silent in this crisis, relief and deliverance will come to the Jews from
another quarter, while you and your father's house will perish. And who
knows, perhaps you have attained to royal position for just such a crisis."
15 Then Esther sent back this answer to Mordechai: 16 "Go, assemble all
the Jews who live in Shushan, and fast in my behalf; do not eat or drink
for three days, night or day. I and my maidens will observe the same fast.
Then I shall go to the king, though it is contrary to the law; and if I am to
perish, I shall perish!" 17 So Mordechai went about [the city] and did just
as Esther had commanded him.

Chapter Five

1 On the third day, Esther put on royal apparel and stood in the inner
court of the king's palace, facing the king's palace, while the king was
sitting on his royal throne in the throne room facing the entrance of the
palace. 2 As soon as the king saw Queen Esther standing in the court, she
won his favor. The king extended to Esther the golden scepter which he
had in his hand, and Esther approached and touched the tip of the scepter.
3 "What troubles you, Queen Esther?" the king asked her. "And what is
your request? Even up to half the kingdom, it shall be granted you." 4 "If it
please Your Majesty," Esther replied, "let Your Majesty and Haman come
today to the feast that I have prepared for him." 5 The king commanded,
"Tell Haman to hurry and do Esther's bidding." So the king and Haman
came to the feast that Esther had prepared.

6 At the wine feast, the king asked Esther, "What is your wish? It shall
be granted you. And what is your request? Even up to half the kingdom,
it shall be fulfilled." 7 "My wish," replied Esther, "my request – 8 if Your
Majesty will do me the favor, if it please Your Majesty to grant my wish
and accede to my request – let Your Majesty and Haman come to the feast
which I will prepare for them; and tomorrow I will do Your Majesty's
bidding."

9 That day Haman went out happy and lighthearted. But when Haman
saw Mordechai in the palace gate, and Mordechai did not rise or even
stir on his account, Haman was filled with rage at him. 10 Nevertheless,
Haman controlled himself and went home. He sent for his friends and his
wife Zeresh, 11 and Haman told them about his great wealth and his many
sons, and all about how the king had promoted him and advanced him
above the officials and the king's courtiers. 12 "What is more," said Haman,
"Queen Esther gave a feast, and besides the king she did not have anyone
but me. And tomorrow too I am invited by her along with the king. 13 Yet
all this is worth nothing to me every time I see that Jew Mordechai sitting
in the palace gate." 14 Then his wife Zeresh and all his friends said to him,

"Let a beam be put up, fifty *amot* high, and in the morning ask the king to have Mordechai hanged on it. Then you can go gaily with the king to the feast." The proposal pleased Haman, and he had the beam put up.

Chapter Six

1 That night, sleep deserted the king, and he ordered the book of records,
the annals, to be brought; and it was read to the king. 2 There it was
found written that Mordechai had denounced Bigtana and Teresh, two
of the king's eunuchs who guarded the threshold, who had plotted to do
away with King Ahashverosh. 3 "What glory or advancement has been
conferred on Mordechai for this?" the king inquired. "Nothing at all has
been done for him," replied the king's servants who were in attendance
on him. 4 "Who is in the court?" the king asked. For Haman had just
entered the outer court of the royal palace, to speak to the king about
having Mordechai hanged on the beam he had prepared for him. 5 "It is
Haman standing in the court," the king's servants answered him. "Let him
enter," said the king. 6 Haman entered, and the king asked him, "What
should be done for a man to whom the king desires to show prestige?"
Haman said to himself, "Whom would the king desire to show prestige
more than me?" 7 So Haman said to the king, "For the man whom the
king desires to show prestige 8 let royal garb which the king has worn be
brought, and a horse on which the king has ridden and on whose head a
royal diadem has been set; 9 and let the attire and the horse be put in the
charge of one of the king's noble courtiers. And let the man whom the
king desires to honor be attired and paraded on the horse through the
city square, while they proclaim before him: This is what is done for the
man whom the king desires to show prestige!" 10 "Quick, then!" said the
king to Haman. "Get the garb and the horse, as you have said, and do this
to Mordechai the Jew, who sits in the king's gate. Omit nothing of all you
have proposed." 11 So Haman took the garb and the horse and arrayed
Mordechai and paraded him through the city square; and he proclaimed

before him: This is what is done for the man whom the king desires to
show prestige!
12 Then Mordechai returned to the king's gate, while Haman was hurried
home, his head covered in mourning. 13 There Haman told his wife Zeresh
and all his friends all that had happened to him. His advisors and his wife
Zeresh said to him, "If Mordechai, before whom you have begun to fall,
is of Jewish stock, you will not overcome him; you will fall before him to
your ruin."
14 While they were still speaking with him, the king's eunuchs arrived and
hurriedly brought Haman to the banquet which Esther had prepared.

Chapter Seven

1 So the king and Haman came to drink with Queen Esther. 2 On the
second day, the king again asked Esther at the wine feast, "What is your
wish, Queen Esther? It shall be granted you. And what is your request?
Even up to half the kingdom, it shall be fulfilled." 3 Queen Esther replied:
"If Your Majesty will do me the favor, and if it pleases Your Majesty, let my
life be granted me as my wish, and my people as my request. 4 For we have
been sold, my people and I, to be destroyed, massacred, and exterminated.
Had we only been sold as bondmen and bondwomen, I would have kept
silent; for no such distress is worthy of the king's trouble."
5 Thereupon King Ahashverosh demanded of Queen Esther, "Who is he?
Who dared to do this?" 6 "The man is an adversary and enemy," replied
Esther, "it is this evil Haman!" And Haman cringed in terror before the
king and the queen. 7 The king, in his fury, left the wine feast for the
palace garden, while Haman remained to plead with Queen Esther for
his life; for he saw that the king had resolved to destroy him. 8 When the
king returned from the palace garden to the banquet room, Haman was
falling on the couch on which Esther reclined. "Does he also mean," cried
the king, "to conquer the queen in my own palace?" No sooner did these
words leave the king's lips than Haman's face was covered. 9 Then Harvona,

one of the eunuchs in attendance on the king, said, "What is more, a beam
is standing at Haman's house, fifty cubits high, which Haman made for
Mordechai – the man whose words saved the king." "Hang him on it!" the
king ordered. 10 So they hanged Haman on the beam which he had put up
for Mordechai, and the king's fury abated.

Chapter Eight

1 That very day King Ahashverosh gave the property of Haman, the enemy
of the Jews, to Queen Esther. Mordechai presented himself to the king, for
Esther had revealed how he was related to her. 2 The king slipped off his
ring, which he had taken back from Haman, and gave it to Mordechai; and
Esther put Mordechai in charge of Haman's property.
3 Esther spoke to the king again, falling at his feet and weeping, and
beseeching him to avert the evil plotted by Haman the Agagite against the
Jews. 4 The king extended the golden scepter to Esther, and Esther arose
and stood before the king. 5 "If it please Your Majesty," she said, "and if I
have won your favor and the proposal seems right to Your Majesty, and
if I am pleasing to you – let dispatches be written countermanding those
which were written by Haman son of Hammedata the Agagite, embodying
his plot to annihilate the Jews throughout the king's provinces. 6 For how
can I bear to see the disaster which will befall my people! And how can I
bear to see the destruction of my kindred!"
7 Then King Ahashverosh said to Queen Esther and Mordechai the Jew,
"I have given Haman's property to Esther, and he has been hanged on the
beam for doing violence to the Jews. 8 And you may further write with
regard to the Jews as you see fit. [Write it] in the king's name and seal it
with the king's signet, for an edict that has been written in the king's name
and sealed with the king's signet may not be revoked."
9 So the king's scribes were summoned at that time, on the twenty-third
day of the third month, that is, the month of Sivan; and letters were written,
at Mordechai's dictation, to the Jews and to the satraps, the governors and

the officials of the one hundred and twenty-seven provinces from India
to Ethiopia: to every province in its own script and to every people in its
own language, and to the Jews in their own script and language. 10 He
had them written in the name of King Ahashverosh and sealed with the
king's signet. Letters were dispatched by mounted couriers, riding steeds
used in the king's service, bred of the royal stud, 11 to this effect: The
king has permitted the Jews of every city to assemble and fight for their
lives; if any people or province attacks them, they may destroy, massacre,
and exterminate its armed force together with women and children, and
plunder their possessions – 12 on a single day in all the provinces of King
Ahashverosh, namely, on the thirteenth day of the twelfth month, that is,
the month of Adar. 13 The text of the document was to be issued as a law
in every single province: it was to be publicly displayed to all the peoples,
so that the Jews should be ready for that day to avenge themselves on their
enemies. 14 The couriers, mounted on royal steeds, went out in urgent
haste at the king's command; and the decree was proclaimed in Shushan
the capital.

15 Mordechai left the king's presence in royal robes of blue wool and fine
white linen, with a magnificent crown of gold and a mantle of fine linen
and purple wool. And the city of Shushan rang with joyous cries. 16 The
Jews enjoyed light and gladness, happiness and honor. 17 And in every
province and in every city, when the king's command and decree arrived,
there was gladness and joy among the Jews, a feast and a holiday. And
many of the people of the land professed to be Jews, for the fear of the Jews
had fallen upon them.

Chapter Nine

1 And so, on the thirteenth day of the twelfth month – that is, the month
of Adar – when the king's command and decree were to be executed, the
very day on which the enemies of the Jews had expected to get them in
their power, the opposite happened, and the Jews got their enemies in

their power. 2 Throughout the provinces of King Ahashverosh, the Jews
assembled in their cities to do violence to those who sought their hurt;
and no one stood in their way, for the fear of them had fallen upon all
the peoples. 3 Indeed, all the officials of the provinces – the satraps, the
governors, and the king's stewards – championed to the Jews, because
the fear of Mordechai had fallen upon them. 4 For Mordechai was now
powerful in the royal palace, and his fame was spreading through all the
provinces; the man Mordechai was growing ever more powerful. 5 So the
Jews struck at their enemies with the sword, slaying and destroying; they
wreaked their will upon their enemies.

6 In Shushan the capital the Jews killed a total of five hundred men. 7 They
also killed Parshandata, Dalphon, Aspata, 8 Porata, Adalia, Aridata,
9 Parmashta, Arisai, Aridai, and Vayzata, 10 the ten sons of Haman son of
Hammedata, the foe of the Jews. But they did not lay hands on the spoil.
11 When the number of those slain in Shushan the capital was reported on
that same day to the king, 12 the king said to Queen Esther, "In Shushan
the capital alone the Jews have killed a total of five hundred men, as well as
the ten sons of Haman. What then must they have done in the provinces of
the realm! What is your wish now? It shall be granted you. And what else
is your request? It shall be fulfilled." 13 "If it please Your Majesty," Esther
replied, "let the Jews in Shushan be permitted to act tomorrow also as
they did today; and let Haman's ten sons be hanged on the beam." 14 The
king ordered that this should be done, and the decree was proclaimed
in Shushan. Haman's ten sons were hanged: 15 and the Jews in Shushan
assembled again on the fourteenth day of Adar and slew three hundred
men in Shushan. But they did not lay hands on the spoil.

16 The rest of the Jews, those in the king's provinces, likewise assembled
and fought for their lives. They disposed of their enemies, killing seventy-
five thousand of their foes; but they did not lay hands on the spoil. 17 That
was on the thirteenth day of the month of Adar; and they rested on the
fourteenth day and made it a day of feasting and merrymaking. (18 But

the Jews in Shushan gathered on both the thirteenth and fourteenth
days, and so rested on the fifteenth, and made it a day of feasting and
merrymaking.) 19 That is why village Jews, who live in unwalled towns,
observe the fourteenth day of the month of Adar and make it a day of
merrymaking and feasting, and as a holiday and an occasion for sending
gifts to one another.
20 Mordechai recorded these events. And he sent dispatches to all the Jews
throughout the provinces of King Ahashverosh, near and far, 21 charging
them to observe the fourteenth and fifteenth days of Adar, every year –
22 the same days on which the Jews enjoyed relief from their foes and
the same month which had been transformed for them from one of grief
and mourning to one of festive joy. They were to observe them as days of
feasting and merrymaking, and as an occasion for sending gifts to one
another and presents to the needy. 23 The Jews accordingly assumed as an
obligation that which they had begun to practice and which Mordechai
prescribed for them.
24 For Haman son of Hammedata the Agagite, the foe of all the Jews, had
plotted to destroy the Jews, and had cast pur – that is, the lot – with intent
to crush and exterminate them. 25 But when [Esther] came before the
king, he commanded: "With the promulgation of this decree, let the evil
plot, which he devised against the Jews, recoil on his own head!" So they
hanged him and his sons on the beam. 26 For that reason they called these
days Purim, after the *pur*. For that reason, of all the instructions in the
said letter and of what they had experienced in that matter and what had
befallen them – 27 the Jews undertook and obligated themselves and their
descendants that it cannot be abrogated, to observe these two days in the
manner prescribed and at the proper time each year. 28 And these days are
recalled and observed in every generation: by every family, every province,
and every city. And these days of Purim shall never cease among the Jews,
and the memory of them shall never perish among their descendants.
29 Then Queen Esther daughter of Avichayil wrote a second letter of Purim

for the purpose of confirming with full authority the aforementioned
one of Mordechai the Jew. 30 Dispatches were sent to all the Jews in the
hundred and twenty-seven provinces of the realm of Ahashverosh with
an ordinance of integrity and honesty. 31 These days of Purim shall be
observed at their proper time, as Mordechai the Jew – and now Queen
Esther – has obligated them to do, and just as they have assumed for
themselves and their descendants the obligation of the fasts with their
lamentations.
32 And Esther's ordinance validating these observances of Purim was
recorded in a scroll.

Chapter Ten

1 King Ahashverosh imposed tribute on the mainland and the islands.
2 All his mighty and powerful acts, and a full account of the greatness to
which the king advanced Mordechai, are recorded in the Annals of the
Kings of Media and Persia. 3 For Mordechai the Jew ranked next to King
Ahashverosh and was highly regarded by the Jews and popular with the
multitude of his brethren; he sought the good of his people and interceded
for the welfare of all his descendants.

וּמֵאָה מְדִינָה—מַלְכוּת, אֲחַשְׁוֵרוֹשׁ: דִּבְרֵי שָׁלוֹם, וֶאֱמֶת. לא לְקַיֵּם אֶת־יְמֵי הַפֻּרִים
הָאֵלֶּה בִּזְמַנֵּיהֶם, כַּאֲשֶׁר קִיַּם עֲלֵיהֶם מָרְדֳּכַי הַיְּהוּדִי וְאֶסְתֵּר הַמַּלְכָּה, וְכַאֲשֶׁר קִיְּמוּ
עַל־נַפְשָׁם, וְעַל־זַרְעָם: דִּבְרֵי הַצּוֹמוֹת, וְזַעֲקָתָם. לב וּמַאֲמַר אֶסְתֵּר—קִיַּם, דִּבְרֵי
הַפֻּרִים הָאֵלֶּה; וְנִכְתָּב, בַּסֵּפֶר.

פרק י

א וַיָּשֶׂם הַמֶּלֶךְ אחשרש (אֲחַשְׁוֵרֹשׁ) מַס עַל־הָאָרֶץ, וְאִיֵּי הַיָּם. ב וְכָל־מַעֲשֵׂה תָקְפּוֹ,
וּגְבוּרָתוֹ, וּפָרָשַׁת גְּדֻלַּת מָרְדֳּכַי, אֲשֶׁר גִּדְּלוֹ הַמֶּלֶךְ—הֲלוֹא־הֵם כְּתוּבִים, עַל־סֵפֶר
דִּבְרֵי הַיָּמִים, לְמַלְכֵי, מָדַי וּפָרָס. ג כִּי מָרְדֳּכַי הַיְּהוּדִי, מִשְׁנֶה לַמֶּלֶךְ אֲחַשְׁוֵרוֹשׁ,
וְגָדוֹל לַיְּהוּדִים, וְרָצוּי לְרֹב אֶחָיו—דֹּרֵשׁ טוֹב לְעַמּוֹ, וְדֹבֵר שָׁלוֹם לְכָל־זַרְעוֹ.

הַהוּא, בָּא מִסְפַּר הַהֲרוּגִים בְּשׁוּשַׁן הַבִּירָה—לִפְנֵי הַמֶּלֶךְ. יב וַיֹּאמֶר הַמֶּלֶךְ לְאֶסְתֵּר
הַמַּלְכָּה, בְּשׁוּשַׁן הַבִּירָה הָרְגוּ הַיְּהוּדִים וְאַבֵּד חֲמֵשׁ מֵאוֹת אִישׁ וְאֵת עֲשֶׂרֶת בְּנֵי־
הָמָן—בִּשְׁאָר מְדִינוֹת הַמֶּלֶךְ, מֶה עָשׂוּ; וּמַה־שְּׁאֵלָתֵךְ וְיִנָּתֵן לָךְ, וּמַה־בַּקָּשָׁתֵךְ עוֹד
וְתֵעָשׂ. יג וַתֹּאמֶר אֶסְתֵּר, אִם־עַל־הַמֶּלֶךְ טוֹב—יִנָּתֵן גַּם־מָחָר לַיְּהוּדִים אֲשֶׁר בְּשׁוּשָׁן,
לַעֲשׂוֹת כְּדָת הַיּוֹם; וְאֵת עֲשֶׂרֶת בְּנֵי־הָמָן, יִתְלוּ עַל־הָעֵץ. יד וַיֹּאמֶר הַמֶּלֶךְ לְהֵעָשׂוֹת
כֵּן, וַתִּנָּתֵן דָּת בְּשׁוּשָׁן; וְאֵת עֲשֶׂרֶת בְּנֵי־הָמָן, תָּלוּ. טו וַיִּקָּהֲלוּ היהודיים (הַיְּהוּדִים)
אֲשֶׁר־בְּשׁוּשָׁן, גַּם בְּיוֹם אַרְבָּעָה עָשָׂר לְחֹדֶשׁ אֲדָר, וַיַּהַרְגוּ בְשׁוּשָׁן, שְׁלֹשׁ מֵאוֹת אִישׁ;
וּבַבִּזָּה—לֹא שָׁלְחוּ, אֶת־יָדָם. טז וּשְׁאָר הַיְּהוּדִים אֲשֶׁר בִּמְדִינוֹת הַמֶּלֶךְ נִקְהֲלוּ וְעָמֹד
עַל־נַפְשָׁם, וְנוֹחַ מֵאֹיְבֵיהֶם, וְהָרוֹג בְּשֹׂנְאֵיהֶם, חֲמִשָּׁה וְשִׁבְעִים אָלֶף; וּבַבִּזָּה—לֹא
שָׁלְחוּ, אֶת־יָדָם. יז בְּיוֹם־שְׁלוֹשָׁה עָשָׂר, לְחֹדֶשׁ אֲדָר; וְנוֹחַ, בְּאַרְבָּעָה עָשָׂר בּוֹ, וְעָשֹׂה
אֹתוֹ, יוֹם מִשְׁתֶּה וְשִׂמְחָה. יח והיהודיים (וְהַיְּהוּדִים) אֲשֶׁר־בְּשׁוּשָׁן, נִקְהֲלוּ בִּשְׁלוֹשָׁה
עָשָׂר בּוֹ, וּבְאַרְבָּעָה עָשָׂר, בּוֹ; וְנוֹחַ, בַּחֲמִשָּׁה עָשָׂר בּוֹ, וְעָשֹׂה אֹתוֹ, יוֹם מִשְׁתֶּה
וְשִׂמְחָה. יט עַל־כֵּן הַיְּהוּדִים הפרוזים (הַפְּרָזִים), הַיֹּשְׁבִים בְּעָרֵי הַפְּרָזוֹת—עֹשִׂים אֵת
יוֹם אַרְבָּעָה עָשָׂר לְחֹדֶשׁ אֲדָר, שִׂמְחָה וּמִשְׁתֶּה וְיוֹם טוֹב; וּמִשְׁלֹחַ מָנוֹת, אִישׁ לְרֵעֵהוּ.
כ וַיִּכְתֹּב מָרְדֳּכַי, אֶת־הַדְּבָרִים הָאֵלֶּה; וַיִּשְׁלַח סְפָרִים אֶל־כָּל־הַיְּהוּדִים, אֲשֶׁר בְּכָל־
מְדִינוֹת הַמֶּלֶךְ אֲחַשְׁוֵרוֹשׁ—הַקְּרוֹבִים, וְהָרְחוֹקִים. כא לְקַיֵּם, עֲלֵיהֶם—לִהְיוֹת עֹשִׂים
אֵת יוֹם אַרְבָּעָה עָשָׂר לְחֹדֶשׁ אֲדָר, וְאֵת יוֹם־חֲמִשָּׁה עָשָׂר בּוֹ: בְּכָל־שָׁנָה, וְשָׁנָה. כב
כַּיָּמִים, אֲשֶׁר־נָחוּ בָהֶם הַיְּהוּדִים מֵאֹיְבֵיהֶם, וְהַחֹדֶשׁ אֲשֶׁר נֶהְפַּךְ לָהֶם מִיָּגוֹן לְשִׂמְחָה,
וּמֵאֵבֶל לְיוֹם טוֹב; לַעֲשׂוֹת אוֹתָם, יְמֵי מִשְׁתֶּה וְשִׂמְחָה, וּמִשְׁלֹחַ מָנוֹת אִישׁ לְרֵעֵהוּ,
וּמַתָּנוֹת לָאֶבְיֹנִים. כג וְקִבֵּל, הַיְּהוּדִים, אֵת אֲשֶׁר־הֵחֵלּוּ, לַעֲשׂוֹת; וְאֵת אֲשֶׁר־כָּתַב
מָרְדֳּכַי, אֲלֵיהֶם. כד כִּי הָמָן בֶּן־הַמְּדָתָא הָאֲגָגִי, צֹרֵר כָּל־הַיְּהוּדִים—חָשַׁב עַל־
הַיְּהוּדִים, לְאַבְּדָם; וְהִפִּל פּוּר הוּא הַגּוֹרָל, לְהֻמָּם וּלְאַבְּדָם. כה וּבְבֹאָהּ, לִפְנֵי הַמֶּלֶךְ,
אָמַר עִם־הַסֵּפֶר, יָשׁוּב מַחֲשַׁבְתּוֹ הָרָעָה אֲשֶׁר־חָשַׁב עַל־הַיְּהוּדִים עַל־רֹאשׁוֹ; וְתָלוּ
אֹתוֹ וְאֶת־בָּנָיו, עַל־הָעֵץ. כו עַל־כֵּן קָרְאוּ לַיָּמִים הָאֵלֶּה פוּרִים, עַל־שֵׁם הַפּוּר—עַל־
כֵּן, עַל־כָּל־דִּבְרֵי הָאִגֶּרֶת הַזֹּאת; וּמָה־רָאוּ עַל־כָּכָה, וּמָה הִגִּיעַ אֲלֵיהֶם. כז קִיְּמוּ
וקבל (וְקִבְּלוּ) הַיְּהוּדִים עֲלֵיהֶם וְעַל־זַרְעָם וְעַל כָּל־הַנִּלְוִים עֲלֵיהֶם, וְלֹא יַעֲבוֹר—
לִהְיוֹת עֹשִׂים אֵת שְׁנֵי הַיָּמִים הָאֵלֶּה, כִּכְתָבָם וְכִזְמַנָּם: בְּכָל־שָׁנָה, וְשָׁנָה. כח וְהַיָּמִים
הָאֵלֶּה נִזְכָּרִים וְנַעֲשִׂים בְּכָל־דּוֹר וָדוֹר, מִשְׁפָּחָה וּמִשְׁפָּחָה, מְדִינָה וּמְדִינָה, וְעִיר
וָעִיר; וִימֵי הַפּוּרִים הָאֵלֶּה, לֹא יַעַבְרוּ מִתּוֹךְ הַיְּהוּדִים, וְזִכְרָם, לֹא־יָסוּף מִזַּרְעָם. {ס}
כט וַתִּכְתֹּב אֶסְתֵּר הַמַּלְכָּה בַת־אֲבִיחַיִל, וּמָרְדֳּכַי הַיְּהוּדִי—אֶת־כָּל־תֹּקֶף: לְקַיֵּם, אֵת
אִגֶּרֶת הַפֻּרִים הַזֹּאת—הַשֵּׁנִית. ל וַיִּשְׁלַח סְפָרִים אֶל־כָּל־הַיְּהוּדִים, אֶל־שֶׁבַע וְעֶשְׂרִים

הָרַמָּכִים. יא אֲשֶׁר נָתַן הַמֶּלֶךְ לַיְּהוּדִים אֲשֶׁר בְּכָל־עִיר־וָעִיר, לְהִקָּהֵל וְלַעֲמֹד עַל־
נַפְשָׁם—לְהַשְׁמִיד וְלַהֲרֹג וּלְאַבֵּד אֶת־כָּל־חֵיל עַם וּמְדִינָה הַצָּרִים אֹתָם, טַף וְנָשִׁים;
וּשְׁלָלָם, לָבוֹז. יב בְּיוֹם אֶחָד, בְּכָל־מְדִינוֹת הַמֶּלֶךְ אֲחַשְׁוֵרוֹשׁ—בִּשְׁלוֹשָׁה עָשָׂר לְחֹדֶשׁ
שְׁנֵים־עָשָׂר, הוּא־חֹדֶשׁ אֲדָר. יג פַּתְשֶׁגֶן הַכְּתָב, לְהִנָּתֵן דָּת בְּכָל־מְדִינָה וּמְדִינָה, גָּלוּי,
לְכָל־הָעַמִּים; וְלִהְיוֹת היהודיים (הַיְּהוּדִים) עתודים (עֲתִידִים) לַיּוֹם הַזֶּה, לְהִנָּקֵם
מֵאֹיְבֵיהֶם. יד הָרָצִים רֹכְבֵי הָרֶכֶשׁ, הָאֲחַשְׁתְּרָנִים, יָצְאוּ מְבֹהָלִים וּדְחוּפִים, בִּדְבַר
הַמֶּלֶךְ; וְהַדָּת נִתְּנָה, בְּשׁוּשַׁן הַבִּירָה.
טו וּמָרְדֳּכַי יָצָא מִלִּפְנֵי הַמֶּלֶךְ, בִּלְבוּשׁ מַלְכוּת תְּכֵלֶת וָחוּר, וַעֲטֶרֶת זָהָב גְּדוֹלָה,
וְתַכְרִיךְ בּוּץ וְאַרְגָּמָן; וְהָעִיר שׁוּשָׁן, צָהֲלָה וְשָׂמֵחָה. טז לַיְּהוּדִים, הָיְתָה אוֹרָה
וְשִׂמְחָה, וְשָׂשֹׂן, וִיקָר. יז וּבְכָל־מְדִינָה וּמְדִינָה וּבְכָל־עִיר וָעִיר, מְקוֹם אֲשֶׁר דְּבַר־
הַמֶּלֶךְ וְדָתוֹ מַגִּיעַ, שִׂמְחָה וְשָׂשׂוֹן לַיְּהוּדִים, מִשְׁתֶּה וְיוֹם טוֹב; וְרַבִּים מֵעַמֵּי הָאָרֶץ,
מִתְיַהֲדִים—כִּי־נָפַל פַּחַד־הַיְּהוּדִים, עֲלֵיהֶם.

פרק ט

א וּבִשְׁנֵים עָשָׂר חֹדֶשׁ הוּא־חֹדֶשׁ אֲדָר, בִּשְׁלוֹשָׁה עָשָׂר יוֹם בּוֹ, אֲשֶׁר הִגִּיעַ דְּבַר־הַמֶּלֶךְ
וְדָתוֹ, לְהֵעָשׂוֹת: בַּיּוֹם, אֲשֶׁר שִׂבְּרוּ אֹיְבֵי הַיְּהוּדִים לִשְׁלוֹט בָּהֶם, וְנַהֲפוֹךְ הוּא, אֲשֶׁר
יִשְׁלְטוּ הַיְּהוּדִים הֵמָּה בְּשֹׂנְאֵיהֶם. ב נִקְהֲלוּ הַיְּהוּדִים בְּעָרֵיהֶם, בְּכָל־מְדִינוֹת הַמֶּלֶךְ
אֲחַשְׁוֵרוֹשׁ, לִשְׁלֹחַ יָד, בִּמְבַקְשֵׁי רָעָתָם; וְאִישׁ לֹא־עָמַד לִפְנֵיהֶם, כִּי־נָפַל פַּחְדָּם
עַל־כָּל־הָעַמִּים. ג וְכָל־שָׂרֵי הַמְּדִינוֹת וְהָאֲחַשְׁדַּרְפְּנִים וְהַפַּחוֹת, וְעֹשֵׂי הַמְּלָאכָה
אֲשֶׁר לַמֶּלֶךְ—מְנַשְּׂאִים, אֶת־הַיְּהוּדִים: כִּי־נָפַל פַּחַד־מָרְדֳּכַי, עֲלֵיהֶם. ד כִּי־גָדוֹל
מָרְדֳּכַי בְּבֵית הַמֶּלֶךְ, וְשָׁמְעוֹ הוֹלֵךְ בְּכָל־הַמְּדִינוֹת: כִּי־הָאִישׁ מָרְדֳּכַי, הוֹלֵךְ וְגָדוֹל.
ה וַיַּכּוּ הַיְּהוּדִים בְּכָל־אֹיְבֵיהֶם, מַכַּת־חֶרֶב וְהֶרֶג וְאַבְדָן; וַיַּעֲשׂוּ בְשֹׂנְאֵיהֶם, כִּרְצוֹנָם.
ו וּבְשׁוּשַׁן הַבִּירָה, הָרְגוּ הַיְּהוּדִים וְאַבֵּד—חֲמֵשׁ מֵאוֹת אִישׁ. ז וְאֵת פַּרְשַׁנְדָּתָא וְאֵת
דַּלְפוֹן, וְאֵת ח אַסְפָּתָא. וְאֵת פּוֹרָתָא וְאֵת
אֲדַלְיָא, {ס} וְאֵת {ר}
אֲרִידָתָא. {ס} ט וְאֵת {ר}
פַּרְמַשְׁתָּא {ס} וְאֵת {ר}
אֲרִיסַי, {ס} וְאֵת {ר}
אֲרִידַי {ס} וְאֵת {ר}
וַיְזָתָא. {ס} י עֲשֶׂרֶת {ר}
בְּנֵי הָמָן בֶּן־הַמְּדָתָא, צֹרֵר הַיְּהוּדִים—הָרָגוּ; וּבַבִּזָּה—לֹא שָׁלְחוּ, אֶת־יָדָם. יא בַּיּוֹם

מְלָאוֹ לִבּוֹ לַעֲשׂוֹת כֵּן. ו וַתֹּאמֶר אֶסְתֵּר–אִישׁ צַר וְאוֹיֵב, הָמָן הָרָע הַזֶּה; וְהָמָן נִבְעַת,
מִלִּפְנֵי הַמֶּלֶךְ וְהַמַּלְכָּה. ז וְהַמֶּלֶךְ קָם בַּחֲמָתוֹ, מִמִּשְׁתֵּה הַיַּיִן, אֶל־גִּנַּת, הַבִּיתָן; וְהָמָן
עָמַד, לְבַקֵּשׁ עַל־נַפְשׁוֹ מֵאֶסְתֵּר הַמַּלְכָּה–כִּי רָאָה, כִּי־כָלְתָה אֵלָיו הָרָעָה מֵאֵת הַמֶּלֶךְ.
ח וְהַמֶּלֶךְ שָׁב מִגִּנַּת הַבִּיתָן אֶל־בֵּית מִשְׁתֵּה הַיַּיִן, וְהָמָן נֹפֵל עַל־הַמִּטָּה אֲשֶׁר אֶסְתֵּר
עָלֶיהָ, וַיֹּאמֶר הַמֶּלֶךְ, הֲגַם לִכְבּוֹשׁ אֶת־הַמַּלְכָּה עִמִּי בַּבָּיִת; הַדָּבָר, יָצָא מִפִּי הַמֶּלֶךְ,
וּפְנֵי הָמָן, חָפוּ. ט וַיֹּאמֶר חַרְבוֹנָה אֶחָד מִן־הַסָּרִיסִים לִפְנֵי הַמֶּלֶךְ, גַּם הִנֵּה־הָעֵץ
אֲשֶׁר־עָשָׂה הָמָן לְמָרְדֳּכַי אֲשֶׁר דִּבֶּר־טוֹב עַל־הַמֶּלֶךְ עֹמֵד בְּבֵית הָמָן–גָּבֹהַּ, חֲמִשִּׁים
אַמָּה; וַיֹּאמֶר הַמֶּלֶךְ, תְּלֻהוּ עָלָיו. י וַיִּתְלוּ, אֶת־הָמָן, עַל־הָעֵץ, אֲשֶׁר־הֵכִין לְמָרְדֳּכָי;
וַחֲמַת הַמֶּלֶךְ, שָׁכָכָה.

פרק ח

א בַּיּוֹם הַהוּא, נָתַן הַמֶּלֶךְ אֲחַשְׁוֵרוֹשׁ לְאֶסְתֵּר הַמַּלְכָּה, אֶת־בֵּית הָמָן, צֹרֵר היהודיים
(הַיְּהוּדִים); וּמָרְדֳּכַי, בָּא לִפְנֵי הַמֶּלֶךְ–כִּי־הִגִּידָה אֶסְתֵּר, מַה הוּא־לָהּ. ב וַיָּסַר הַמֶּלֶךְ
אֶת־טַבַּעְתּוֹ, אֲשֶׁר הֶעֱבִיר מֵהָמָן, וַיִּתְּנָהּ, לְמָרְדֳּכָי; וַתָּשֶׂם אֶסְתֵּר אֶת־מָרְדֳּכַי, עַל־בֵּית
הָמָן.
ג וַתּוֹסֶף אֶסְתֵּר, וַתְּדַבֵּר לִפְנֵי הַמֶּלֶךְ, וַתִּפֹּל, לִפְנֵי רַגְלָיו; וַתֵּבְךְּ וַתִּתְחַנֶּן־לוֹ, לְהַעֲבִיר
אֶת־רָעַת הָמָן הָאֲגָגִי, וְאֵת מַחֲשַׁבְתּוֹ, אֲשֶׁר חָשַׁב עַל־הַיְּהוּדִים. ד וַיּוֹשֶׁט הַמֶּלֶךְ
לְאֶסְתֵּר, אֵת שַׁרְבִט הַזָּהָב; וַתָּקָם אֶסְתֵּר, וַתַּעֲמֹד לִפְנֵי הַמֶּלֶךְ. ה וַתֹּאמֶר אִם־עַל־
הַמֶּלֶךְ טוֹב וְאִם־מָצָאתִי חֵן לְפָנָיו, וְכָשֵׁר הַדָּבָר לִפְנֵי הַמֶּלֶךְ, וְטוֹבָה אֲנִי, בְּעֵינָיו–
יִכָּתֵב לְהָשִׁיב אֶת־הַסְּפָרִים, מַחֲשֶׁבֶת הָמָן בֶּן־הַמְּדָתָא הָאֲגָגִי, אֲשֶׁר כָּתַב לְאַבֵּד אֶת־
הַיְּהוּדִים, אֲשֶׁר בְּכָל־מְדִינוֹת הַמֶּלֶךְ. ו כִּי אֵיכָכָה אוּכַל, וְרָאִיתִי, בָּרָעָה, אֲשֶׁר־יִמְצָא
אֶת־עַמִּי; וְאֵיכָכָה אוּכַל וְרָאִיתִי, בְּאָבְדַן מוֹלַדְתִּי.
ז וַיֹּאמֶר הַמֶּלֶךְ אֲחַשְׁוֵרֹשׁ לְאֶסְתֵּר הַמַּלְכָּה, וּלְמָרְדֳּכַי הַיְּהוּדִי: הִנֵּה בֵית־הָמָן נָתַתִּי
לְאֶסְתֵּר, וְאֹתוֹ תָּלוּ עַל־הָעֵץ–עַל אֲשֶׁר־שָׁלַח יָדוֹ, ביהודיים (בַּיְּהוּדִים). ח וְאַתֶּם
כִּתְבוּ עַל־הַיְּהוּדִים כַּטּוֹב בְּעֵינֵיכֶם, בְּשֵׁם הַמֶּלֶךְ, וְחִתְמוּ, בְּטַבַּעַת הַמֶּלֶךְ: כִּי־כְתָב
אֲשֶׁר־נִכְתָּב בְּשֵׁם־הַמֶּלֶךְ, וְנַחְתּוֹם בְּטַבַּעַת הַמֶּלֶךְ–אֵין לְהָשִׁיב. ט וַיִּקָּרְאוּ סֹפְרֵי־
הַמֶּלֶךְ בָּעֵת־הַהִיא בַּחֹדֶשׁ הַשְּׁלִישִׁי הוּא־חֹדֶשׁ סִיוָן, בִּשְׁלוֹשָׁה וְעֶשְׂרִים בּוֹ, וַיִּכָּתֵב
כְּכָל־אֲשֶׁר־צִוָּה מָרְדֳּכַי אֶל־הַיְּהוּדִים וְאֶל הָאֲחַשְׁדַּרְפְּנִים־וְהַפַּחוֹת וְשָׂרֵי הַמְּדִינוֹת
אֲשֶׁר מֵהֹדּוּ וְעַד־כּוּשׁ שֶׁבַע וְעֶשְׂרִים וּמֵאָה מְדִינָה, מְדִינָה וּמְדִינָה כִּכְתָבָהּ וְעַם וָעָם
כִּלְשֹׁנוֹ; וְאֶל־הַיְּהוּדִים–כִּכְתָבָם, וְכִלְשׁוֹנָם. י וַיִּכְתֹּב, בְּשֵׁם הַמֶּלֶךְ אֲחַשְׁוֵרֹשׁ, וַיַּחְתֹּם,
בְּטַבַּעַת הַמֶּלֶךְ; וַיִּשְׁלַח סְפָרִים בְּיַד הָרָצִים בַּסּוּסִים רֹכְבֵי הָרֶכֶשׁ, הָאֲחַשְׁתְּרָנִים–בְּנֵי,

פרק ו

א בַּלַּיְלָה הַהוּא, נָדְדָה שְׁנַת הַמֶּלֶךְ; וַיֹּאמֶר, לְהָבִיא אֶת־סֵפֶר הַזִּכְרֹנוֹת דִּבְרֵי הַיָּמִים,
וַיִּהְיוּ נִקְרָאִים, לִפְנֵי הַמֶּלֶךְ. ב וַיִּמָּצֵא כָתוּב, אֲשֶׁר הִגִּיד מָרְדֳּכַי עַל־בִּגְתָנָא וָתֶרֶשׁ
שְׁנֵי סָרִיסֵי הַמֶּלֶךְ—מִשֹּׁמְרֵי, הַסַּף: אֲשֶׁר בִּקְשׁוּ לִשְׁלֹחַ יָד, בַּמֶּלֶךְ אֲחַשְׁוֵרוֹשׁ. ג וַיֹּאמֶר
הַמֶּלֶךְ—מַה־נַּעֲשָׂה יְקָר וּגְדוּלָּה לְמָרְדֳּכַי, עַל־זֶה; וַיֹּאמְרוּ נַעֲרֵי הַמֶּלֶךְ, מְשָׁרְתָיו, לֹא־
נַעֲשָׂה עִמּוֹ, דָּבָר. ד וַיֹּאמֶר הַמֶּלֶךְ, מִי בֶחָצֵר; וְהָמָן בָּא, לַחֲצַר בֵּית־הַמֶּלֶךְ הַחִיצוֹנָה,
לֵאמֹר לַמֶּלֶךְ, לִתְלוֹת אֶת־מָרְדֳּכַי עַל־הָעֵץ אֲשֶׁר־הֵכִין לוֹ. ה וַיֹּאמְרוּ נַעֲרֵי הַמֶּלֶךְ,
אֵלָיו—הִנֵּה הָמָן, עֹמֵד בֶּחָצֵר; וַיֹּאמֶר הַמֶּלֶךְ, יָבוֹא. ו וַיָּבוֹא, הָמָן, וַיֹּאמֶר לוֹ הַמֶּלֶךְ,
מַה־לַּעֲשׂוֹת בָּאִישׁ אֲשֶׁר הַמֶּלֶךְ חָפֵץ בִּיקָרוֹ; וַיֹּאמֶר הָמָן, בְּלִבּוֹ, לְמִי יַחְפֹּץ הַמֶּלֶךְ
לַעֲשׂוֹת יְקָר, יוֹתֵר מִמֶּנִּי. ז וַיֹּאמֶר הָמָן, אֶל־הַמֶּלֶךְ: אִישׁ, אֲשֶׁר הַמֶּלֶךְ חָפֵץ בִּיקָרוֹ.
ח יָבִיאוּ לְבוּשׁ מַלְכוּת, אֲשֶׁר לָבַשׁ־בּוֹ הַמֶּלֶךְ; וְסוּס, אֲשֶׁר רָכַב עָלָיו הַמֶּלֶךְ, וַאֲשֶׁר נִתַּן
כֶּתֶר מַלְכוּת, בְּרֹאשׁוֹ. ט וְנָתוֹן הַלְּבוּשׁ וְהַסּוּס, עַל־יַד־אִישׁ מִשָּׂרֵי הַמֶּלֶךְ הַפַּרְתְּמִים,
וְהִלְבִּישׁוּ אֶת־הָאִישׁ, אֲשֶׁר הַמֶּלֶךְ חָפֵץ בִּיקָרוֹ; וְהִרְכִּיבֻהוּ עַל־הַסּוּס, בִּרְחוֹב הָעִיר,
וְקָרְאוּ לְפָנָיו, כָּכָה יֵעָשֶׂה לָאִישׁ אֲשֶׁר הַמֶּלֶךְ חָפֵץ בִּיקָרוֹ. י וַיֹּאמֶר הַמֶּלֶךְ לְהָמָן, מַהֵר
קַח אֶת־הַלְּבוּשׁ וְאֶת־הַסּוּס כַּאֲשֶׁר דִּבַּרְתָּ, וַעֲשֵׂה־כֵן לְמָרְדֳּכַי הַיְּהוּדִי, הַיּוֹשֵׁב בְּשַׁעַר
הַמֶּלֶךְ: אַל־תַּפֵּל דָּבָר, מִכֹּל אֲשֶׁר דִּבַּרְתָּ. יא וַיִּקַּח הָמָן אֶת־הַלְּבוּשׁ וְאֶת־הַסּוּס, וַיַּלְבֵּשׁ
אֶת־מָרְדֳּכָי; וַיַּרְכִּיבֵהוּ, בִּרְחוֹב הָעִיר, וַיִּקְרָא לְפָנָיו, כָּכָה יֵעָשֶׂה לָאִישׁ אֲשֶׁר הַמֶּלֶךְ
חָפֵץ בִּיקָרוֹ. יב וַיָּשָׁב מָרְדֳּכַי, אֶל־שַׁעַר הַמֶּלֶךְ; וְהָמָן נִדְחַף אֶל־בֵּיתוֹ, אָבֵל וַחֲפוּי
רֹאשׁ. יג וַיְסַפֵּר הָמָן לְזֶרֶשׁ אִשְׁתּוֹ, וּלְכָל־אֹהֲבָיו, אֵת, כָּל־אֲשֶׁר קָרָהוּ; וַיֹּאמְרוּ לוֹ
חֲכָמָיו וְזֶרֶשׁ אִשְׁתּוֹ, אִם מִזֶּרַע הַיְּהוּדִים מָרְדֳּכַי אֲשֶׁר הַחִלּוֹתָ לִנְפֹּל לְפָנָיו לֹא־תוּכַל
לוֹ—כִּי־נָפוֹל תִּפּוֹל, לְפָנָיו. יד עוֹדָם מְדַבְּרִים עִמּוֹ, וְסָרִיסֵי הַמֶּלֶךְ הִגִּיעוּ; וַיַּבְהִלוּ
לְהָבִיא אֶת־הָמָן, אֶל־הַמִּשְׁתֶּה אֲשֶׁר־עָשְׂתָה אֶסְתֵּר.

פרק ז

א וַיָּבֹא הַמֶּלֶךְ וְהָמָן, לִשְׁתּוֹת עִם־אֶסְתֵּר הַמַּלְכָּה. ב וַיֹּאמֶר הַמֶּלֶךְ לְאֶסְתֵּר גַּם בַּיּוֹם
הַשֵּׁנִי, בְּמִשְׁתֵּה הַיַּיִן—מַה־שְּׁאֵלָתֵךְ אֶסְתֵּר הַמַּלְכָּה, וְתִנָּתֵן לָךְ; וּמַה־בַּקָּשָׁתֵךְ עַד־חֲצִי
הַמַּלְכוּת, וְתֵעָשׂ. ג וַתַּעַן אֶסְתֵּר הַמַּלְכָּה, וַתֹּאמַר—אִם־מָצָאתִי חֵן בְּעֵינֶיךָ הַמֶּלֶךְ,
וְאִם־עַל־הַמֶּלֶךְ טוֹב: תִּנָּתֶן־לִי נַפְשִׁי בִּשְׁאֵלָתִי, וְעַמִּי בְּבַקָּשָׁתִי. ד כִּי נִמְכַּרְנוּ אֲנִי
וְעַמִּי, לְהַשְׁמִיד לַהֲרוֹג וּלְאַבֵּד; וְאִלּוּ לַעֲבָדִים וְלִשְׁפָחוֹת נִמְכַּרְנוּ, הֶחֱרַשְׁתִּי—כִּי אֵין
הַצָּר שֹׁוֶה, בְּנֵזֶק הַמֶּלֶךְ.

ה וַיֹּאמֶר הַמֶּלֶךְ אֲחַשְׁוֵרוֹשׁ, וַיֹּאמֶר לְאֶסְתֵּר הַמַּלְכָּה: מִי הוּא זֶה וְאֵי־זֶה הוּא, אֲשֶׁר־

שַׁרְבִיט הַזָּהָב, וְחָיָה; וַאֲנִי, לֹא נִקְרֵאתִי לָבוֹא אֶל־הַמֶּלֶךְ—זֶה, שְׁלוֹשִׁים יוֹם. יב וַיַּגִּידוּ
לְמָרְדֳּכָי, אֵת דִּבְרֵי אֶסְתֵּר. יג וַיֹּאמֶר מָרְדֳּכַי, לְהָשִׁיב אֶל־אֶסְתֵּר: אַל־תְּדַמִּי בְנַפְשֵׁךְ,
לְהִמָּלֵט בֵּית־הַמֶּלֶךְ מִכָּל־הַיְּהוּדִים. יד כִּי אִם־הַחֲרֵשׁ תַּחֲרִישִׁי, בָּעֵת הַזֹּאת—רֶוַח
וְהַצָּלָה יַעֲמוֹד לַיְּהוּדִים מִמָּקוֹם אַחֵר, וְאַתְּ וּבֵית־אָבִיךְ תֹּאבֵדוּ; וּמִי יוֹדֵעַ—אִם־לְעֵת
כָּזֹאת, הִגַּעַתְּ לַמַּלְכוּת. טו וַתֹּאמֶר אֶסְתֵּר, לְהָשִׁיב אֶל־מָרְדֳּכָי. טז לֵךְ כְּנוֹס אֶת־כָּל־
הַיְּהוּדִים הַנִּמְצְאִים בְּשׁוּשָׁן, וְצוּמוּ עָלַי וְאַל־תֹּאכְלוּ וְאַל־תִּשְׁתּוּ שְׁלֹשֶׁת יָמִים לַיְלָה
וָיוֹם—גַּם־אֲנִי וְנַעֲרֹתַי, אָצוּם כֵּן; וּבְכֵן אָבוֹא אֶל־הַמֶּלֶךְ, אֲשֶׁר לֹא־כַדָּת, וְכַאֲשֶׁר
אָבַדְתִּי, אָבָדְתִּי. יז וַיַּעֲבֹר, מָרְדֳּכָי; וַיַּעַשׂ, כְּכֹל אֲשֶׁר־צִוְּתָה עָלָיו אֶסְתֵּר.

פרק ה

א וַיְהִי בַּיּוֹם הַשְּׁלִישִׁי, וַתִּלְבַּשׁ אֶסְתֵּר מַלְכוּת, וַתַּעֲמֹד בַּחֲצַר בֵּית־הַמֶּלֶךְ הַפְּנִימִית,
נֹכַח בֵּית הַמֶּלֶךְ; וְהַמֶּלֶךְ יוֹשֵׁב עַל־כִּסֵּא מַלְכוּתוֹ, בְּבֵית הַמַּלְכוּת, נֹכַח, פֶּתַח הַבָּיִת.
ב וַיְהִי כִרְאוֹת הַמֶּלֶךְ אֶת־אֶסְתֵּר הַמַּלְכָּה, עֹמֶדֶת בֶּחָצֵר—נָשְׂאָה חֵן, בְּעֵינָיו; וַיּוֹשֶׁט
הַמֶּלֶךְ לְאֶסְתֵּר, אֶת־שַׁרְבִיט הַזָּהָב אֲשֶׁר בְּיָדוֹ, וַתִּקְרַב אֶסְתֵּר, וַתִּגַּע בְּרֹאשׁ הַשַּׁרְבִיט.
ג וַיֹּאמֶר לָהּ הַמֶּלֶךְ, מַה־לָּךְ אֶסְתֵּר הַמַּלְכָּה; וּמַה־בַּקָּשָׁתֵךְ עַד־חֲצִי הַמַּלְכוּת, וְיִנָּתֵן
לָךְ. ד וַתֹּאמֶר אֶסְתֵּר, אִם־עַל־הַמֶּלֶךְ טוֹב—יָבוֹא הַמֶּלֶךְ וְהָמָן הַיּוֹם, אֶל־הַמִּשְׁתֶּה
אֲשֶׁר־עָשִׂיתִי לוֹ. ה וַיֹּאמֶר הַמֶּלֶךְ—מַהֲרוּ אֶת־הָמָן, לַעֲשׂוֹת אֶת־דְּבַר אֶסְתֵּר; וַיָּבֹא
הַמֶּלֶךְ וְהָמָן, אֶל־הַמִּשְׁתֶּה אֲשֶׁר־עָשְׂתָה אֶסְתֵּר. ו וַיֹּאמֶר הַמֶּלֶךְ לְאֶסְתֵּר בְּמִשְׁתֵּה
הַיַּיִן, מַה־שְּׁאֵלָתֵךְ וְיִנָּתֵן לָךְ; וּמַה־בַּקָּשָׁתֵךְ עַד־חֲצִי הַמַּלְכוּת, וְתֵעָשׂ. ז וַתַּעַן אֶסְתֵּר,
וַתֹּאמַר: שְׁאֵלָתִי, וּבַקָּשָׁתִי. ח אִם־מָצָאתִי חֵן בְּעֵינֵי הַמֶּלֶךְ, וְאִם־עַל־הַמֶּלֶךְ טוֹב, לָתֵת
אֶת־שְׁאֵלָתִי, וְלַעֲשׂוֹת אֶת־בַּקָּשָׁתִי—יָבוֹא הַמֶּלֶךְ וְהָמָן, אֶל־הַמִּשְׁתֶּה אֲשֶׁר אֶעֱשֶׂה
לָהֶם, וּמָחָר אֶעֱשֶׂה, כִּדְבַר הַמֶּלֶךְ. ט וַיֵּצֵא הָמָן בַּיּוֹם הַהוּא, שָׂמֵחַ וְטוֹב לֵב; וְכִרְאוֹת
הָמָן אֶת־מָרְדֳּכַי בְּשַׁעַר הַמֶּלֶךְ, וְלֹא־קָם וְלֹא־זָע מִמֶּנּוּ—וַיִּמָּלֵא הָמָן עַל־מָרְדֳּכַי,
חֵמָה. י וַיִּתְאַפַּק הָמָן, וַיָּבוֹא אֶל־בֵּיתוֹ; וַיִּשְׁלַח וַיָּבֵא אֶת־אֹהֲבָיו, וְאֶת־זֶרֶשׁ אִשְׁתּוֹ.
יא וַיְסַפֵּר לָהֶם הָמָן אֶת־כְּבוֹד עָשְׁרוֹ, וְרֹב בָּנָיו; וְאֵת כָּל־אֲשֶׁר גִּדְּלוֹ הַמֶּלֶךְ וְאֵת אֲשֶׁר
נִשְּׂאוֹ, עַל־הַשָּׂרִים וְעַבְדֵי הַמֶּלֶךְ. יב וַיֹּאמֶר, הָמָן—אַף לֹא־הֵבִיאָה אֶסְתֵּר הַמַּלְכָּה עִם־
הַמֶּלֶךְ אֶל־הַמִּשְׁתֶּה אֲשֶׁר־עָשָׂתָה, כִּי אִם־אוֹתִי; וְגַם־לְמָחָר אֲנִי קָרוּא־לָהּ, עִם־הַמֶּלֶךְ.
יג וְכָל־זֶה, אֵינֶנּוּ שֹׁוֶה לִי: בְּכָל־עֵת, אֲשֶׁר אֲנִי רֹאֶה אֶת־מָרְדֳּכַי הַיְּהוּדִי—יוֹשֵׁב,
בְּשַׁעַר הַמֶּלֶךְ. יד וַתֹּאמֶר לוֹ זֶרֶשׁ אִשְׁתּוֹ וְכָל־אֹהֲבָיו, יַעֲשׂוּ־עֵץ גָּבֹהַּ חֲמִשִּׁים אַמָּה,
וּבַבֹּקֶר אֱמֹר לַמֶּלֶךְ וְיִתְלוּ אֶת־מָרְדֳּכַי עָלָיו, וּבֹא־עִם־הַמֶּלֶךְ אֶל־הַמִּשְׁתֶּה שָׂמֵחַ;
וַיִּיטַב הַדָּבָר לִפְנֵי הָמָן, וַיַּעַשׂ הָעֵץ.

ח וַיֹּאמֶר הָמָן, לַמֶּלֶךְ אֲחַשְׁוֵרוֹשׁ—יֶשְׁנוֹ עַם־אֶחָד מְפֻזָּר וּמְפֹרָד בֵּין הָעַמִּים, בְּכֹל
מְדִינוֹת מַלְכוּתֶךָ; וְדָתֵיהֶם שֹׁנוֹת מִכָּל־עָם, וְאֶת־דָּתֵי הַמֶּלֶךְ אֵינָם עֹשִׂים, וְלַמֶּלֶךְ
אֵין־שֹׁוֶה, לְהַנִּיחָם. ט אִם־עַל־הַמֶּלֶךְ טוֹב, יִכָּתֵב לְאַבְּדָם; וַעֲשֶׂרֶת אֲלָפִים כִּכַּר־כֶּסֶף,
אֶשְׁקוֹל עַל־יְדֵי עֹשֵׂי הַמְּלָאכָה, לְהָבִיא, אֶל־גִּנְזֵי הַמֶּלֶךְ. י וַיָּסַר הַמֶּלֶךְ אֶת־טַבַּעְתּוֹ,
מֵעַל יָדוֹ; וַיִּתְּנָהּ, לְהָמָן בֶּן־הַמְּדָתָא הָאֲגָגִי—צֹרֵר הַיְּהוּדִים. יא וַיֹּאמֶר הַמֶּלֶךְ לְהָמָן,
הַכֶּסֶף נָתוּן לָךְ; וְהָעָם, לַעֲשׂוֹת בּוֹ כַּטּוֹב בְּעֵינֶיךָ. יב וַיִּקָּרְאוּ סֹפְרֵי הַמֶּלֶךְ בַּחֹדֶשׁ
הָרִאשׁוֹן, בִּשְׁלוֹשָׁה עָשָׂר יוֹם בּוֹ, וַיִּכָּתֵב כְּכָל־אֲשֶׁר־צִוָּה הָמָן אֶל אֲחַשְׁדַּרְפְּנֵי־הַמֶּלֶךְ
וְאֶל־הַפַּחוֹת אֲשֶׁר עַל־מְדִינָה וּמְדִינָה וְאֶל־שָׂרֵי עַם וָעָם, מְדִינָה וּמְדִינָה כִּכְתָבָהּ
וְעַם וָעָם כִּלְשׁוֹנוֹ: בְּשֵׁם הַמֶּלֶךְ אֲחַשְׁוֵרֹשׁ נִכְתָּב, וְנֶחְתָּם בְּטַבַּעַת הַמֶּלֶךְ. יג וְנִשְׁלוֹחַ
סְפָרִים בְּיַד הָרָצִים, אֶל־כָּל־מְדִינוֹת הַמֶּלֶךְ—לְהַשְׁמִיד לַהֲרֹג וּלְאַבֵּד אֶת־כָּל־הַיְּהוּדִים
מִנַּעַר וְעַד־זָקֵן טַף וְנָשִׁים בְּיוֹם אֶחָד, בִּשְׁלוֹשָׁה עָשָׂר לְחֹדֶשׁ שְׁנֵים־עָשָׂר הוּא־חֹדֶשׁ
אֲדָר; וּשְׁלָלָם, לָבוֹז. יד פַּתְשֶׁגֶן הַכְּתָב, לְהִנָּתֵן דָּת בְּכָל־מְדִינָה וּמְדִינָה, גָּלוּי, לְכָל־
הָעַמִּים—לִהְיוֹת עֲתִדִים, לַיּוֹם הַזֶּה. טו הָרָצִים יָצְאוּ דְחוּפִים, בִּדְבַר הַמֶּלֶךְ, וְהַדָּת
נִתְּנָה, בְּשׁוּשַׁן הַבִּירָה; וְהַמֶּלֶךְ וְהָמָן יָשְׁבוּ לִשְׁתּוֹת, וְהָעִיר שׁוּשָׁן נָבוֹכָה.

פרק ד

א וּמָרְדֳּכַי, יָדַע אֶת־כָּל־אֲשֶׁר נַעֲשָׂה, וַיִּקְרַע מָרְדֳּכַי אֶת־בְּגָדָיו, וַיִּלְבַּשׁ שַׂק וָאֵפֶר;
וַיֵּצֵא בְּתוֹךְ הָעִיר, וַיִּזְעַק זְעָקָה גְדוֹלָה וּמָרָה. ב וַיָּבוֹא, עַד לִפְנֵי שַׁעַר־הַמֶּלֶךְ: כִּי
אֵין לָבוֹא אֶל־שַׁעַר הַמֶּלֶךְ, בִּלְבוּשׁ שָׂק. ג וּבְכָל־מְדִינָה וּמְדִינָה, מְקוֹם אֲשֶׁר דְּבַר־
הַמֶּלֶךְ וְדָתוֹ מַגִּיעַ—אֵבֶל גָּדוֹל לַיְּהוּדִים, וְצוֹם וּבְכִי וּמִסְפֵּד; שַׂק וָאֵפֶר, יֻצַּע לָרַבִּים.
ד ותבואינה (וַתָּבוֹאנָה) נַעֲרוֹת אֶסְתֵּר וְסָרִיסֶיהָ, וַיַּגִּידוּ לָהּ, וַתִּתְחַלְחַל הַמַּלְכָּה, מְאֹד;
וַתִּשְׁלַח בְּגָדִים לְהַלְבִּישׁ אֶת־מָרְדֳּכַי, וּלְהָסִיר שַׂקּוֹ מֵעָלָיו—וְלֹא קִבֵּל. ה וַתִּקְרָא
אֶסְתֵּר לַהֲתָךְ מִסָּרִיסֵי הַמֶּלֶךְ, אֲשֶׁר הֶעֱמִיד לְפָנֶיהָ, וַתְּצַוֵּהוּ, עַל־מָרְדֳּכָי—לָדַעַת מַה־
זֶּה, וְעַל־מַה־זֶּה. ו וַיֵּצֵא הֲתָךְ, אֶל־מָרְדֳּכָי—אֶל־רְחוֹב הָעִיר, אֲשֶׁר לִפְנֵי שַׁעַר־הַמֶּלֶךְ.
ז וַיַּגֶּד־לוֹ מָרְדֳּכַי, אֵת כָּל־אֲשֶׁר קָרָהוּ; וְאֵת פָּרָשַׁת הַכֶּסֶף, אֲשֶׁר אָמַר הָמָן לִשְׁקוֹל
עַל־גִּנְזֵי הַמֶּלֶךְ ביהודיים (בַּיְּהוּדִים)—לְאַבְּדָם. ח וְאֶת־פַּתְשֶׁגֶן כְּתָב־הַדָּת אֲשֶׁר־נִתַּן
בְּשׁוּשָׁן לְהַשְׁמִידָם, נָתַן לוֹ—לְהַרְאוֹת אֶת־אֶסְתֵּר, וּלְהַגִּיד לָהּ; וּלְצַוּוֹת עָלֶיהָ, לָבוֹא
אֶל־הַמֶּלֶךְ לְהִתְחַנֶּן־לוֹ וּלְבַקֵּשׁ מִלְּפָנָיו—עַל־עַמָּהּ. ט וַיָּבוֹא, הֲתָךְ; וַיַּגֵּד לְאֶסְתֵּר,
אֵת דִּבְרֵי מָרְדֳּכָי. י וַתֹּאמֶר אֶסְתֵּר לַהֲתָךְ, וַתְּצַוֵּהוּ אֶל־מָרְדֳּכָי. יא כָּל־עַבְדֵי הַמֶּלֶךְ
וְעַם־מְדִינוֹת הַמֶּלֶךְ יֹדְעִים, אֲשֶׁר כָּל־אִישׁ וְאִשָּׁה אֲשֶׁר יָבוֹא־אֶל־הַמֶּלֶךְ אֶל־הֶחָצֵר
הַפְּנִימִית אֲשֶׁר לֹא־יִקָּרֵא אַחַת דָּתוֹ לְהָמִית, לְבַד מֵאֲשֶׁר יוֹשִׁיט־לוֹ הַמֶּלֶךְ אֶת־

מְרוּקֵיהֶן: שִׁשָּׁה חֳדָשִׁים, בְּשֶׁמֶן הַמֹּר, וְשִׁשָּׁה חֳדָשִׁים בַּבְּשָׂמִים, וּבְתַמְרוּקֵי הַנָּשִׁים.
יג וּבָזֶה, הַנַּעֲרָה בָּאָה אֶל־הַמֶּלֶךְ—אֵת כָּל־אֲשֶׁר תֹּאמַר יִנָּתֵן לָהּ, לָבוֹא עִמָּהּ, מִבֵּית
הַנָּשִׁים, עַד־בֵּית הַמֶּלֶךְ. יד בָּעֶרֶב הִיא בָאָה, וּבַבֹּקֶר הִיא שָׁבָה אֶל־בֵּית הַנָּשִׁים שֵׁנִי,
אֶל־יַד שַׁעַשְׁגַז סְרִיס הַמֶּלֶךְ, שֹׁמֵר הַפִּילַגְשִׁים: לֹא־תָבוֹא עוֹד אֶל־הַמֶּלֶךְ, כִּי אִם־
חָפֵץ בָּהּ הַמֶּלֶךְ וְנִקְרְאָה בְשֵׁם. טו וּבְהַגִּיעַ תֹּר־אֶסְתֵּר בַּת־אֲבִיחַיִל דֹּד מָרְדֳּכַי אֲשֶׁר
לָקַח־לוֹ לְבַת לָבוֹא אֶל־הַמֶּלֶךְ, לֹא בִקְשָׁה דָּבָר—כִּי אִם אֶת־אֲשֶׁר יֹאמַר הֵגַי סְרִיס־
הַמֶּלֶךְ, שֹׁמֵר הַנָּשִׁים; וַתְּהִי אֶסְתֵּר נֹשֵׂאת חֵן, בְּעֵינֵי כָּל־רֹאֶיהָ. טז וַתִּלָּקַח אֶסְתֵּר
אֶל־הַמֶּלֶךְ אֲחַשְׁוֵרוֹשׁ, אֶל־בֵּית מַלְכוּתוֹ, בַּחֹדֶשׁ הָעֲשִׂירִי, הוּא־חֹדֶשׁ טֵבֵת—בִּשְׁנַת־
שֶׁבַע, לְמַלְכוּתוֹ. יז וַיֶּאֱהַב הַמֶּלֶךְ אֶת־אֶסְתֵּר מִכָּל־הַנָּשִׁים, וַתִּשָּׂא־חֵן וָחֶסֶד לְפָנָיו
מִכָּל־הַבְּתוּלוֹת; וַיָּשֶׂם כֶּתֶר־מַלְכוּת בְּרֹאשָׁהּ, וַיַּמְלִיכֶהָ תַּחַת וַשְׁתִּי. יח וַיַּעַשׂ הַמֶּלֶךְ
מִשְׁתֶּה גָדוֹל, לְכָל־שָׂרָיו וַעֲבָדָיו—אֵת, מִשְׁתֵּה אֶסְתֵּר; וַהֲנָחָה לַמְּדִינוֹת עָשָׂה, וַיִּתֵּן
מַשְׂאֵת כְּיַד הַמֶּלֶךְ. יט וּבְהִקָּבֵץ בְּתוּלוֹת, שֵׁנִית; וּמָרְדֳּכַי, יֹשֵׁב בְּשַׁעַר־הַמֶּלֶךְ. כ אֵין
אֶסְתֵּר, מַגֶּדֶת מוֹלַדְתָּהּ וְאֶת־עַמָּהּ, כַּאֲשֶׁר צִוָּה עָלֶיהָ, מָרְדֳּכָי; וְאֶת־מַאֲמַר מָרְדֳּכַי
אֶסְתֵּר עֹשָׂה, כַּאֲשֶׁר הָיְתָה בְאָמְנָה אִתּוֹ. כא בַּיָּמִים הָהֵם, וּמָרְדֳּכַי יֹשֵׁב בְּשַׁעַר־
הַמֶּלֶךְ; קָצַף בִּגְתָן וָתֶרֶשׁ שְׁנֵי־סָרִיסֵי הַמֶּלֶךְ, מִשֹּׁמְרֵי הַסַּף, וַיְבַקְשׁוּ לִשְׁלֹחַ יָד, בַּמֶּלֶךְ
אֲחַשְׁוֵרֹשׁ. כב וַיִּוָּדַע הַדָּבָר לְמָרְדֳּכַי, וַיַּגֵּד לְאֶסְתֵּר הַמַּלְכָּה; וַתֹּאמֶר אֶסְתֵּר לַמֶּלֶךְ,
בְּשֵׁם מָרְדֳּכָי. כג וַיְבֻקַּשׁ הַדָּבָר וַיִּמָּצֵא, וַיִּתָּלוּ שְׁנֵיהֶם עַל־עֵץ; וַיִּכָּתֵב, בְּסֵפֶר דִּבְרֵי
הַיָּמִים—לִפְנֵי הַמֶּלֶךְ.

פרק ג

א אַחַר הַדְּבָרִים הָאֵלֶּה, גִּדַּל הַמֶּלֶךְ אֲחַשְׁוֵרוֹשׁ אֶת־הָמָן בֶּן־הַמְּדָתָא הָאֲגָגִי—וַיְנַשְּׂאֵהוּ;
וַיָּשֶׂם, אֶת־כִּסְאוֹ, מֵעַל, כָּל־הַשָּׂרִים אֲשֶׁר אִתּוֹ. ב וְכָל־עַבְדֵי הַמֶּלֶךְ אֲשֶׁר־בְּשַׁעַר
הַמֶּלֶךְ, כֹּרְעִים וּמִשְׁתַּחֲוִים לְהָמָן—כִּי־כֵן, צִוָּה־לוֹ הַמֶּלֶךְ; וּמָרְדֳּכַי—לֹא יִכְרַע, וְלֹא
יִשְׁתַּחֲוֶה. ג וַיֹּאמְרוּ עַבְדֵי הַמֶּלֶךְ, אֲשֶׁר־בְּשַׁעַר הַמֶּלֶךְ—לְמָרְדֳּכָי: מַדּוּעַ אַתָּה עוֹבֵר,
אֵת מִצְוַת הַמֶּלֶךְ. ד וַיְהִי, באמרם (כְּאָמְרָם) אֵלָיו יוֹם וָיוֹם, וְלֹא שָׁמַע, אֲלֵיהֶם;
וַיַּגִּידוּ לְהָמָן, לִרְאוֹת הֲיַעַמְדוּ דִּבְרֵי מָרְדֳּכַי—כִּי־הִגִּיד לָהֶם, אֲשֶׁר־הוּא יְהוּדִי. ה וַיַּרְא
הָמָן—כִּי־אֵין מָרְדֳּכַי, כֹּרֵעַ וּמִשְׁתַּחֲוֶה לוֹ; וַיִּמָּלֵא הָמָן, חֵמָה. ו וַיִּבֶז בְּעֵינָיו, לִשְׁלֹחַ
יָד בְּמָרְדֳּכַי לְבַדּוֹ—כִּי־הִגִּידוּ לוֹ, אֶת־עַם מָרְדֳּכָי; וַיְבַקֵּשׁ הָמָן, לְהַשְׁמִיד אֶת־כָּל־
הַיְּהוּדִים אֲשֶׁר בְּכָל־מַלְכוּת אֲחַשְׁוֵרוֹשׁ—עַם מָרְדֳּכָי. ז בַּחֹדֶשׁ הָרִאשׁוֹן, הוּא־חֹדֶשׁ
נִיסָן, בִּשְׁנַת שְׁתֵּים עֶשְׂרֵה, לַמֶּלֶךְ אֲחַשְׁוֵרוֹשׁ: הִפִּיל פּוּר הוּא הַגּוֹרָל לִפְנֵי הָמָן, מִיּוֹם
לְיוֹם וּמֵחֹדֶשׁ לְחֹדֶשׁ שְׁנֵים־עָשָׂר—הוּא־חֹדֶשׁ אֲדָר.

הַמַּלְכָּה: כִּי עַל־כָּל־הַשָּׂרִים, וְעַל־כָּל־הָעַמִּים, אֲשֶׁר, בְּכָל־מְדִינוֹת הַמֶּלֶךְ אֲחַשְׁוֵרוֹשׁ.
יז כִּי־יֵצֵא דְבַר־הַמַּלְכָּה עַל־כָּל־הַנָּשִׁים, לְהַבְזוֹת בַּעְלֵיהֶן בְּעֵינֵיהֶן: בְּאָמְרָם, הַמֶּלֶךְ
אֲחַשְׁוֵרוֹשׁ אָמַר לְהָבִיא אֶת־וַשְׁתִּי הַמַּלְכָּה לְפָנָיו—וְלֹא־בָאָה. יח וְהַיּוֹם הַזֶּה תֹּאמַרְנָה
שָׂרוֹת פָּרַס־וּמָדַי, אֲשֶׁר שָׁמְעוּ אֶת־דְּבַר הַמַּלְכָּה, לְכֹל, שָׂרֵי הַמֶּלֶךְ; וּכְדַי, בִּזָּיוֹן
וָקָצֶף. יט אִם־עַל־הַמֶּלֶךְ טוֹב, יֵצֵא דְבַר־מַלְכוּת מִלְּפָנָיו, וְיִכָּתֵב בְּדָתֵי פָרַס־וּמָדַי,
וְלֹא יַעֲבוֹר: אֲשֶׁר לֹא־תָבוֹא וַשְׁתִּי, לִפְנֵי הַמֶּלֶךְ אֲחַשְׁוֵרוֹשׁ, וּמַלְכוּתָהּ יִתֵּן הַמֶּלֶךְ,
לִרְעוּתָהּ הַטּוֹבָה מִמֶּנָּה. כ וְנִשְׁמַע פִּתְגָם הַמֶּלֶךְ אֲשֶׁר־יַעֲשֶׂה בְּכָל־מַלְכוּתוֹ, כִּי רַבָּה
הִיא; וְכָל־הַנָּשִׁים, יִתְּנוּ יְקָר לְבַעְלֵיהֶן—לְמִגָּדוֹל, וְעַד־קָטָן. כא וַיִּיטַב, הַדָּבָר, בְּעֵינֵי
הַמֶּלֶךְ, וְהַשָּׂרִים; וַיַּעַשׂ הַמֶּלֶךְ, כִּדְבַר מְמוּכָן. כב וַיִּשְׁלַח סְפָרִים, אֶל־כָּל־מְדִינוֹת
הַמֶּלֶךְ—אֶל־מְדִינָה וּמְדִינָה כִּכְתָבָהּ, וְאֶל־עַם וָעָם כִּלְשׁוֹנוֹ: לִהְיוֹת כָּל־אִישׁ שֹׂרֵר
בְּבֵיתוֹ, וּמְדַבֵּר כִּלְשׁוֹן עַמּוֹ.

פרק ב

א אַחַר, הַדְּבָרִים הָאֵלֶּה, כְּשֹׁךְ, חֲמַת הַמֶּלֶךְ אֲחַשְׁוֵרוֹשׁ—זָכַר אֶת־וַשְׁתִּי וְאֵת אֲשֶׁר־
עָשָׂתָה, וְאֵת אֲשֶׁר־נִגְזַר עָלֶיהָ. ב וַיֹּאמְרוּ נַעֲרֵי־הַמֶּלֶךְ, מְשָׁרְתָיו: יְבַקְשׁוּ לַמֶּלֶךְ נְעָרוֹת
בְּתוּלוֹת, טוֹבוֹת מַרְאֶה. ג וְיַפְקֵד הַמֶּלֶךְ פְּקִידִים, בְּכָל־מְדִינוֹת מַלְכוּתוֹ, וְיִקְבְּצוּ אֶת־
כָּל־נַעֲרָה־בְתוּלָה טוֹבַת מַרְאֶה אֶל־שׁוּשַׁן הַבִּירָה אֶל־בֵּית הַנָּשִׁים, אֶל־יַד הֵגֶא סְרִיס
הַמֶּלֶךְ שֹׁמֵר הַנָּשִׁים; וְנָתוֹן, תַּמְרוּקֵיהֶן. ד וְהַנַּעֲרָה, אֲשֶׁר תִּיטַב בְּעֵינֵי הַמֶּלֶךְ—תִּמְלֹךְ,
תַּחַת וַשְׁתִּי; וַיִּיטַב הַדָּבָר בְּעֵינֵי הַמֶּלֶךְ, וַיַּעַשׂ כֵּן.
ה אִישׁ יְהוּדִי, הָיָה בְּשׁוּשַׁן הַבִּירָה; וּשְׁמוֹ מָרְדֳּכַי, בֶּן יָאִיר בֶּן־שִׁמְעִי בֶּן־קִישׁ—אִישׁ
יְמִינִי. ו אֲשֶׁר הָגְלָה, מִירוּשָׁלַיִם, עִם־הַגֹּלָה אֲשֶׁר הָגְלְתָה, עִם יְכָנְיָה מֶלֶךְ־יְהוּדָה—
אֲשֶׁר הֶגְלָה, נְבוּכַדְנֶאצַּר מֶלֶךְ בָּבֶל. ז וַיְהִי אֹמֵן אֶת־הֲדַסָּה, הִיא אֶסְתֵּר בַּת־דֹּדוֹ—כִּי
אֵין לָהּ, אָב וָאֵם; וְהַנַּעֲרָה יְפַת־תֹּאַר, וְטוֹבַת מַרְאֶה, וּבְמוֹת אָבִיהָ וְאִמָּהּ, לְקָחָהּ
מָרְדֳּכַי לוֹ לְבַת. ח וַיְהִי, בְּהִשָּׁמַע דְּבַר־הַמֶּלֶךְ וְדָתוֹ, וּבְהִקָּבֵץ נְעָרוֹת רַבּוֹת אֶל־
שׁוּשַׁן הַבִּירָה, אֶל־יַד הֵגָי; וַתִּלָּקַח אֶסְתֵּר אֶל־בֵּית הַמֶּלֶךְ, אֶל־יַד הֵגַי שֹׁמֵר הַנָּשִׁים.
ט וַתִּיטַב הַנַּעֲרָה בְעֵינָיו, וַתִּשָּׂא חֶסֶד לְפָנָיו, וַיְבַהֵל אֶת־תַּמְרוּקֶיהָ וְאֶת־מָנוֹתֶהָ
לָתֵת לָהּ, וְאֵת שֶׁבַע הַנְּעָרוֹת הָרְאֻיוֹת לָתֶת־לָהּ מִבֵּית הַמֶּלֶךְ; וַיְשַׁנֶּהָ וְאֶת־נַעֲרוֹתֶיהָ
לְטוֹב, בֵּית הַנָּשִׁים. י לֹא־הִגִּידָה אֶסְתֵּר, אֶת־עַמָּהּ וְאֶת־מוֹלַדְתָּהּ: כִּי מָרְדֳּכַי צִוָּה
עָלֶיהָ, אֲשֶׁר לֹא־תַגִּיד. יא וּבְכָל־יוֹם וָיוֹם—מָרְדֳּכַי מִתְהַלֵּךְ, לִפְנֵי חֲצַר בֵּית־הַנָּשִׁים:
לָדַעַת אֶת־שְׁלוֹם אֶסְתֵּר, וּמַה־יֵּעָשֶׂה בָּהּ. יב וּבְהַגִּיעַ תֹּר נַעֲרָה וְנַעֲרָה לָבוֹא אֶל־
הַמֶּלֶךְ אֲחַשְׁוֵרוֹשׁ, מִקֵּץ הֱיוֹת לָהּ כְּדָת הַנָּשִׁים שְׁנֵים עָשָׂר חֹדֶשׁ—כִּי כֵּן יִמְלְאוּ, יְמֵי

מגילת אסתר

פרק א

א וַיְהִי, בִּימֵי אֲחַשְׁוֵרוֹשׁ: הוּא אֲחַשְׁוֵרוֹשׁ, הַמֹּלֵךְ מֵהֹדּוּ וְעַד־כּוּשׁ–שֶׁבַע וְעֶשְׂרִים
וּמֵאָה, מְדִינָה. ב בַּיָּמִים, הָהֵם–כְּשֶׁבֶת הַמֶּלֶךְ אֲחַשְׁוֵרוֹשׁ, עַל כִּסֵּא מַלְכוּתוֹ, אֲשֶׁר,
בְּשׁוּשַׁן הַבִּירָה. ג בִּשְׁנַת שָׁלוֹשׁ, לְמָלְכוֹ, עָשָׂה מִשְׁתֶּה, לְכָל־שָׂרָיו וַעֲבָדָיו: חֵיל פָּרַס
וּמָדַי, הַפַּרְתְּמִים וְשָׂרֵי הַמְּדִינוֹת–לְפָנָיו. ד בְּהַרְאֹתוֹ, אֶת־עֹשֶׁר כְּבוֹד מַלְכוּתוֹ, וְאֶת־
יְקָר, תִּפְאֶרֶת גְּדוּלָּתוֹ; יָמִים רַבִּים, שְׁמוֹנִים וּמְאַת יוֹם. ה וּבִמְלוֹאת הַיָּמִים הָאֵלֶּה,
עָשָׂה הַמֶּלֶךְ לְכָל־הָעָם הַנִּמְצְאִים בְּשׁוּשַׁן הַבִּירָה לְמִגָּדוֹל וְעַד־קָטָן מִשְׁתֶּה–שִׁבְעַת
יָמִים: בַּחֲצַר, גִּנַּת בִּיתַן הַמֶּלֶךְ. ו חוּר כַּרְפַּס וּתְכֵלֶת, אָחוּז בְּחַבְלֵי־בוּץ וְאַרְגָּמָן,
עַל־גְּלִילֵי כֶסֶף, וְעַמּוּדֵי שֵׁשׁ; מִטּוֹת זָהָב וָכֶסֶף, עַל רִצְפַת בַּהַט־וָשֵׁשׁ–וְדַר וְסֹחָרֶת.
ז וְהַשְׁקוֹת בִּכְלֵי זָהָב, וְכֵלִים מִכֵּלִים שׁוֹנִים; וְיֵין מַלְכוּת רָב, כְּיַד הַמֶּלֶךְ. ח וְהַשְּׁתִיָּה
כַדָּת, אֵין אֹנֵס: כִּי־כֵן יִסַּד הַמֶּלֶךְ, עַל כָּל־רַב בֵּיתוֹ–לַעֲשׂוֹת, כִּרְצוֹן אִישׁ־וָאִישׁ.
ט גַּם וַשְׁתִּי הַמַּלְכָּה, עָשְׂתָה מִשְׁתֵּה נָשִׁים–בֵּית, הַמַּלְכוּת, אֲשֶׁר, לַמֶּלֶךְ אֲחַשְׁוֵרוֹשׁ.
י בַּיּוֹם, הַשְּׁבִיעִי, כְּטוֹב לֵב־הַמֶּלֶךְ, בַּיָּיִן–אָמַר לִמְהוּמָן בִּזְּתָא חַרְבוֹנָא בִּגְתָא
וַאֲבַגְתָא, זֵתַר וְכַרְכַּס, שִׁבְעַת הַסָּרִיסִים, הַמְשָׁרְתִים אֶת־פְּנֵי הַמֶּלֶךְ אֲחַשְׁוֵרוֹשׁ.
יא לְהָבִיא אֶת־וַשְׁתִּי הַמַּלְכָּה, לִפְנֵי הַמֶּלֶךְ–בְּכֶתֶר מַלְכוּת: לְהַרְאוֹת הָעַמִּים וְהַשָּׂרִים
אֶת־יָפְיָהּ, כִּי־טוֹבַת מַרְאֶה הִיא. יב וַתְּמָאֵן הַמַּלְכָּה וַשְׁתִּי, לָבוֹא בִּדְבַר הַמֶּלֶךְ, אֲשֶׁר,
בְּיַד הַסָּרִיסִים; וַיִּקְצֹף הַמֶּלֶךְ מְאֹד, וַחֲמָתוֹ בָּעֲרָה בוֹ.
יג וַיֹּאמֶר הַמֶּלֶךְ, לַחֲכָמִים יֹדְעֵי הָעִתִּים: כִּי־כֵן, דְּבַר הַמֶּלֶךְ, לִפְנֵי, כָּל־יֹדְעֵי דָּת
וָדִין. יד וְהַקָּרֹב אֵלָיו, כַּרְשְׁנָא שֵׁתָר אַדְמָתָא תַרְשִׁישׁ, מֶרֶס מַרְסְנָא, מְמוּכָן–
שִׁבְעַת שָׂרֵי פָּרַס וּמָדַי, רֹאֵי פְּנֵי הַמֶּלֶךְ, הַיֹּשְׁבִים רִאשֹׁנָה, בַּמַּלְכוּת. טו כְּדָת,
מַה־לַּעֲשׂוֹת, בַּמַּלְכָּה, וַשְׁתִּי–עַל אֲשֶׁר לֹא־עָשְׂתָה, אֶת־מַאֲמַר הַמֶּלֶךְ אֲחַשְׁוֵרוֹשׁ,
בְּיַד, הַסָּרִיסִים.
טז וַיֹּאמֶר מומכן (מְמוּכָן), לִפְנֵי הַמֶּלֶךְ וְהַשָּׂרִים, לֹא עַל־הַמֶּלֶךְ לְבַדּוֹ, עָוְתָה וַשְׁתִּי